Soldiers, Martyrs, Traitors, and Exiles

THE ETHNOGRAPHY OF POLITICAL VIOLENCE

Cynthia Keppley Mahmood, Series Editor

A complete list of books in the series is available from the publisher.

Soldiers, Martyrs, Traitors, and Exiles

Political Conflict in Eritrea
and the Diaspora

Tricia Redeker Hepner

PENN

University of Pennsylvania Press

Philadelphia

Published by
University of Pennsylvania Press
Philadelphia, Pennsylvania 19104-4112

Printed in the United States of America on acid-free paper

10   9   8   7   6   5   4   3   2   1

Library of Congress Cataloging-in-Publication Data

Redeker Hepner, Tricia M.
  Soldiers, martyrs, traitors, and exiles : political conflict in Eritrea and the diaspora / Tricia Redeker Hepner.
      p.   cm. — (The ethnography of political violence)
  Includes bibliographical references and index.
  ISBN 978-0-8122-4171-6 (alk. paper)
    1. Eritrea—Emigration and immigration.   2. United States—Emigration and immigration.   3. Nationalism—Eritrea.   4. Eritreans—United States—Social conditions.   5. Eritreans—United States—Political activity.   6. Civil society—Eritrea.   7. Transnationalism.   8. Eritrea—Politics and government.   I. Title.
JV8996.5.R43   2009
305.892′89—dc22

                                                                    2009001008

In memoriam
Fessehaye "Joshua" Yohannes
1959–2007

Contents

Abbreviations

AES	Association of Eritrean Students
AESNA	Association of Eritrean Students in North America
AEWNA	Association of Eritrean Women in North America
BMA	British Military Administration
CCE	Constitutional Commission of Eritrea
DENA	Democratic Eritreans in North America
EDM	Eritrean Democratic Movement
EFLNA	Eritreans for Liberation in North America
ELF	Eritrean Liberation Front
ELF-RC	Eritrean Liberation Front–Revolutionary Council
ELM	Eritrean Liberation Movement
EPLF	Eritrean Peoples Liberation Front
EPLF-DP	Eritrean Peoples Liberation Front–Democratic Party
EPRDF	Ethiopian Peoples Revolutionary Democratic Front
EPRP	Ethiopian Peoples Revolutionary Party
ERA	Eritrean Relief Association
ESUNA	Ethiopian Students Union in North America
GONGO	government-organized nongovernmental organization
NCEW	National Confederation of Eritrean Workers
NGO	nongovernmental organization
NUES	National Union of Eritrean Students
NUEW	National Union of Eritrean Women
NUEY	National Union of Eritrean Youth
NUEYS	National Union of Eritrean Youth and Students
NUEYS-NA	National Union of Eritrean Youth and Students–North America
PFDJ	Peoples Front for Democracy and Justice
PGE	Provisional Government of Eritrea
RC	Revolutionary Council
TPLF	Tigrayan Peoples Liberation Front
UNHCR	United Nations High Commissioner for Refugees
USCR	United States Committee for Refugees

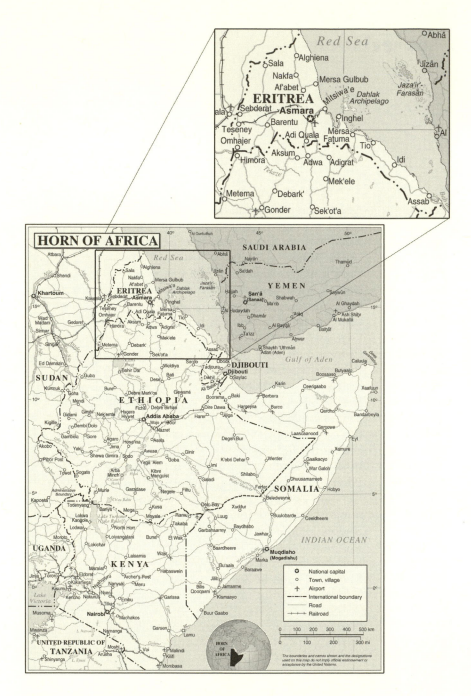

Map 1. Eritrea, in the Horn of Africa. Based on a UN map available at www.un.org.

Preface

As a multisited study undertaken in both Eritrea and the United States, this book represents an effort to move beyond the insularism and exceptionalism characterizing both Eritrean studies and Eritrean nationalism itself. Because Eritrea has largely been inaccessible to researchers for much of its recent history, few sustained ethnographic analyses of Eritrea or its diasporas yet exist. The majority of research to date has focused, rather narrowly, on the historical and political conditions surrounding the thirty-year struggle for independence from Ethiopia (1961–91). Many scholars have written with a particular objective in mind, that is, to legitimize (or dismiss) Eritrean nationalist claims. Few contemporary and critical ethnographic studies have yet appeared, including those addressing the diaspora as a key sector of the Eritrean nation-state. Moreover, the Eritrean leadership has long cultivated an image of Eritrea as inscrutable, misunderstood, and perpetually threatened by enemies within and without. Reinforcing and perhaps even exploiting the classic view of the Horn of Africa as a world apart, this image underpins nationalist narratives of isolation and the turn toward authoritarianism.

Among the first generation of anthropologists to study the country after independence, I am convinced that ethnography is needed perhaps nowhere so urgently as it is in Eritrea today. As access to information and the country itself becomes increasingly restricted, it is vital to record and reconstruct people's actual encounters with the past, present, and future. As anthropologist Donald Donham (1999b) has shown for Ethiopia, revolutionary movements rapidly repress diverse, locally constructed understandings, smoothing the ineffable contingencies of political transformation into homogenized, linear inevitabilities. Recovering the multidimensional human experiences that accompany dramatic change is vital for a richer and more accurate comprehension of the sociopolitical conditions that follow. Moreover, analytical abstractions from the Eritrean case are valuable precisely because they enable new contextualizations, defusing the exceptionalist logic that feeds intolerance, xenophobia, and militarization.

The approach taken in this book is therefore one of witnessing the subjective life experiences of Eritrean people. Many of these experiences seem to brush history against the grain, thus countering official, homogenizing nationalist narratives that euphemize and justify the tragedies of war, political repression, forced migration, and human rights abuses. However, this was not the original intention of this study. Rather, my goal was to interpret the successes and challenges of what in the mid-1990s still seemed to many observers a progressive and deeply inspiring African liberation movement and to chart the development of a euphoric new state once referred to as a leader in the (erstwhile) African Renaissance. In particular, I hoped to account for how the Eritrean diaspora in the United States had contributed to the independence movement historically and to assess their participation in nation building relative to the new government's goals and policies.

One of my initial hypotheses was that exile communities had considerable power and autonomy vis-à-vis the party-state. However, I soon discovered that the former revolutionary guerrilla movement, the Eritrean Peoples Liberation Front (EPLF), and now the government of Eritrea (known as the Peoples Front for Democracy and Justice, or PFDJ), had long been at the center of transnational relationships, and indeed bore down heavily from above as well as laterally through its own deterritorialized institutions, policies, and the people who carried out state functions and party orders. In developing a more complex understanding of how the Eritrean state and its transnational society related to one another, I realized I had underestimated the role of the state as a major structural force shaping transnational institutions and the communities and people who participated in them (or, conversely, rejected them). I had also not anticipated the intense fragmentation within exile communities or the repressive elements of transnationalism that so disempowered people even as they pursued spaces for resistance and autonomy. I was also surprised to discover that the rising debates about democracy and civil society that emerged following the 1998–2000 border war with Ethiopia were expressing as much about the historic grievances lodged deep within Eritrean society and culture and the nationalist revolution itself as they were about the dilemmas facing Eritrea as a new state in a rapidly globalizing world. Those historic grievances were soon overlaid by newer ones related to the retrenchment of nationalism and the intensified militarism and repression that arose after 2001, precipitating a new level of violence by the state and pushing more and more soldiers to become traitors and exiles despite the state's forceful appeals to honor the glorious sacrifices of the martyrs with obedience and self-sacrifice.

Clearly, crafting an analysis of Eritrea and exile is rife with challenges.

Some of these are related to the objective difficulties of researching and writing about a relatively closed, postrevolutionary society where inquiry and discussion are potentially dangerous pursuits for both the researcher and the researched. Other challenges are related to the as yet unknown quality of Eritrean history, culture, and society. Not only are sources (whether archival or ethnographic) often difficult to access, but also the unfamiliarity of Eritrea to most audiences usually requires that substantial background information be provided in order to make sense of contemporary conditions. Finally, because Eritrea's quest for national identity and statehood has been so marked by internal conflicts and power struggles, multiple clashing narratives of the past and present compete at every turn, rendering truth and fact maddeningly elusive.

In many ways, this is a work of critical social history, structured by anthropological methods and analysis. While my chief concern is actually the contemporary dilemmas associated with transnational political struggle and the encounter between territorial nationalism and globally constructed models of political and social power, I discovered through the course of field research that none of these made much sense unless carefully situated within the historical context of the Eritrean revolution and forced migration. Scholars have pointed out the necessity of historicizing transnationalism and the context of forced migration in order to better understand the implications of transnational processes for migrating communities and sending and receiving states. Similarly, some Africanists (like Mahmoud Mamdani 1996) have argued that current claims to democratization and civil society require a historical analysis in order to comprehend how analogies and differences between Africa and the North/West have been constructed. In addition, taking a historical approach can be an effective research strategy under conditions of political instability and in settings where trust between research participants is compromised. Addressing events or debates that occurred in the past allowed people to discuss issues or answer questions that had a direct bearing on current events, but in a way that seemed safer due to the removal from the immediate present. It also helped me identify the way in which competing narratives or clashing views on the present had emerged out of conflicts within the historic nationalist movement itself.

Finally, a historical focus speaks to the anguish I observed among so many Eritreans as they wrestled with the same dilemmas in their communities and relationship to the Eritrean nation-state that my research aimed to address in a different way. While most Eritreans with whom I spoke at length revealed a well-developed consciousness of the national past as they had personally experienced it, a collective disorientation also clouded their gaze, engendering confusion, misunderstanding, and hostility within the diaspora and transnational social field. The sense of fragmentation Eritreans seemed to feel, and particularly those whose lives had been rent asunder by both war and exile, appeared to me to find its coherence only by reaching back to a time—if ever it existed— when the pieces were not yet so broken, when dreams of neither unity nor independence had been achieved and certainly not transformed into the stuff of fear and nightmares.

In assembling the pieces and narratives I have gathered among Eritreans into my own narrative, I have been continually reminded how all cultural processes, all histories, all political struggles, and all texts are essentially composites of competing memories of the past and dynamic perspectives on the present. Eritreans, both those in exile and those at home, have remembered events and narrated them to me and to one another in ways that serve contemporary political purposes. Moreover, my own memories of Eritrea intervene continually, forcing me to respond to those of my counterparts and perhaps betraying my own political and humanitarian concerns. Throughout this study I have tried to carefully balance the different interpretations of the past and present I discovered and to avoid deliberately staking a position on what does or does not constitute truth. It is hardly an original proposition that truth, fact, and objectivity are all relative, and perhaps nowhere is this more salient than during times of massive social and political upheaval, such as during revolutions and wars. It is my hope that the narrative I contribute here may possibly help Eritreans to view their own in new ways.

This is a pragmatic analytical strategy attuned to a complicated, emotionally fraught subject more than it is a theoretical commitment to postmodernism, however. I want to carefully avoid the sense in which "narratives" are formed and articulated in a space that is somehow distanced from concrete political experiences. Narratives, for Eritreans and others, are not just stories to be told and retold. Nor are all narratives equal. Each is a perspective that emerges from a unique location within a collective, yet differentiated, political undertaking. Some are formed within the very grip of violence and dislocation, others from the communal comfort of university campuses, yet all are structured by the intense pressures of collective and individual survival. The tales of exhilaration recounted by radicalized students living in the United States, far from the trauma of war at home, are no less Eritrean than those that recall the smells and sounds of solitary confinement in a prison cell. But they are most certainly different tales indeed.

Chapter 1
Eritrea and Exile

Hailu

"Hello?"

A crackle, a pause, and a voice through the wire.

"Terhas? It is Hailu. From Asmara."

"Hailu!" Another pause. Then a breath: mine. "My God! How *are* you?"

The delay on the telephone captured and collapsed the distance between us all at once. How many years had gone by? Two? Four? My world seemed to freeze. Time and space folded momentarily.

Palm trees swayed against the sky above me, and the diesel fumes of a nearby truck left traces in the air. Asmara came rushing back, channeled through Hailu's guttural voice. Such few words spoken, and already he sounded repressed. I battled the urge to babble the banalities of old friends suddenly catching up.

"How is Asmara? Where are you calling from? Is everything all right?"

"I am at home. It's late," he said, keeping his voice hushed.

"How have you been?"

"Still a soldier," he replied, tension lacing the edges of what he meant to sound normal, even lighthearted.

I flashbacked to an evening promenade down Liberation Avenue, Asmara, summer 2001, the midst of my fieldwork, and Hailu talking with matter-of-fact pathos about the circumscriptions of life in postrevolutionary Eritrea.

"Maybe there will be war, maybe there will be peace. Maybe I will live, maybe I will die," I heard him say.

"*Que será, será*, whatever will be will be," he singsonged in Semitic-inflected Spanglish. I could see his lanky shoulders shrug, weighted down with a self-conscious resignation he couldn't throw off.

Five years later, and Hailu was still working for pocket change in

National Service, an agent of the state, low level, unimportant, vulnerable. It had been a decade for him now, I realized.

"Still?" I managed, my throat feeling thick. "I thought you were supposed to be demobilized. . . ."

"Not yet." The words were clipped, distinct, not like the slur of native-spoken English.

He continued. "Girmay-*Shikor* moved into my building. Right next door." He laughed, sort of. "Girmay-*Shikor* and I are best friends now."

I blurted and regretted, "How better to keep an eye on those who associate with dangerous outsiders."

It was stupid and I wanted to backpedal. To where?

Maybe Hailu could wax amused about a security agent formerly assigned to investigate me, my research, and Hailu's role in it. But not me, not on the phone, not after all this time. I had long since moved back to my own reality, having abandoned Hailu to cope with his.

I listened for the telltale click of an unwanted listener—were those real, or just rumors?—and reflected on the uncircumscribed choice made by Hailu to help me with my research. Once, I asked him why he did it, when I had little to offer in return.

He answered simply: "It's something to do. It breaks up the routine of my days."

Days he lived in the cracks and crevices of neither war nor peace, waiting, like all Eritreans, for one or the other to appear.

Hailu still answered every day for that casual choice he made, in friendly, ominous chitchat with his next-door neighbor. "Girmay-Sweetie" was a silly moniker we invented to deflate the fear in some small way.

"You have finished your research project. I am sorry I didn't e-mail to say *yohana*. The Internet here is . . . you know, it is difficult."

"I know, I know. It's okay. Yes, I finished the project. I'm living in California. I'm actually sitting by the pool right now. It's lovely."

Immediately, the breach of distance between us yawned into the gaping chasm it was.

He rushed to offer me a bridge. "I'd like to read your work. Can you send me something?"

"Yes, I'd love you to read it. Can I mail you some papers? Or how about I send you a CD?"

"No, there are censors. They will open it and look. Better to send e-mail attachments. I will read them at work."

It's because the Internet connections are better in government offices, but Hailu's solution seemed more subversive to me. In person, I would have pointed that out, and we would have laughed, again chipping at the fear. We would have taken dark delight in the small ways we might outwit the state; we would have felt exhilarated by our ability to maneuver so close to it. But from my distance the danger now seemed paradoxically more real.

"No. I'll send something with a colleague going to Asmara. Can you meet her and get it?"

"Yes. I will like to see your work, after all this time."

"I would like you to have it. You were a part of it, after all."

Hailu changed the subject. I sensed he was ready to conclude our conversation.

"Did you hear from my brother in San Diego? I told him to call you. He has his own phone number now. Maybe you can find him?"

"I will get in touch with him for sure, Hailu. E-mail me his number, I don't have a pen and paper here. And tell the rest of your family that I send my greetings."

"*Haray*, Terhasina," he sighed, using a diminutive of my Tigrinya name, *our Terhas*. "We will talk again soon. I will go now. *Ciao*."

"*Ciao*, Hailu."

A click, and the thread between us was severed.

The palm trees rustled against a pure and cloudless coastal California sky. Two teenage girls in bikinis giggled from the pool. I laid back on my chaise lounge. All was quiet and peaceful from without, but within a tsunami roared. Teardrops magnified the scene before my eyes, then overflowed rapidly down my cheeks, their ticklish tracks reminding me to unclench my jaw and stop grinding my teeth. For the rest of the day, my world was tipped askew, surreal. Hailu's voice echoed in my head. But it was the things he didn't say that bothered me the most.

Two days later I received an e-mail. I didn't recognize the name of the sender, but it was Eritrean, so I opened it immediately.

It was Hailu. He wrote in lowercase letters, terse and rushed: "here as you know no free press, human rights violations at highest levels, round up by military police, no elections, chaos in economic policy, unpaid national service continues, no peace no war situation (war is more likely to come), military personnel are taking the office of the civil servants—in other words military regime is prevailing, every one striving to survive, this generalizes the situation here. some time soon i will e-mail you every thing on what is going on here."

I imagined him sitting at his military post, plain khaki fatigues clinging to his slight frame, typing with two fingers, glancing over his shoulder. One click, and the message was sent. One more, and it was deleted.

When I first met Hailu, soon after the thirty-year war for Eritrean independence had ended, he was twenty-four, three years older than I was at the time. He wore his hair in a mini-Afro and sported sideburns, looking a bit like a Black Panther in ill-fitting, First World hand-me-downs. Eritrea was a different place then, and Hailu and I both different people.

He was passionate in his patriotism, dedicated to a free Eritrea. The war of independence from Ethiopia had begun a decade before he was born and ended when he was twenty. In 1995 he was assigned as a liaison between the transitional government and well-meaning but unprepared visitors like me. His English was impeccable, his manner shy and retiring.

I was one of seven American volunteers sent to Eritrea by a nongovernmental organization (NGO) to participate in postwar reconstruction. Fresh from university, a newly minted idealism hammering in my head and overflowing from my heart, I sought confirmation of my most earnest conviction: that humanity's essence emerged from a wellspring of goodness and justice. The Eritrea I saw reflected in Hailu's eyes drew me inexorably toward it and held me captive.

It was but a glimpse we caught back then, when Eritrea had finally emerged from three decades of suffering and upheaval in the longest and most painful birth in African history. The slate had been wiped clean. No crippling debt cast long shadows over the fledgling country. The men in power were dedicated servants to the cause, steeped in idealism and pragmatism. It was a time of delirious hope, when virtually anything seemed possible in the pursuit of modernity, prosperity, and social justice. Eritrea was proclaimed the bright new future of Africa: a beacon in the continent's approaching renaissance. We were all seduced by that moment in time: four million Eritreans, scores of foreign observers, Hailu, and me.

Fifteen years later and delusions of limitless power have replaced the humility of the hardened freedom-fighters-turned-statesmen. Dreams of peace and justice have morphed into the nightmare of chronic emergency for the *Hafash,* "the broad masses," in whose name the struggle was waged. My naïveté has given way to darkly intimate knowledge, a lacerated heart, and a host of disturbing familiars. The latter haunt my own memories of Eritrea and taunt me for sharing the collective dream with Eritreans.

As for Hailu, today he is a reluctant soldier indentured to a freedom he serves but cannot define. A freedom whose essence has been sucked dry, leaving only the husk. His nationalist zeal has deflated, imploded into itself. He mutters that the certain years of war were preferable to the precarious days of peace, that the oppression of the Ethiopian Derg regime was less shameful than the repression of the Peoples Front for Democracy and Justice (PFDJ). From the view of Girmay-*Shikor* and other government loyalists, this makes Hailu a traitor.

When another war breaks out, Hailu could end up a martyr as well.

Unless, of course, he makes it into exile first. He's afraid of the hyenas in the desert, though. He told me that twelve years ago, as we stood looking up together at the dusty, denuded mountain ranges I was there to help reforest. The hyenas developed a taste for human flesh, he said, because of the bodies left lying around. Now they'll attack and kill a lone person wandering through the lowlands toward Sudan. Better to hire a merchant with a camel caravan and with experience smuggling refugees.

That night I read and reread Hailu's e-mail. Then I slept fitfully and dreamt, again, of Eritrea.

Summer 2005. I could hardly believe I was back in Asmara. My senses were overwhelmed, assaulted with sights, smells, and sounds that seemed both intimately familiar and yet removed, as if from another lifetime.

Dust from the potholed streets combined with the odor of diesel in a bitter drip down my throat. A thousand smoldering coal fires cast their musty odor to the wind. Donkey-drawn carts jostled with taxicabs and white SUVs marked "UN" in black. Muslim women in heavy black *hijab* strolled side by side with Christian women in gauzy white *tilfi*. Their henna-stained hands flashed with Arab gold, their feet with Italian leather.

Old men in cotton *gabis* wandered through the winding streets, looking like gnarled prophets from antiquity. Handsome youths in black leather jackets smiled broadly and bumped shoulders in greeting, their clasped hands soaked with the scent of spiced butter and *berbere* pepper. Lithe, ethereal beauties, gums tattooed blue against brilliant white teeth, peered through beaded curtains from the dark interior of shops.

Children crowded around me, too young to feign the proud indifference to foreigners cultivated by their elders. They tugged my clothing and called me Taliano, "Italian," offering chewing gum, tissues, and prickly cactus fruit called *beles*. But the hiss of cappuccino machines and the hum of conversation drew me instead toward the doors of so many European-style cafés.

I wondered if this was how exiles felt returning home. I felt like an exile myself in some ways. My last memories of Asmara remained a hasty departure: a tearful farewell gathering with friends and fictive kin, polluted by the intense fear that someone or something would prevent me from either leaving now or ever coming back again.

I had battled a migraine as I sat in the Asmara airport, glancing over both shoulders for Girmay-*Shikor*. I felt nauseated, weak, beyond spooked. I didn't have faith in any god but prayed anyway, covering all my bases.

Less than two days before, Girmay-*Shikor* had finally threatened me openly. His lip had curled into a sneer over his yellowish teeth, a tooth-pick clamped between molars and poking out at me. He laughed grittily at my mounting frustration, relishing the fear I tried to hide. It was barely dawn when he came to my house, banging on the gate until I emerged in pajamas. I suggested the teahouse next door but found myself ushered into his car instead, the door decisively slammed shut beside me.

"If you have not done anything wrong, Doctor, why are you so upset?" he said. "If none of those people were important, why won't you give me their names?"

I stared him hard in the eye, trying to muster genuine defiance. "You're right. I did nothing wrong. I have all the necessary permits to be here. It's not my problem that you don't understand the concept of confidentiality in research. I will *not* give you names of people I inter-viewed, and I will, in fact, report this to the American embassy."

The last bit escaped as a symbolic gesture, and it sickened me to find myself invoking it. I was wielding my own nationality as though it made me untouchable, as though it would deter Girmay-*Shikor* or his superiors from making an example of me, another nosy foreigner who might sow discord among the people with her endless questions and alien ideas.

Instead, Girmay-*Shikor* sneered again and pushed the toothpick from one side of his mouth to the other.

"Go. Your American government can do nothing for you," he said, calling my bluff. He knew I was a hypocrite and had little faith in the embassy to save me from anything. Once, in one of our half-dozen previ-ous "interviews," as he called them, he had maneuvered me into a cri-tique of American politics. At the time, I had stupidly imagined it would build solidarity between us: a critical-minded American is somehow closer to an Eritrean, I had thought. More sympathetic, more under-standing of the plight of oppressed peoples, more of a comrade in struggle.

But my assumption had only betrayed my practical ignorance of the political environment I was studying. I had blathered aimlessly about the superficiality of American democracy, corporate corruption, structural racism, and systemic inequality. Girmay-*Shikor*, I now understood, had processed that conversation differently. If I was contrary about my own society and government, how disloyal would I be to Eritrea? Appealing to the American embassy as I squirmed under Girmay-*Shikor*'s thumb just made him gleeful. And it made me more suspect, more opportunis-tic in his eyes.

As I rode low and incognito in a taxicab later that afternoon to the American embassy compound, a white cotton *netsela* wrapped around my head and shoulders, I warily watched out the windows for Girmay-

Shikor's green sedan. When I arrived at the embassy, with its garrison walls and drooping bougainvillea, I was shuffled into a room with a well-scrubbed, fresh-faced white American man, barely older than I. He had been in Eritrea two weeks and seemed baffled by my tear-streaked face and saga with *wushtawi gudayat*, internal security.

"I'm sorry, ma'am," he drawled. "I'm afraid there's not much we can do for you. If you are arrested or separated from your passport by anyone or anything, please be sure to call me." He handed me a glossy white business card with the seal of the United States of America. I stared at it in disbelief. Then he continued, "I just find this little country so charming. The city is so safe and peaceful. You can walk about at any time of night. Not what I pictured for, you know, *Africa*."

I departed the embassy knowing I would have to leave Asmara as soon as possible. Otherwise there was no telling what Girmay-*Shikor* might be ordered to do. I held the secrets of hundreds of lives. What would I become responsible for should those secrets and the identities of their tellers be extracted from me? I could feel myself starting to break. Nothing about my life experience, or my training in anthropology, had quite prepared me for this.

I hailed another cab and went directly to the Lufthansa booking office. Eight hours later I was curled in a chair in the airport, clutching my head in my hands, fending off the pain that pounded my skull and the fear that roiled my guts.

And so it seemed surreal that I should find myself back in Asmara four years later, strolling past colonial Italian villas as though I had never left like that. I had returned for some follow-up data, an interview here and there, a look at some archival materials, a refresher on the reality to which I had bound myself, for better or worse.

I was enjoying an oddly flavored Chinese meal in an Asmara restaurant. The ingredients were authentic, but the local spices gave the meal a distinctively *Habesha*, "Abyssinian," cast: spicy red pepper with hints of cardamom and cloves. Sharing my table was Percy Alexander, a longtime journalist and near-veteran of the Eritrean liberation war. Canadian in origin and employed by the British, Percy had lived in foxholes and traveled by night with the guerrilla soldiers since the 1970s, personally recording the history of major battles from Barentu to Nakfa. He was jaded, arrogant, unimpressible.

"You need to watch it, Doc," he commented, between bites of an egg roll. "I've heard some things." Grease oozed at the corner of his mouth, and he swiped at it with the back of his hand.

"What things? What do you mean? From whom?" I knew Percy had extensive internal connections and was privy to the rumor mill, or *bado-seleste*, of the government.

"You know, the usual. *Wushtawi gudayat,* internal security. You know how researchers are disliked around here. They know you're here again."

"Of course they know I'm here," I almost snapped. "I came through customs, went to the university, asked for permission to visit the archives. What am I supposed to do, skulk around and pretend I'm on vacation?" I jabbed at the crucial differences I perceived between ethnographic and journalistic methods. Percy was unruffled.

"Well, I'm only trying to tell you, you know. Just be careful. Call on me if you need to." Then he got up abruptly from the table, wiped his mouth on a napkin, slung a backpack over his shoulder, traipsed outside to his motorcycle, mounted it, zoomed off.

I paid for the meal and stepped outside into the overcast afternoon. It was *keremti,* the rainy season, and I could smell the gathering clouds. A few drops began to splatter around me. I decided on an after-lunch macchiato at Sunshine Hotel to wait it out.

A snuffling whimper stopped me in my tracks. Backing up a few steps, I peered down a narrow, rocky alley. A shape was clinging to the wall, ghostly. I stepped toward it, and it moved away, covering its face. Its nearly white hair hung in long, stringy tangles.

"Hey," I said softly. "Hey. Do you speak English?"

The creature peered at me over curled fingers. It was a little white girl, towheaded, blue-eyed. Maybe six or seven. Dirty. Her ragged dress hung off one shoulder, and streaks of dust ran the length of her pale legs, which grew filthier at her feet. Except for her ghostly skin and hair, she looked rather like a local child.

"Hey. Are you lost?" I reached out to touch her. She shrank away but lowered her hands and looked me in the face. I was disturbed to see that she bore an uncanny resemblance to me, when I was child. Her eyebrows and eyelashes were so blonde they were nearly invisible, her new front teeth too large for her head.

"You must be lost, sweetheart. Where are your parents?" I looked around, searching for signs of other white people. What on earth was this little girl doing here, by herself? Not even in the company of other children? I stepped back into the street to glance in all directions. But when I turned back to the alley the little girl had vanished, darting back into the maze of residential neighborhoods that branched off the main thoroughfares.

For a moment I stood frozen and baffled. Then I remembered what Percy Alexander had said, and a wave of urgency closed in on me. Clearly, the little white child must belong here somehow; she couldn't possibly be lost and abandoned. And anyway, I had to get on with my task as quickly as possible. Whatever that was.

I walked on through the downtown area, past the little shaded cabana in the roundabout, known simply as City Park. White-shirted baristas blended mango and guava juices in the cabana, and young people sat eating gelato, finishing hurriedly before the rains began. And then I heard a familiar voice calling to me, somewhere beyond.

I craned my neck, looking around for the source, when suddenly Dr. Gergish Woldeselassie appeared in front of me. I started, not sure where he had come from.

"Hallo there," he said quickly, in the clipped, almost British English that distinguished him plainly. He was short and stocky, light skinned, impish, well dressed. Bushy gray curls spouted from his temples, and thick glasses magnified his eyes. He was standing very close to me, holding some object between us. A bag of some sort, blue canvas, with a zipper.

"Dr. Gergish! My gosh, you surprised me! I heard you but didn't see you till just now. How have you been?"

Back in 2001, Dr. Gergish had been, I thought, an ally. Something between a government official and an academic, he worked at the university but was also a power player in the ruling party. He occupied an interesting position: a keeper of documents and spokesperson for official social and historical pronouncements, tacking between scholar and politico. Despite the power he held, he came across as relaxed, fair-minded, perhaps even a bit critical. He was masterful in his language and diplomatic in his dealings.

I liked Dr. Gergish and wanted to trust him. I had even interviewed him at length one rainy afternoon, as the drops beat loudly and relentlessly against the metallic roof of his institutional office, the maps of Eritrea damp and peeling from the concrete walls. Like most of our conversations, our interview had been relaxed and easy. But in the end I always left his company wondering, had I said the wrong thing? Raised a red flag? Even more effectively than Girmay-*Shikor,* and much more subtly, Gergish could bring me to a grinding halt.

He wasted no time, speaking to me conspiratorially. "Look here," he said, as he hastily unzipped the bag. "Look inside."

I peered into the bag, a moment later catching my breath as my heartbeat skipped and quickened. It was a stack of compact discs, maybe twenty or thirty of them. The plain silvery sort that you buy in bulk at office supply stores. The kind you carry into the field to save and back up all your precious documents, mailing copies home at intervals.

Written in black ink, curving around the edges of each CD, were labels indicating their contents. "Interview transcripts." "Archival Data Back-up." "Fieldnotes I, Fieldnotes II, Fieldnotes III." The writing looked eerily like my own. I started again, my eyes darting to Gergish's.

"What are *these?* Oh, my God."

"It's your work," he hissed. "All of it. All of your field notes, all of your interviews, all of your notes on your archival research. Everything you collected on Eritrea, from the beginning."

"But how . . . ?" I asked in disbelief.

"Don't mind that," Gergish whispered hurriedly. "We have it now, and we plan to discuss it thoroughly with you and with everyone who participated in your research. But first we need you to sort the data for us. Sort the materials from your research with Eritreans in the United States from the materials you collected here in Eritrea. Wherever else in the world you went and talked to Eritreans."

I was confused. Why would Gergish give me back my data if the government was planning to use it against me and all my research participants? I opened my mouth to ask, but Gergish's eyes supplied the answer. So he wasn't so far removed from the world of independent thought and inquiry. He still remembered and cared. It passed for a moment between us, silently, that acknowledgment. Gergish was trying to help me and trying to protect everyone who had been part of my research.

Dumbly, I took the bag from his hands. And then he was gone.

The next thing I knew I was speeding along in my friend Semere's car. The car was a tiny Italian thing Semere had inherited from his grandfather, who had owned it since the 1960s. It ran like a charm, though Semere looked absolutely ridiculous driving it.

Semere was, without a doubt, the tallest man in Eritrea. His friends called him Te'qes, short for *semay-teqes,* or "skyscraper." His knees bent up round the steering wheel, making the car look like a toy. The whole thing was cartoonish: our bodies nearly squished together, heads inches apart, Semere's knees and elbows making him look like a grasshopper in a go-cart.

On my lap was the blue canvas bag with the zipper, containing all my work, all the hopes and dreams and doubts and nightmares I had recorded from Eritrean people across two continents. We sped along the potholed street and screeched around corners, jostling like sardines in a can being shaken by the trembling of the country beneath us.

It occurred to me then that drive-by shootings might happen in Asmara, although I had never heard of it before. Not random shootings for the hell of it, gang or political party warfare (there were no parties save the ruling one), but the exacting sniper sort. A quick pickoff, clean and understated. Probably I had been living in Los Angeles too long already and was mixing up my cultural paranoias. But I couldn't help thinking about our two heads so close together in that tiny car, how a shot meant for me could easily take out Semere. Or vice versa. I felt awful. I was a menace to myself and everyone around me. I was reminded of Hortense Powdermaker, who a half-century earlier had realized that just being seen with her informants in the Jim Crow South endangered their very lives. Why hadn't I done something safe, like gone to law school? Or focused on Caribbean studies and worked in Puerto Rico, as I'd once planned, where I'd conduct my studies in the idyllic comfort of the tropics, Spanish rolling off my tongue, and home but a hop across the blue-green sea?

I think I trusted Semere. It was hard to tell sometimes who you could trust and who you couldn't. I had learned that uncertainty and suspicion from Eritreans, although clearly I had been slow on the uptake. Semere had been good to me in the past, driving me up to the mental institution in 2001 so I could find an interview subject, a psychologist, for whom I had long been searching. He hadn't wanted me to be by myself there, and so he had waited several hours until at last I emerged, my mission accomplished.

I had only just gotten back to Eritrea and already I was caught up in a goose chase, dragging people into things because of my research. What did this work of mine matter anyway? Who really cared about what was happening in this tiny African country and what I had to say about it? Perhaps Girmay-*Shikor* and his superiors were right: maybe I was just a troublemaker, a nosy outsider, a *ferenji* exploiting powerless people for information and, ultimately, her own gain.

"Dammit!" I cursed aloud, slapping my thigh hard enough to hurt.

I had long ago forsaken the childhood impression that being an anthropologist would resemble an Indiana Jones movie, and now here I was, feeling like a cross between a spy and a damn fool. I wasn't being paid for this work, and I didn't have important state secrets. I had simply held intimate conversations with people whose thoughts and feelings and experiences might run contrary to the official story. Surely countless anthropologists before me had faced this too, and yet I could summon none of the lessons of their experience now. All I knew was that my status made me dangerous and made everyone who knew me a potential dissident.

Inside the bag, my hand ran along the CDs, flipping through each one. A piece of paper brushed my fingers, and I took it out. A receipt. Twenty U.S. dollars. The price of my work? Someone had paid 300 nakfa for these copies of my files. Had they been pilfered at the post office? From my room, and I hadn't noticed? And who purchased them back again? Dr. Gergish? I wasn't sure if I should be impressed or insulted. On the one hand, 300 nakfa was a pittance. On the other, it was half what a National Service conscript earned in a whole month, and more than what many families lived on for longer than that.

"Semere. *N'tay meselkha?*" I said, peering at his enormous profile. "What do you think I should do?"

I was hoping I would agree with whatever he had to say. Eritreans could give weird answers to dilemmas sometimes. It was as though the decades of war and upheaval had shaped their conception of danger so much that their perceptions seemed distorted and unpredictable to people like me.

So I was hoping Semere wouldn't say, as I had heard before when I was scared and confused by undercurrents of impending violence, "*Shiger yellen. Normaaal,*" "No problem, everything's normal." It was the flip side of fear: the naturalization of instability and denial of any danger at all.

I was surprised when Semere replied, "You need to get out. I am taking you to the Lufthansa office in Tiravolo, where you will go in there and say it's a family emergency and you need to change your air ticket. Get on the plane to Germany tonight, and take those CDs with you. Gergish was giving you that chance. Better to take it."

I knew Semere was right, but I was worried sick about all of it. If I left suddenly like that, wasn't it an admittance of guilt somehow? If I stayed and held my ground, wasn't that proof I was doing nothing wrong? I could no longer understand the nature of my own role in Eritrea. From my own perspective, that of a social scientist, I was merely collecting data and following procedures, protecting people's confidentiality, and thinking critically. But those seemingly clear-cut methods turned out to mean something else altogether in Eritrea.

The only thing that did seem clear was that my own ideas of right and wrong, guilty and innocent, did not apply. Not here, not now. It was just not up to me. As we sped along toward the Lufthansa office, I tried to think of what to tell the family I lived with in Asmara. Should I tell them anything at all? Would it be safer if they didn't know? Should I . . . ?

And then, in a flash of darkness, a screech, a slam, and a jolt.

In an instant, my eyes were open again. But the scene was different, nothing like the inside of Semere's tiny Italian car.

My gaze met the pale, buttery yellow of drapes fluttering in the dawn breeze. Beaming red numbers stared back from the clock on the dresser: 4:48 AM. I was in my bed, at home in California. It was summer 2005, and I had not returned to Eritrea at all.

So it was all a dream then. This last trip to Asmara. Percy Alexander and the Chinese food. The lost white child. My stolen data and Gergish's last chance. I got out of bed and padded silently into my library, flopped down on the couch, and rubbed my eyes. Taking up a pad and pencil, I recorded the images throbbing in my head. Contained within that dream—or nightmare, perhaps—had been the kernel of reality as I had come to know it, a reality I shared while documenting it as an anthropologist. Here follows that reality, as best as I can render it, in all its duality of sublime dreams and terrible nightmares.

Eritrea and Exile

On the coastal Horn of Africa, jutting heavenward from south to north with the last staggering peaks of the Great Rift, falling away to the salty moonlike deserts of the east and the fertile plains and colorless sands to the west, sits the northeast African nation of Eritrea. Despite securing independence from Ethiopia in 1993, thus ending three decades of warfare with that legendary empire-state, the country remains much as it has always been—a lonely wedge of rugged, embattled terrain.

Further war with Ethiopia in 1998–2000 over the common border precipitated new levels of political and economic hardship for people of both countries, though especially for Eritreans. Other related challenges confront the small Red Sea state. Deeply ingrained patterns of militarism and political intolerance produced by one of modern Africa's longest wars have come to dominate the polity as well as everyday life. Now adding to the legacies of sacrifice and social suffering that accompanied the independence struggle and subsequent border conflict are widespread human rights violations committed by a government that once heroically brought liberation to its citizens. This in turn has generated new flows of refugees, as younger, educated men and women in particular have left Eritrea in ever-increasing numbers. Fleeing conflict and repression just as their parents' generation once did, these sojourners join a global diaspora that still seems more closely tied to the home country than to the international and national spaces in which Eritreans have settled.

Meanwhile, the Eritrean nation-state has become ever more embroiled in turbulent regional and global dynamics. The continuing standoff with Ethiopia perpetually threatens further war, and perhaps Eritrea's hard-won independence itself. The United States currently supports Ethiopia as one of its most important allies in Africa, while bloodshed and misery wracks neighboring Somalia as battles are waged by U.S.-backed Ethiopian forces in the latest front in the ill-conceived war on terror. Defiant Eritrea seems to beckon a crisis of global proportions as the government allegedly supports Somali Islamists against Ethiopia, challenging the latter's dominance in the Horn of Africa and, by proxy, American hegemony. Viewing even mediating bodies such as the United Nations as hostile to its national interests, it steadily alienates much of the international community, and especially the nations of the North and West, while strengthening ties with Iran and China.

Existing precariously amid the turbulence of a past marked by war, the cyclical and emergent conflicts of the present, and the trepidation of an uncertain future, is Eritrean society itself. From the flashpoint of the Horn of Africa to the urban centers of the United States, where Eritreans have long resided and continue to arrive today, the legacies of political violence spin on. Yet so too do other legacies—those of hopefulness, resilience, and the stubborn belief that inalienable rights and dignity also belong to Eritreans, wherever they may be and whatever that might mean in practice. Across great distances and "against all odds" (Connell 1997), Eritreans continue to struggle for a freedom that has not yet materialized. And thus things remain much as they have always been.

This is a historical ethnography about the lesser-known ways that Eritreans have struggled throughout the long war for independence and afterward, not only against Ethiopia but also with respect to one another. It is a story about the pain and paradox of transnational political struggle as it played out among the people of this troubled northeast African nation both at home and in diaspora, in a context defined by displacement, betrayal, and long-distance nationalism. In telling the story, I analyze how often violent efforts to construct national identity and control territory unfolded through space and time, drawing diverse and dispersed populations into a contentious but compelling political process. By emphasizing how everyday people experienced political transformation within the institutions formulated for that purpose, I try to capture the dilemmas faced by a modern nation-state emerging during the postmodern era of globalization, midwifed by the multistranded cross-border practices known as transnationalism. My goal is to document how a territorial regime incorporated its subjects in far-flung worlds, and how those subjects, in turn, entrenched and defied official definitions of the person, the citizen, the community, the society, and the nation-state itself.

Eritrea is the youngest country in Africa and a striking example of what Nina Glick-Schiller and Georges Eugene Fouron (2001) have called a "transnational nation-state." Small, postcolonial, and controversial for its government's uncompromising approach to national development and state building (see O'Kane and Hepner 2009), the country has embodied trends associated with contemporary globalization since the early years of the armed struggle for independence from Ethiopia (1961–91). Some of these trends include large-scale forced migration within the context of Cold War alliances and alienations, anticolonial ideologies and confrontations, and policies developed after World War II to manage refugee flows in a world partitioned into nation-state units (Malkki 1995b). Accompanying large-scale migration was the propagation of nationalist sentiment among a scattered people who shared a common (if contested) historical experience, signaling another trend associated with globalization: the ongoing importance of national identity alongside the reshaping and respatialization of nation-states, political communities, and governments.

While taking place across the global milieu, these trends have unfolded for Eritreans almost exclusively in localized terms. That is, they have long been dominated by the ideologies and institutions of the nationalist guerrilla movement that carried the struggle for independence to fruition. This movement was known as the Eritrean Peoples Liberation Front (EPLF) until the early 1990s, when the political transition to independence then created the current single-party government, the PFDJ. The transnational dimensions of the independence struggle were created both by refugees and other migrants who settled in places such as the urban United States during the long war, and by cadres or officials within the EPLF and PFDJ, who used various institutions, organizations, and ideologies to mobilize people at home and abroad. But the transnational movement that helped secure independence also extended the power and cultural logic of militarized, authoritarian rule. This latter characteristic of the EPLF and PFDJ became clearer after independence but, as this study documents, has its foundations in the institutionalized patterns of transnational politics as early as the 1970s.

Because of the transnational manner in which the independence struggle took shape, Eritrea today is comprised not only of its Red Sea territory but also of vast and intricate networks that span multiple national settings. The penetration of dominant nationalist ideology and state power into these networks is evident. So is the influence of the cultural, political, and economic settings they cut across. Less clear but equally compelling, however, is how these networks impact Eritrea itself. The power structure that rules through the mechanisms of the PFDJ party-state cultivates impenetrability to external pressures, including those exerted by transnational networks of citizens living in diaspora. Ironically, however, that power structure transgresses territorial boundaries of governance itself, extending its administrative reach and repressive capacities across great distances, reaching into the daily lives of citizens who live thousands of miles from the country itself. At home, the party-state dominates even more intensely the bodies, minds, and everyday realities of its citizens, crippling any form of activity or organization that is not initiated by the PFDJ itself.

As a result, contemporary Eritrea is characterized by a jarring blend of xenophobic localism and cosmopolitan globalism. Pragmatic guerrilla fighters turned political elites have long exploited opportunities presented by war, migration, and the new technological and communicative potentials of globalization to cultivate their administrative and coercive capacities and control much of what enters and exits the country. As they expand across diasporic spaces, the institutions of the party-state move like glaciers, crushing dispersed citizens' efforts to forge or retain autonomous organizations or identities apart from PFDJ control and discouraging their identification with international, "un-Eritrean" organizations or identities. Sustained by webs spun from the sacrifices of its scattered people, the PFDJ now hangs heavy and vigilant in the center, poised to devour the foreign, the external, the disruptive, and the uninvited. This privileging of a state whose existence is predicated on a dislocated society is implicated in how and why Eritrea presents us with so many troubling dilemmas. Along with many Eritreans, I address several pressing yet controversial questions: How is it that the great promise of national liberation and the singular reason for so much sacrifice has become a source of further suffering and limitation for so many? What patterns in the past and present, internal and external to Eritrea, help make sense of how dreams can morph into nightmares? And how do we balance this critical inquiry with careful recognition of the structural constraints imposed on small, poor nation-states like Eritrea within a global hierarchy dominated by neoliberal approaches to political economy and development?

At the core of this dilemma, and of the Eritrean story told here, are two intimately related facets. One is that of violence, betrayal, and loss endured by people who have long played roles in a passionate political drama that most have neither authored nor controlled. From rural farmers and nomadic pastoralists to urban workers and intellectuals, generations of Eritreans have lived amid the precarious distinctions drawn among soldiers, martyrs, traitors, and exiles. These have defined more than social and political positions during times of revolutionary upheaval. They have become ingrained in the very subjectivity of men and women, for whom these roles, and the distinctions drawn between them, are about more than just belonging. They are often matters of life and death. For while the official nationalist imaginary (and the state's security apparatus) distinguishes clearly between soldiers, martyrs, traitors, and exiles, the differences are much less certain in lived reality. Underpinning the ambiguity is the ever-present possibility that one role may rapidly transform into another with dramatic and often irreversible consequences.

The other facet of the story is that of dispersion: refugees and other migrants who left Eritrea during the long war with Ethiopia never to return permanently. Together with those who continue to flee from militarism, political repression, and further war, they comprise a globally differentiated diaspora whose incorporation into the nation-state is ambivalent at best. From colonialism to revolution to the attainment of independence in the early 1990s, the development of Eritrean national-ism necessarily includes the forced migration of approximately one-quarter of its total population and their simultaneous gathering-in again through transnational institutions and relationships. In one respect, this facet of the story emphasizes the sacrifices and commitment of four mil-lion people who achieved the unity of purpose to survive and triumph in their quest for a state over nearly a half-century of upheaval. In another, it highlights the great prices paid for the sake of sovereignty and the ways that Eritreans have inflicted and endured violence and injustice on one another in the quest for *hadde hizbi, hadde libi,* "One People, One Heart." Perhaps more than anything else, the Eritrean case illustrates how territorial nationalism thrives in a de-territorialized world, and how those at the margins—in this case, in exile—remain "a necessary entailment of the state" (Das and Poole 2004:4). And, finally, as the lives and words of Eritrean men and women so powerfully demon-strate, it reveals how political struggle may literally constitute culture and personhood (see Aretxaga 1997, 2003; Donham 1999b), indelibly shaping society and the institutions and individuals that comprise it.

Haunted by Battles: History, Politics, and Culture

Although a full-fledged member of the international community since the national referendum that established independent statehood in 1993, Eritrea remains unfamiliar to many people throughout the world. Thus it seems nearly impossible to write anything about Eritrea's pres-ent, let alone hazard conjectures about its future, without laying out in detail the historic struggle for nationhood that so defines it. The pri-mary narrative that characterizes most accounts of Eritrean history and politics focuses on how the territory became distinguished from the expanding Ethiopian empire-state due to its strategic and desirable loca-tion on the coast of Red Sea. Beginning with Ottoman and Egyptian occupations from the sixteenth to the nineteenth centuries, Eritrea's modern claim to a separate territorial and national identity is based on the successive external powers who sought to achieve or maintain con-trol over the region. This narrative of conquest and occupation contin-ues in a more or less unbroken historical chain, from Italian colonialism (1890–1941) and British Military Administration (BMA; 1941–52) to a tenuous autonomy within the Ethio-Eritrean Federation (1952–61) to ultimately the Ethiopian annexation, which sparked the armed move-ment for liberation. Even sixteen years after independence, anxieties about occupation and external control still drive domestic and foreign policies and patterns of governance. Underpinning this narrative is the emotional weight and collective memory of the tens of thousands of people who died—in nationalist parlance, the "martyrs"—as a result of the struggle. Thus Eritrea truly appears, in the words of historian Richard Reid, "a nation haunted by battle and indeed governed by the dead" (2005:480).

These battles, and the accompanying arguments and evidence that support, reject, and critique Eritrea's claims to a national identity and territory apart from Ethiopia are well documented by scholars and journalists alike. I will not recount them here, nor will I offer a sustained discussion of Eritrea's "official" history, which is also readily available in any number of works.[1] Rather, my intention is to offer, in ethnographically thicker and geographically unbounded terms, aspects of Eritrea's political history that remain largely absent from the existing literature and yet crucial to understanding the country, its ongoing struggles, and its place in the world. As an anthropologist, my goal is also to animate the study of Eritrean politics as a cultural and subjective phenomenon rather than as purely one of institutions and policies (Verdery 1999) by rendering it accessible through the lives and experiences of men and women.[2]

However, two interrelated elements of the well-told tale of the nationalist struggle for independence are important to acknowledge in greater detail at this juncture, because they are foundational to the primary concerns of this book. The first is the early role of Eritreans living outside the territory—in other words, in temporary or permanent exile—in building the nationalist movement and thus forging some of its initial transnational features institutionally and ideologically. The second is what I will call political identity, or the way in which national identity is culturally configured and made subjectively meaningful to people by participation and socialization in organizations and ideological frameworks and through ritualized, structured practices that order everyday life. Many authors have noted the importance and success of the EPLF's mass organizations, or collective associations set up to mobilize different sectors of society during the social revolution that accompanied the independence struggle. However, the EPLF's organizations were not the only ones that mattered. As I argue in the following chapter, they were but one piece (albeit a major one) of a larger, variegated process in which nationalism became configured relative to specific political experiences, perspectives, and institutionalized patterns.

This is because the struggle for independence was not initiated by the EPLF, but rather by the Eritrean Liberation Front (ELF), the original guerrilla front that formed in 1960. The ELF itself was preceded by civil associations of students, workers, and other political activists who began mobilizing in the 1950s. Only in the mid to late 1970s did the EPLF become the dominant fighting force, after which it gradually established exclusive domain over the nationalist movement until independence. Nationalism itself traces its roots to the 1940s, when Eritrea was controlled by the BMA, and for the first (and to date, last) time in its history witnessed the growth of a lively public sphere replete with contending parties, labor unions, and voluntary associations, or what is typically referred to as "civil society." This period was also marked by rising political violence against Eritrean citizens and political leaders, perpetrated by the Ethiopian regime and those who remained loyal to a united Eritrea and Ethiopia. In the latter 1950s, after Eritrea was federated back to Ethiopia by a fateful decision of the United Nations (Negash 1997), this violence provoked widespread unrest, as the general strike of 1958 and the growing activism of urban university students, teachers, and workers so clearly illustrated (see Ammar 1997; Killion 1997). During this same time period, nationalist leaders such as Woldeab Woldemariam and Ibrahim Sultan spent time abroad, where organizations of radical university students and workers began articulating and organizing a pro-independence movement.

In fact, the origins of the civil wings of the nationalist movement for independence themselves lie largely in exile, and particularly with Muslim students and workers. Eritrea, like Ethiopia, is divided roughly equally among Muslims and Christians, and Islam was an important basis for early nationalist mobilization in Eritrea itself as well as in exile. Indeed, the armed ELF formed in the western, Muslim-dominated lowlands, and for much of its life remained unable to shake its image as Arab or Islamist (though, as we will see in the next chapter, this is not an accurate characterization). Prior to the ELF's formation, and nourishing the front's roots, was the activism of Eritrean students attending Al-Azhar University in Cairo, Egypt. After Woldeab Woldemariam's arrival in 1953, the city became a hub for nationalist organizing, and in 1955 the Egyptian government subsidized the Eritrean Students' Club, where leaders of political groups and their followers gathered to discuss the Eritrean situation (Saulsberry 2002:236). Among members of the club were several young men who later helped form the ELF. By 1959, the student activists, now numbering several hundred, were joined by other exiled leaders such as Ibrahim Sultan and Idris Mohamed Adem (Killion 1998:130–31).

However, the first formal pro-independence organization in exile was the Eritrean Liberation Movement (ELM), formed in 1958 in Sudan. Known in Arabic as Harakat Tahrir Eritrea, or in Tigrinya as MaHber Show'ate ("association of seven," for the ELM's tendency to establish secret cells of seven members each), the ELM professed a kind of secular, socialist nationalism similar to that emerging in other Arab nations at the time (see Pratt 2006). Founded by Muslim Eritrean workers in Port Sudan, ELM sought to bridge the increasingly fractious Muslim-Christian divide emerging in Eritrea (Saulsberry 2002:245), precipitated by Ethiopian and other loyalist efforts to foment discord among Eritreans and retard the growth of a common unifying identity. The founders of ELM traveled to Eritrea to organize their cells of seven with the goal of building a popular, secular nationalist movement from the ground up. In September 1960, ELM held its first congress clandestinely in Eritrea's capital city, Asmara, hoping to attract mass support. But already the ELF had begun organizing in the western lowlands, and by 1962 ELM had lost many members to the emergent armed guerrilla movement (see Killion 1998:195–96).

Although most of the ELF's early networks focused on the western lowlands and among Beni 'Amer clans in particular, it also attracted some support from Christian activists in Eritrean towns who communicated with their counterparts in Cairo. Other recruits to the ELF included Eritrean lowlanders who had been serving in the Sudan Defense Force. In 1962, the ELF consisted of twenty-five armed soldiers, one of whom, Hamid Idris Awate, is said to have fired the first shot of the armed struggle. As the ELF developed, its headquarters moved from Cairo to Kassala in Sudan, with further offices in Khartoum. The strategy of leadership in exile became a central feature of the ELF's organizational structure, thus transnationalizing the nationalist movement from its very beginnings.

Nationalist organizing in exile was not limited to Egypt and Sudan. In Ethiopia, Eritrean students became involved in both the nationalist movement and changes taking place in Ethiopia itself. The latter included events fueling the Ethiopian revolution of 1974, which deposed Emperor Haile Sellassie and led to the rise of the Stalinist military regime known as the Derg, under Colonel Mengistu Haile Mariam. Although the Ethiopian revolution aggravated the Eritrean nationalist struggle rather than resolved it, prior to that, Eritrean students participated in the political transformations throughout the entire region and, indeed, globally. In Damascus, Syria, the General Union of Eritrean Students formed in 1968, a pro-independence organization with links to the ELF. By 1970, such groups were forming anywhere Eritreans could be found, often influenced by other struggles and other nationalisms. Similar developments took place in North America and Europe, though these diasporic locations mainly became the province of the EPLF rather than the ELF, as we shall see.

The transnational origins of the Eritrean nationalist movement are thus historically significant, as is the role of the ELF and its civic predecessors in forging the kinds of organizational and institutional practices that have been central to Eritrean political life ever since. However, these elements of the Eritrean story have been largely unaddressed in much of the existing literature, which until very recently, reflected almost exclusively an EPLF, and territorial, perspective. While researchers and observers have commented extensively on the EPLF's capacity to mobilize Eritreans through popular mass organizations as mechanisms for both governance and political socialization, far less attention has been given to how these were always transnational phenomena. Similarly, almost no attention has been paid to how popular participation in the two fronts and its mass organizations resulted in different formulations of political identity. That so many Eritreans experienced nationalism itself through the institutions and ritualized behaviors structured by either ELF or EPLF organizational forms is undeniable and helps to explain the tenacious internal political conflicts among Eritreans today. This subject, and the impact of the civil war waged between the ELF and the EPLF for control over the nationalist movement, is addressed in Chapter 2.

Transnational Governance and Civil Society

The central argument advanced in this book is that Eritrea is a transnational entity and has been so since the inception of the nationalist movement for independence. As a result, the country today exemplifies forms of state power and sociopolitical action that are simultaneously centralizing and diffuse, authoritarian and democratizing, nationalist and internationalist (Hepner 2008). Through the transnational social field—an arena of historically constituted but unevenly developed institutions, organizations, and relationships—the PFDJ (initially the EPLF) has deployed modes of governance that operate extraterritorially in order to consolidate its territorial power and reinforce a particular nationalist orientation. At the same time, citizens have mobilized global networks at the grassroots of Eritrea and exile (though increasingly just the latter) to formulate a public sphere that has been purged from the country itself. Shaped by their simultaneous experiences as Eritreans and as denizens of the North and West, and resonating with rights and freedoms evocative of erstwhile nationalist dreams, contemporary transnational citizens today articulate a distinctive, yet conflicted, vision for Eritrea's development within the global system of nation-states. Interpenetrated by the party-state and its policies, and saddled with painful historical legacies and political grievances related especially to the tension between EPLF and ELF political identities, transnational civil society is a fraught and contentious arena where the center, and the margins, of the nation-state converge. To explore how this pattern came about and evolved over time is to bring many contemporary dilemmas into focus, including the pressing and controversial questions noted earlier. That is, how did a liberation movement replete with the promise and apparent praxis of democracy become an authoritarian, militarized, single-party regime? And how have citizens both enabled and resisted this development?

While the history of transnational political struggle in Eritrea and exile has roots in the 1940s and 1950s, it gathered momentum in the 1970s when Eritrean students and workers in the United States and Europe, and the EPLF in Eritrea, together mapped out a sociopolitical arena defined by ideological relationships and institutional linkages that connected the front and its supporters abroad discursively and materially (Hepner 2005). Following the lead of early ELF organizing in exile, the objective behind this arrangement was to further the goals of the nationalist revolution under the EPLF and, ultimately, secure independence. While these linkages began with the EPLF's mass organizations of students, workers, women, and youth, they later grew to include entities as varied as churches, nongovernmental organizations, extended kin and fictive kin networks, coalitions of "civic societies," political groups, and cyberspatialized communities. These entities have structured the Eritrean transnational social field over the past nearly forty years.

This historically constituted transnational social field was essential to the success of the independence struggle under the EPLF. It has also been a key part of the maintenance and increasing centralization of the PFDJ. Today the transnational social field is the primary arena where the Eritrean state and its partially de-territorialized society struggle to create or repress avenues for sociopolitical belonging and power. In their unequivocal support for an independent Eritrea, and in both their loyalty to the PFDJ party and their opposition to it, Eritreans participating in the transnational social field act as a transnational civil society. But they are a particular kind of civil society, one that has emerged not from the liberal social contract, as in the democratic states of the industrial North and West, but rather from the starkness of colonialism, warfare, political repression, and, more recently, human rights abuses. As the party-state eradicates any autonomous public sphere within Eritrea, resists building institutions not contained within the state apparatus (Bundegaard 2004:46), and erodes older institutions that once mediated citizens' relationship with government (Tronvoll 1998a, 1998b, 1999), longtime and recent exiles seek to fill the vacuum in diaspora, as they anticipate a future beyond the present.[3] Yet others work to expedite the government's hegemony, driven by visceral fears of national disintegration and unable to imagine possible alternatives to the current political configuration. This raises the following questions: If transnationalism has simultaneously been central to the success and power of the EPLF/PFDJ, and to the goal of independence overall, why is it also seen as problematic by both the state and by so many citizens? How and why does the state seek to control its citizens both at home and abroad so effectively, and with what consequences for whom?

From an actor-centered perspective, transnationalism has been broadly defined (in now classic terms) as "processes by which immigrants forge and sustain multi-stranded social relations that link together their societies of origin and settlement" (Basch, Glick-Schiller, and Blanc 1994:7). In this approach, transnationalism evokes the "social field" identified by Max Gluckman (1940; see also Turner 1969) as an uneven layering of contradictory and unequal social relations structured by changing political economies and state frameworks. From an institutional or structural perspective, transnationalism also refers to the practices, strategies, organizations, policies, and institutions by which governments, nongovernmental bodies, and/or corporate entities sustain their interests while shaping the social realities of the people who act within them and are acted upon by them (see Callaghy, Kassimir, and Latham 2002; Levitt and de la Dehesa 2003; Itzigsohn 2000). The institutional and structural aspects of transnationalism are therefore entangled with those of the global political-economic order, and neoliberalism especially. Characteristic of the political-economic policies and assumptions of powerful countries of the global North (or West) who provide development lending, investment, and other incentives to poor countries of the global South, neoliberalism typically entails a loss of control by developing governments over matters of national political-economy, and a "strings-attached" relationship with foreign or international governments and agencies. This gives rise to the phenomenon of "apparent states" (Glick-Schiller and Fouron 2001), or weak nation-states whose control over domestic policy and economy are increasingly hollowed out by foreign interests, NGOs, multilateral agencies, and multinational capital (see also Ferguson 2006; Hansen and Stepputat 2006).

Indeed, becoming such an "apparent state" is one of the fears held by Eritreans of all political persuasions and by the party-state itself. The transnational configuration that characterizes the Eritrean nation-state, and the continuing importance of the diaspora politically and economically, means that Eritrea's own structural composition exposes it to significant "interference" by external agendas, capital, and interests. At the same time, because exiles have long been necessary to—and explicitly claimed by—the EPLF/PFDJ, their particular interests and demands are difficult for the state to both fully control and ignore. Where the EPLF once depended upon exiles' financial support and access to external resources during the independence struggle, the PFDJ now draws an estimated one-third to one-half of the country's gross national product (GNP) from remittances and other kinds of investments such as government bonds or donations, as well as an annual 2 percent tax levied on all Eritrean adults (see Bernal 2004; Fessehatzion 2005). These practices dominated the Eritrean transnational social field until quite recently, when the 1998–2000 Ethiopian-Eritrean border war shifted and fractured the priorities of both party-state and society in ways that will be documented in subsequent chapters.

As important as transnationalism proved to be for the attainment of independence, it has therefore also been an unpredictable, potential liability for the party-state. As the following chapters will detail, exiles have long adopted ideas, identities, and practices that conflicted with the narrower objectives of first the EPLF and later the PFDJ. Similarly, the nationalist struggle is itself historically contested, and this too has had transnational manifestations and consequences. Following the political conflict and intermittent warfare waged between the EPLF and the ELF in the 1970s, the latter was ultimately defeated and driven across the western border into Sudan in 1981. A considerable portion of former fighters and civilian members of the ELF then made their way as internationally recognized refugees to different countries around the world, including the United States. This complicated the transnational social field dominated by the EPLF and its supporters in the 1970s and presented obstacles to the EPLF's nationalist objectives before and after independence. Many ELF-affiliated exiles and others resisted the deterritorialized authority and administrative control of the EPLF, and now the PFDJ, in their communities and lives. And while all exiles remain linked in some ways to Eritrea via the transnational social field mapped out during the nationalist revolution, they have also mobilized other kinds of resources, identities, or agendas to intervene into Eritrean society or to resist the party-state's authority. As Smith and Guarnizo noted (1998:9), the incorporation of transnational subjects into sending states inadvertently "opens up interstitial spaces which create multiple possibilities for novel forms of human agency" and "provide[s] possibilities for resistance as well as accommodation to power 'from above.'"

In recent years, and especially since the border war with Ethiopia from 1998 to 2000, the PFDJ has intensified the militarization of society and tightened its control over citizens abroad to retard the flow of "social remittances" (Levitt 2001), if not financial ones, into Eritrean society. As the PFDJ party purges dissidents from its midst and detains without charge citizens perceived to threaten both national security and sovereignty, disaffections fester within the military, in prisons, in the crushed vestiges of an emergent public sphere, and especially in exile.

Official obsessions with national security and sovereignty feed the ever present threat of war with Ethiopia and heighten anxieties about "foreign" interventions, which are defined mainly in terms of imperialism, cultural pollution, and dependency (see also Reid 2005). Many Eritreans at home and abroad grow restless, fearful, and disillusioned. New flows of refugees leave the country almost daily, undertaking dangerous journeys across seas of sand and water (see Bariagaber 2006; Bundegaard 2004:37; Kibreab 2005, 2006), driven by fantasies of peace and a "good life" abroad (Treiber 2005). Meanwhile, the *warsay*, the inheritors of the EPLF's heroic struggle for freedom, swell the ranks of an army increasingly admonished to recall the sacrifices of the martyrs and the *yike'alo*, their all-powerful fighting forebears. With Ethiopia as "the dark presence squatting on the Eritrean national horizon" (Reid 2005:481), these soldiers may soon become martyrs if another war begins. Thus many pine for exile, as their fears and desires—and those of the party-state—draw them closer to the realm of traitors.

The historic transnational social field has today become a battleground for the definitions and practices of nationalism, state jurisdiction, governance, political economy, and citizenship. It is also a kind of laboratory for the cultural adaptation and deployment of ideas and practices associated with democracy, civil society, and rights with which exiles have engaged abroad and now seek to apply to Eritrea. As they vernacularize ideologies and models of "democratic" governance, rights, and social power that have become dominant—if not uncontested—across the globe (Merry 2006; Paley 2002), many Eritreans both at home and abroad utilize the transnational social field to push the state toward the forms and practices deemed most desirable in the contemporary world (and which often suit particular political agendas, including the neoliberal one). Yet others seek to delay or redefine democratization and to maintain the existing power structure, appealing to Eritrea's nationalist past as the only blueprint for the future. Thus, in both their discursive and practical pursuits, exiles merge imperfectly with one another and with local counterparts to both reproduce the power of the nationalist state and defy it. State and citizenry become ever more entangled, and alienated, in the quest of each to define the other. The wider implications of these processes, and how the Eritrean case provides valuable insight into larger global political-economic trends and their cultural expressions, are taken up in the final chapter of this book.

Chapter 2
A Tale of Two Fronts
Nationalism and Political Identity in the ELF and EPLF

> If the purpose of history is the description of the flux of humanity and of peoples, the first question to be answered, unless all the rest is to remain unintelligible, will be: What is the power that moves nations?
>
> —Leo Tolstoy, *War and Peace*

Asgedom

The first few times I met Asgedom Abraham he seemed like an ageless giant. It was only some time later, as we stood talking face to face one day, that I suddenly realized he was not a very tall man and probably twenty years my senior.

Standing very straight and carrying himself with striking dignity, attired in a houndstooth jacket and slim black turtleneck that lent him a modern, stylish effect, Asgedom seemed to me both youthful and wizened all at once. Like many *habesha* men he wore a small mustache and kept his hair shaved close. His skin was pale and rough. On the days he sported spectacles he bore a resemblance to the great sociologist W. E. B. Du Bois. A passionate energy emanated from him and surrounded him like an aura. Merely sitting in his presence and preparing for the first of what would be a series of three lengthy interviews, I felt myself absorbing his energy and radiating it back. Unlike many Eritreans I coaxed into structured conversation, Asgedom was unreserved. He was articulate and engaged, stimulated by my interest in his country, and eager to speak. As we sat chitchatting in his office, he glanced repeatedly at my tape recorder.

"Are we recording?" he asked.

"No, we haven't started the interview yet." I replied, reaching for the printout of my carefully prepared questions.

"We need to record everything," he said.

I was slightly taken aback. "Oh, absolutely we will. I'm glad you're so comfortable with it."

"I've tried to record things too, you know," he said. "I've tried to keep records of our past. Do you see those notebooks there?"

He motioned to haphazard stacks of papers and spiral-bound composition books on the shelf behind him.

"Those are all pieces of the story. The story of ELF. No one has really written it. We don't even know it. You see, Eritreans don't know our own history, our own story. We all think we know one another better than we do. I've tried to get it down a hundred times. . . ." His voice trailed off.

I contemplated the notebooks, imagining the pieces they contained, pieces of the history of the ELF that Asgedom had tried to record and abandoned. His eagerness to begin the interview suddenly made more sense, and so did the role I would play.

"Well, let's begin then." I pressed the red button and the recorder whirred to life.

Asgedom was not afraid to talk freely. Unlike those who belonged to the EPLF or PFDJ, staying within party lines was not a concern. Rather, as a soldier on the losing side of the ELF-EPLF civil war and a member of the current political opposition (or a "traitor," depending on whom you talked to), Asgedom's only objective was to begin telling what now formed part of the underbelly of nationalist history. His gaze locked onto mine, and I listened carefully, paying close attention to how he constructed his story.

It was a subtle recognition of my own knowledge that Asgedom did not try to begin, as others often did, by justifying the liberation war to me. Nor did he pause to explain the political intricacies of the movement—the tortured birth of the EPLF out of the ELF, and the parricide of sorts that brought him bewildered and nearly broken to the United States almost twenty years ago. Sitting across the table from him, the recorder between us, I felt like the latest notebook inscribed with his memories.

We began at the beginning, in standard life history interview format, with where he was born and raised. But almost immediately he jumped to his political involvement with the ELF as a student at Asmara University in 1973, then called Santa Famiglia for the Catholic missionaries who founded it. The first in all generations of his family to attend college, he soon jettisoned his mother's hopes that he would secure a good job and instead was drawn into the rebel movement. He started out running literature underground for the fighters and soon became a clandestine organizer sent regularly from Asmara to his former high school in an outlying town. Within a year or two he had abandoned the university to join the ELF in the field.

"Once you get involved in politics," he said, "once you get involved in the issue of nationalism, it takes over. There was nothing that could put that in second place for me then, not even my mother's dreams."

I tried to guide him back again, probing for patterns in what drew some people toward perilous politics in the first place—"What work did your father do? Was your mother educated?"—but he resisted. This is what defined his life: political activism, self-sacrifice, being a freedom fighter. Soon I surrendered my interview design and relinquished control. He was going to tell his story, and I could prompt and seek clarification, but I could not direct its flow. Only once did I try again, asking him to jump from his time as a fighter to his arrival in the United States as a refugee. He stopped and looked at me, interrupted. The jump was too great. There was a long story behind his exile that he must develop before it even made sense to address it.

And his was unequivocally exile. Asgedom had joined the ELF three years after the EPLF had formed out of a series of breakaway groups. It was neither by conscious choice nor by design—it was simply the ELF he found first, and which found him. In fact, some of his earliest political memories involved the fragmentation of the armed nationalist movement into two rival fronts. Even as a highland Christian urbanite, Asgedom felt none of the religious sectarianism, regionalism, and Islamic chauvinism that had supposedly haunted the ELF, and to which the formation of the EPLF in 1970 was typically attributed. Instead, what he recalled was the pain of internal nationalist alienations.

"It's a—I can feel it as if it was last year, two years ago, last Saturday—it's so vivid, it's something that when you look back to say what went wrong, you only see how politics is so dirty that you can betray the trust of what the people were looking for in you. And the people! The people tried! In every village, over the entire country, from every corner, people organized themselves into committees for national dialogue, to bring the ELF and EPLF back together again. Our own parents did that. Everywhere you went, they said, 'You should conquer this. You should be together.'"

But Asgedom knew, and his story illustrated at every turn, that the split between the ELF and the EPLF was never conquered. It was a split he felt not only with his compatriots who belonged to the opposing front but also within the ELF itself, within the Eritrean community he came to reside in many years later in the United States, and, ultimately, within himself.

"It was August. It started in August 1980. ELF was finally driven out in 1981."

His voice, which carried a softened edge unusual in most Tigrinya speakers, was punctuated with long pauses I wasn't sure how to interpret. Was he thinking and choosing words carefully? Searching for the right word? Sometimes I felt his emotion spilling over and beckoning my own, and I swallowed hard against it.

He rubbed his eyes hard, and I wondered if the memories were painful, or moving, or overwhelming. But his voice never betrayed him; it didn't crack or waver. He just fell silent for long moments, his chest rising and falling.

"We were in Sudan. I mean, the whole entire organization of ELF went to Sudan. Most of our army disintegrated, by an estimated eighteen to twenty thousand. Some were left behind, some went over to EPLF. But when you are unable to fight as an army, it doesn't matter how many are left behind, you have lost the battle. The leadership has lost the ability to keep the army together to fight. And so we went to Sudan, to the places known as Korokan and Tahaday, and that is when we began this process of soul searching, assessing what went wrong." He was almost whispering now. "We had enough time. I mean, we had a whole year to think it over."

"And so was this when you finally came to the United States?" I asked.

He leaned forward and backward, fidgeted with the cuff of his pants, scratched his knees, crossed and uncrossed his legs.

"Not yet, not yet." His voice began rising again. "We were freedom fighters, you know, but we could not be that as individuals. How were we to continue fitting in as a group? How were we to keep fighting for Eritrea? The whole of ELF was scattered now, fragmented. So we began reorganizing. You know, it's at this time when you are just sitting there, you have nothing else to do, and you start to challenge yourself and challenge the organization, going through every detail, asking who we are and what's our part, how are we—as ELF—going to work together next time? That is our organization, ELF, for now and forever. We all had different ideas about what was best for ELF, we all had different ways of seeing it. Everyone had their own agendas for how to change. That's what's in politics!"

He was almost shouting now. His hand slapped the table, making the tape recorder jump.

"So what did you do?" I asked, riveted.

"Well, there were other reorganizations happening at that time too. I belonged to a group that would later become the one called Saghem. Then there was Abdallah Idris's group, and—well, it gets complicated. We forced the leadership to accept our demands for an organizational congress, a meeting to get together for an assessment. Others warned us not to go there. Abdallah wouldn't accept this, they said. No, we said, we are here and we want this meeting to happen. But Abdallah was one step ahead. He had the security chief killed and then he arrested some top executives and six or seven other cadres. Unfortunately, I was one of them."[1]

"One of the ones arrested?"

"Arrested." The word came out with finality. He paused for long time and rubbed his eyes again. "That was the first—." He sighed and paused again.

"We were never prepared for that," he continued. "For some strange reason it never occurred to us that Abdallah would do that."

"So what happened to you then?"

"Tcchht! Now we were taken to some remote Sudanese prison—who knows where. You wouldn't know where they were taking you. You'd go by night in a Land Cruiser, and for months at a time or a whole entire year maybe they'd just take you from place to place. You wouldn't know if you'd be alive, if you'd survive this. I mean, there's nothing, there's no communication, not from the day you were taken hostage to the day they let you out. No one tells you what they want or what you have done. It's just political—they could kill you at any time. We were lucky! Those of us in this emerging group that would become known as Saghem, you know, Abdallah Idris had a focus, and that focus was to eliminate us."

"When did they let you out? And why?"

"March 1983. Who knows why? The decision can come—we were expecting anything. They can come one day and kill you, or they can say you are free to go. Maybe there was enough pressure that Abdallah was forced to take that step. For whatever reason, who knows what rationale came to his mind, but he let us go. Otherwise—well, at one point, one of us escaped. It was an amazing thing to do. I mean, this place is nowhere, it's no man's land, it's in the desert, it's hot, you try to escape and you die. But he managed to escape. He was later killed in Kassala. But I was let go. My mother came there looking for me."

"Your mother?" I asked, surprised.

"Yeah, my mother!" He smiled for the first time in a long while. His shoulders relaxed, the climactic moment of his imprisonment by his own erstwhile comrades now over.

"She had heard on the Ethiopian radio that there was a crisis in ELF and some people had been arrested. Rumors were out, and some of the names were out too. And so my mother came from Asmara—this unbelievable thing. Imagine! She was about sixty-one. She went from Asmara first to Keren, then went six or seven days on camel and on foot, until she reached Kassala. She was going everyday to Abdallah's deputies, asking them to free me. By then they had brought a Land Rover and were taking us to Kassala. I met her there. And she just cried and cried. She died in 1995." He shook his head and smiled again.

Even after being driven from Eritrea in the civil conflict between the fronts, even following his imprisonment by other factions of the ELF in Sudan, Asgedom's exile did not end there. Rather, it was just beginning.

In 1984 he came to the United States under the Family Reunification Program: his wife's brother, already in the United States, had petitioned for the whole family as they sojourned in Kassala. Asgedom was reluctant to go. He was still holding out hope not only for the reunification of the ELF but also for the whole Eritrean nationalist movement. He was a soldier, after all, even if he was also already an exile and, to some on both sides, a traitor.

Up to this point in our conversation I could see that Asgedom needed to tell this story as a linear progression, to pull through the single thread of his life that he had lost again and again in all those notebooks halffilled with other threads. As if to sort them out, he deliberately recounted the names of each of his comrades who were arrested and imprisoned in Sudan with him. They had gone to Sweden, Ontario, Munich, California, Washington, D.C., perhaps one to Atlanta or to Philadelphia. They may remember the names of all the secret prisons they were taken to by night, he said, the names he can no longer recall. He was extremely cognizant and conscious of his own past, his history and experiences, and yet caught by surprise by it still, full of wonderment and questions about how the pieces fit together and made sense. And along with the pieces of his own life, he wondered how the pieces of other lives and stories fit together and made sense, how they might form a whole out there in the world, a whole known as Eritrea.

But just as Asgedom seemed to achieve a kind of coherence—"I've never told the story this way before," he said, perhaps a bit shyly—we arrived at his decision (if one could call it that) to resettle in the United States. It was here that Asgedom seemed to lose himself again entirely, the year between his release from prison and his migration to the United States still a confounding blur.

"I was released from prison in March 1983. And I came here to the U.S. in May 1984. See, this is where sometimes I have a hard time making sense of it—maybe when you rewind the tape and listen again to the months in between you can see—You know, those of us in Saghem, we were like a small family. We knew each other from Asmara University. We joined ELF together, and then created Saghem together. I mean, there was no conflict or contradiction among us that made me want to leave. But when I was in Sudan—you never think of your other family before, but now I have this other family, my wife and children—maybe there was pressure, people saying, 'What will you do now? This crisis will never be resolved.' 'Asgedom,' they said, 'you should take your family and just go somewhere now.' But coming out of this agonizing experience—maybe your mind is not clear. I mean, I don't know, this all kind of collected at once. Otherwise, I don't think I would have left Sudan."

He was flailing, not with the memories themselves but with the memories of choices he had made.

I reached out with a question. "So, it was your experience in prison maybe—"

"I'm trying to make sense of it because—"

"—that made you vulnerable to the idea of leaving?"

"—because I never would have left them."

"Your ELF comrades?"

"Yeah." His voice dropped low, the starkness of exile told complete.

It was poignant and powerful to observe Asgedom struggling to pull it all together. At times he seemed more lost than I in his labor to understand Eritreanness. Slowly, through the course of our interview I began to see that he was using me as a way to take apart his pain and narrate it into coherence, for himself as an individual, as a member of an organization struggling to build a revolution, as an Eritrean, as an exile, and as a member of a community of exiles.

Reflecting on the telling of this one man's story and the other subtle indicators of his thoughts and feelings, those fleeting asides and gestures, small word choices that revealed barely tangible shades of being and experience, I understood that Asgedom wanted to see this story reflected back to him from me. Maybe this was one way that he sought to achieve perspective.

Later I would see that it was not just Asgedom. Later I would think that maybe all Eritreans, so deeply affected and transformed collectively by war, revolution, exile, and marginality—as a nation and as a community of dispersed communities—themselves were striving to "see" what happened to them, to find the sense and wholeness in the fragmented, yet somehow hopeful history and reality they inhabited so intensely. In telling those stories of themselves and their country ("When you ask an Eritrean about himself, he will only tell you about Eritrea," a man in Detroit said quietly to me as we gazed together at photographs of Eritrean deportees from Ethiopia praying in the desert), they were reaching for its reflection of wholeness, searching for the unity they know must be there. Not just the reflection held up by outsiders but in the mutual recognitions between Eritreans as well.

And as I came to know the politics of the diaspora community better, I also saw another dimension of Asgedom's exile. His commitment to bridging divisions between ELF factions and with the EPLF/PFDJ never ceased. He tried, again and again, through many different avenues, to draw his compatriots together while remaining an independent and critical thinker. And for that he was cursed, spurned, and hated as well as admired, respected, and needed.

At the time I interviewed Asgedom, I did not yet understand the tension between cohesion and fragmentation in the collective Eritrean experience and in the lives of individual men and women. Neither did most Eritreans, although like Asgedom, many were acutely aware of it in their lived experiences. At first glance, and by their own descriptions, Eritreans exuded an uncanny uniformity of identity and purpose, which I once heard described as a kind of "monocular ultra-nationalism." So what was at the heart of this tension I observed in Asgedom and countless others after him? What did he mean by, "We don't know our own story, our own history?" Whose story? Whose history? How many were there? How could Eritreans simultaneously appear to themselves and to others as so unified and yet remain so tormented, so fragmented, in their communities and inner lives? Was this unity merely a hollow, self-told tale, or did it exist somewhere out there in space and time? What historical or structural developments accounted for this? How could I interpret anthropologically the intensely personal experience of the political I observed in Asgedom and so many others?

Divergent Nationalisms and Political Identities

Upon returning home from the first part of a six-hour interview conducted with Asgedom Abraham, a former member of the ELF and a leader in the midwestern diaspora community I was studying, I realized the magnitude of what he had shared with me. Through him, I glimpsed the depths of Eritrean nationalism, political identity, and exile not as abstract phenomena but as lived experiences constitutive of one's very humanity. He had demonstrated to me how, under certain historical conditions, politics might literally constitute personhood and that reified concepts like "nation-states" and "refugees" merely conceal and technify the roiling human drama from whence these categories emerge (see Malkki 1995b; Thieman-Dino and Schechter 2004). On a methodological level, I was also firmly convinced that "the connections between the political restructuring of states and personal and collective subjectivity and agency are accessible to ethnographic methods" (Greenhouse 2002:2). As several scholars have shown, states and political movements are not static entities in neutral space, removed from everyday lives and experiences.[2] Rather, they are "shifting complexes of people and roles" (Herzfeld 1997:5) that actively intersect with—and emerge from—consciousness, culture, social action, and place. In that glimpse into

Asgedom's subjectivity, his personhood, I discovered that which is frequently absent in scholarly discussions of nation-states and political transformations, and yet lies at the very heart of why such abstractions remain compelling to real men and women.

Indeed, it is the primary bond between nationalist and political identity that helps explain the tension between unity and fragmentation in Eritrea and its transnational exile communities both historically and today. One of the key patterns to emerge in my work, dramatically understated in the literature on Eritrea, is that the ELF and EPLF fashioned and inculcated in their members distinctive forms of nationalist identity out of the prevailing sociocultural conditions facing Eritrean society. Through the process of recruitment, political indoctrination, and incorporation into the daily life of the fronts in the areas they liberated and administered, political identity coconstituted, and coevolved with, national identity. But becoming a fighter or civilian member of the ELF or the EPLF did more than shape Eritreanness. For many, the nexus of national and political identification helped constitute personhood itself by dramatically altering the collective social context in which individuals became identity-bearing subjects. This bond between contrasting political and nationalist identities, and the intermittent, violent civil war waged between the ELF and the EPLF from 1972 to 1981, left lasting marks on individual psyches, collective identities, and Eritrean exile communities. Its legacy continues to shape Eritrean society as the transnational project unfolds.

In this chapter I explore the close linkage between political and national identity common to both the ELF and the EPLF. In so doing, I analyze how nationalism was internally diverse, based on the preexisting cultural backgrounds of Eritrean people, and how it became subjectively meaningful for those who were resocialized within organizational or institutional mechanisms. Those mechanisms were aspects of the fronts themselves, including their organizational features, their particular ideologies, and the kinds of structured practices through which they ordered peoples' lives, marked crucial events, and oriented the nation toward the future. More abstractly, I characterize the ELF's nationalism as pluralist and the EPLF's as synthetic (Medina 1997) in their encounters with competing subnational identities such as gender, religion, ethnicity, or region. I addressed in Chapter 1 the formation of the ELF and the role played by exiles in Egypt, Sudan, and other locations. Thus the initial focus is on the ELF's construction of nationalism and the relationship between the front's structure, ideology, and existing Eritrean sociocultural patterns. Next, I analyze the EPLF's emergence as a coalition of splinter groups from the ELF and how it configured its nationalism and political agenda vis-à-vis both the ELF and Eritrean society. In the penultimate section I draw on ethnographic data to probe the origins and depths of nationalism and political identity in the lives of Eritrean people, particularly in terms of the links between kinship, nationalism, and political affiliation. Finally, I address the role of the ELF-EPLF civil war in shaping national and political subjectivities and structuring mass migration, as it was largely ELF affiliates who went into exile in the 1980s and became resettled refugees in the United States and elsewhere.

It is important to grasp these links between nationalism, political identity, and exile prior to turning our attention to Eritrean communities in the United States. Other authors have broached the idea that the ELF and the EPLF related differently to Eritrean society (Pool 2001; Woldemikael 1993) and noted the important connections between nationalist and political identity (Matsuoka and Sorenson 2001:49). None, however, have explored the depth and enduring significance of this bond for Eritrean people and communities and the nation-state. In fact, it has indelibly marked community relations in places such as the United States as well as ongoing transnational debates about national belonging and the meanings ascribed to concepts such as citizenship, democracy, civil society, and rights by Eritreans today.

Nationalism and "The Politics of Exclusion": The Eritrean Liberation Front

Origins and Structure

The origins of the ELF (often referred to as Jebha) among lowland Muslim communities, students, and exiles in Egypt and Sudan, and the early expression of nationalism through Islam all proved decisive in the life, death, and legacy of the front. Despite the fact that little has been written about the continuity between Eritrean Islam and nationalism (Pool 2001:47) and that numerous Christians joined the front after 1968, since its inception the ELF has been viewed in both Eritreanist scholarship and in Ethiopian narratives (especially propaganda of the period) as Islamist in its nature and goals. Indeed, the front's 1962 clash with the ELM was largely over religion: ELM's staunch secularism confronted the Islamism of early ELF leaders who shared links to powerful *tariqas*, or brotherhoods, of the western lowlands like the al-Mirghani Khatmiyya (Killion 1998; Iyob 1995; Pool 2001:48). Moreover, the earliest roots of pro-independence sentiment were among Muslim lowland serfs who rallied to Islamic notions of egalitarianism during the BMA years. These principles remained important to the Cairo-based founders of the ELF in 1960 and shaped the front's development.

The ELF's structure and ideological contours can be traced largely to the three founding individuals that dominated its first executive committee and the social milieus from which they came. Idris Mohammed Adem, Idris Osman Galawdewos, and Osman Saleh Sabbe each took up different posts in the leadership of the front, with Adem as the head and spokesman; Galawdewos directing military operations from Kassala, Sudan; and Sabbe claiming responsibility for foreign relations and fundraising (Pool 2001:49). Beginning in the western Beni 'Amer regions and fanning east toward Keren, the leaders drew upon their own clan-based connections, ethnic and regional solidarities, and connections with religious brotherhoods or *tariqas*, to recruit early fighters and win local support. Abroad, they appealed to Muslim Eritrean students and workers in Sudan, Egypt, Saudi Arabia, and the Gulf States for external material and political support and developed good relations with leaders such as Jamal Abdel Nasser in Egypt, Maummar al-Gaddafi in Libya, and the Ba'athist Party in Syria and Iraq (Iyob 1995:108; Markakis 1987:111). Inspired by the Arab nationalism of Nasser's Egypt and the Algerian revolution, as well as other political trends in the wider Muslim world (Pratt 2006), the early ELF leadership articulated Eritrean liberation largely in terms of Islam. Indeed, these individuals viewed Eritrea as more closely linked to the Arab world than to Africa. However, for many early ELF fighters this emphasis on pan-Arabism and Islam appears to have been mainly an expression of the front's cultural continuity with the communities from which it was emerging, for whom Islam had been a unifying force.

Contrasting Nationalist Grains

Because of the historical continuities among the Orthodox Christian-dominated highland regions of Ethiopia and what is now Eritrea (Levine 1974; Marcus 1994), lowland Muslim communities in Eritrea were variously excluded, marginalized, and feared by the expanding imperial center. Moreover, the lowland regions bore much of the brunt of violence and devastation during the successive colonial periods and especially the Ethio-Eritrean Federation (Murtaza 1998). The deployment of Islam and ethnic or kin-based recruitment strategies in the ELF was thus hardly surprising (Markakis 1987:117). Most early Muslim nationalists made little distinction between highland Christian Eritreans and their Ethiopian counterparts, viewing them as part of a single political and cultural entity. This lack of differentiation between Eritrean and Ethiopian highland Christians in the minds of many early Muslim nationalists highlights the incipience of national identity in the early 1960s despite certain common experiences among Eritreans. This hostility toward highland Christians, as well as the ELF's reproduction of lowland clan, class, and regional segmentation within its organization, has led Iyob (1995) and others (Connell 1997, 2005a; Gebremedhin 1989; Pateman 1998) to characterize the ELF as practicing a "politics of exclusion". (Iyob 1995:108).

A different interpretive tack could suggest that the ELF's orientation was partly a response to the historic politics of exclusion practiced by the Ethiopian imperial state and the Eritrean highland Christian culture linked to it through religion, political economy, language, and kinship. Because lowland Muslim communities were heavily influenced by the Ottoman Turks, Egyptians, and the Sudanese Beja populations to the west, with whom they shared much in common, they experienced the encroaching highland Orthodox Christian empire as a foreign influence in many ways. The analysis of the ELF as inherently exclusionary thus seems embedded within the assumption that lowland Muslims' separatism was self-imposed rather than historically determined. Reframed, however, the linkage between pro-independence nationalism, Islam, and regionally specific ethnic and clan identities actually appears a politics of inclusion from the vantage point of lowland Muslim communities excluded and dominated by highland power structures. Its basis in broader Islamic identities and structures also reveals other early transnational influences at the core of Eritrean nationalism, in this case, pan-Arabism.

As I argue here, drawing largely upon the work of Markakis (1987) and Pool (2001), The ELF's policies and structure initially and cyclically excluded highland Christians because it remained deeply embedded in prenationalist patterns and historical experiences common to the Muslim, lowland regions. It drew upon religious, regional, ethnic, and kin-based solidarities as an early recruitment technique, a pattern that has repeated itself often in diverse societies in Africa and elsewhere. Only later did it find itself reproducing and entrenching politically sectarian identities and power struggles. While these features created intractable problems for the ELF as a nationalist movement and guerrilla army, they also accommodated a more diverse range of identities and political positions within the ELF's construction of nationalism (see Connell 1997:75; Pool 2001:142). The incorporation of large numbers of highland Christians in the late 1960s and early 1970s actually highlights this flexibility, even as many scholars have focused solely on the discrimination and exclusion faced by early Christian recruits and viewed the ELF's expansion into the highlands as largely an attempt to thwart the emergent EPLF.

Today many Eritreans—both Christian and Muslim—retain an emotional connection to the ELF (if not always a political, programmatic one) but have found little in official narratives of nationalism or nationalist history that genuinely values the ELF's contributions to the independence struggle and the nation-state. Rather, the ELF remains woefully underexamined in the scholarly literature except as a negative foil for the EPLF. By attempting to write against this trend, I seek to uncover deeper complexities in the "cultural construction of Eritrean nationalism" (Woldemikael 1993) and contribute to a research agenda that accounts for marginalized histories and identities rather than assumes the vantage point of the dominant perspective.[3] I also do so because rendering the politics of transnationalism and the experience of exile intelligible requires first a careful interrogation of the ELF and EPLF divide.

This is not to obscure or deny the hostility and mistrust faced by early Christian recruits into the ELF, however. Certainly, some Christians suffered as a result of the ELF's own origins and orientation. Nor is my intention to uncritically celebrate the ELF's flexibility and accommodation of subnational loyalties and identities within its nationalist framework, for these competing interests often aggravated existing tensions between Eritreans and weakened both the front and the independence movement as a whole. However, most treatments of the ELF to date emerge from the standpoint of those whose political allegiance resides overtly or tacitly with the EPLF, which has itself defined the parameters of dominant analysis. Contemporary, official nationalist discourse tends to reduce the ELF's complexities and contradictions to simple failures and, ultimately, devalues the role of the ELF in helping construct the nation-state. Yet the legacy of the ELF endures in the hearts and minds of millions of Eritreans and continues to represent an alternative nationalist subject position and political framework for the nation-state. For all of these reasons it deserves serious attention, despite the dearth of reliable sources.

Sectarianism and Fragmentation

The western lowland communities in which the ELF took hold and from whom its first leaders were drawn had a long tradition of patronage based on ethnic and kinship ties within a caste-like class structure. Idris Mohammed Adem, Idris Osman Galawdewos, and Osman Saleh Sabbe drew upon this pattern as a tool of early recruitment and support as well as a source of power for themselves. After establishing cells of fighters in the regions they hailed from, as well as in exile locations such as Sudan, Egypt, Saudi Arabia, Syria (and clandestinely in Addis Ababa and Asmara), they linked these directly to Cairo through their own personalities and ethno-regional or kin relationships. The attachment of fighter cells to the leadership structure in Cairo was informal and flexible, and each leader became a kind of "patron" for the zone of command in his native region. This ethno-regional and kinship-based patronage system worked well initially but later presented problems as the zones became "competing fiefs" with little to unify them in terms of consciousness, strategy, or objectives (Markakis 1987:115; see also Pool 2001:49–50).

Modeling the ELF on the Algerian National Liberation Front (AFLN), the leadership created a four-zone structure corresponding to regions and populations. The first, strongest, and most populous zone was the western lowlands and consisted largely of Beni 'Amer and Nara men who shared a patron-client linkage to Mohammed Idris Adem. The second zone was the northern highland regions, encompassing Keren and part of Sahel Province. The majority of fighters came from the Bilien population and were connected to Idris Osman Galawdewos. The third zone consisted of the central highland regions of Akele Guzai, Seraye, and Hamasien. This zone indicated the ELF's interest in eventually recruiting Christians; however, due to clashes between local Christians and Muslims as well as the political fragmentation of the BMA and Federation periods, the zone remained weak until the late 1960s and early 1970s when the number of Christian recruits increased dramatically. Consisting mostly of fighters from Muslim Saho communities, zone 3 also lacked a patron among the leadership. Finally, zone 4 covered the eastern lowlands of Semhar and Denkel provinces and was dominated by the personality of Osman Saleh Sabbe and local Saho and Afar recruits (see Markakis 1987:113–15).

Zone commanders were appointed by the Cairo leadership from among the local populations and used their own kin and ethno-regional connections to recruit additional fighters and members (Pool 2001:50). Loosely linked to the Revolutionary Command, established in Kassala in 1962, each zone remained largely autonomous; commanders had a great deal of flexibility in designing and implementing military, administrative, and economic activities. The Command's intended role was to administer the zones centrally and then link them back to the leadership in Cairo. However, as each zone competed for more patronage-based privileges from the leadership, including munitions, funds, and supplies, competition between zones soon devolved into power struggles among ethno-regional and clan populations as well as the leadership itself. Individual ELF fighters also became embroiled in local community struggles and took sides with different groups. In the western and southeastern lowlands, some even participated in attacks on Kunama and Afar groups (Markakis 1987:116). The zonal organization therefore entrenched long-standing hostilities among communities who held historic grievances against those from which the fighters were drawn. For example, Christian peasants in Akele Guzai, zone 4, saw the Saho ELF fighters as extensions of their longtime enemies (Pool 2001:51–52). Moreover, the leadership had not developed a firm political ideology to guide the struggle. They espoused a loose nationalism undergirded only by the goal of independence and pan-Arabism.

When disaffected Christian students and workers started favoring independence in the late 1960s and looking to join the armed struggle, the ELF had no formula or structure in place to absorb them. Secret cells existed in Asmara and Addis Ababa, and gradually these began incorporating Christian members who donated funds, distributed nationalist literature, and joined the fighters in the field (Markakis 1987:118). Accordingly, a fifth zone was set up to accommodate the waves of new recruits and became known as "the Christian zone." The strategy of creating a separate Christian zone was partly intended to alleviate tensions among Tigrinya peasants whose clashes with Muslim Saho neighbors had made them recalcitrant toward the ELF fighters of Saho background.

The long history of mistrust between Muslims and Christians engendered by the expansion of the Orthodox Christian imperial center surfaced powerfully in the ELF during the years of initial highland recruitment.[4] In 1967, ELF fighters killed fifty Christian peasants migrating to the western regions to farm on the suspicion that they were spies for Ethiopia, upsetting many Christian recruits. Most of the new recruits came from urban backgrounds and had never lived under conditions of rural hardship or met face to face the kinds of people from whom they now received orders. Older generations of fighters from the rural lowlands also viewed the younger, educated urbanites with suspicion and disdain. Patterns of social distance between Christians and Muslims, such as the mutual taboo on consuming meats prepared by the other, created logistical problems in the field and led to further alienation. Overwhelmed, many early Christian recruits defected from the ELF. Some later took up starring roles in Ethiopian propaganda, as newspapers and radio capitalized on their experiences to underscore the "Islamic separatist" agenda of the ELF rebels.

Beginning in 1966, the ELF began sending both Christian and Muslim recruits to China, Cuba, and Syria for training. As the ranks of the front grew, the composition—if not the structure—of the fighting forces changed. The training in Maoist China had a particularly significant impact on the political consciousness of those who received it, leading to the rise of a dissident or reform movement called Eslah among new recruits. This movement included figures who later became leaders in the EPLF, such as Isayas Afwerki, Ramadan Mohammed Nur, Abraham Tewolde, and Mohammed Ali Omero. Eslah advocated a complete overhaul of the zonal structure and criticized the ethnoregional and kin-based sectarianism in the ELF. It also demanded that the leadership come out of exile where it would not be so divorced from developments on the ground. Most of the reformers happened to be Christian; however, they had numerous allies in other zones that together comprised a diverse ethno-regional and religious cross-section of Eritrean society.

In 1967 Ethiopian forces launched their first assault on the ELF to devastating effect. The poorly integrated zones and absent leadership highlighted the weaknesses of the ELF's structure, although the widespread violence wreaked on local populations also ensured a massive wave of recruits following the offensive (Markakis 1987:121). Thus, beginning in 1969, major efforts were initiated to address the various problems within the front. The conference, known as Adobha, helped alleviate some of the ELF's problems but it did not root out the sectarianism caused by the early patron-clientism between commanders and leaders or the ethnic or kin-based solidarities among fighters in particular areas.

In 1970, the ELF executed three hundred fighters at a training camp in the western lowlands, all Christian recruits from Addis Ababa, on charges that they were spies for the Ethiopian regime. The move highlighted the enduring lack of trust between the two major religious groups and the failure to differentiate between Eritrean highlanders and Ethiopians in the sectarian Muslim view. Christians interpreted the bloody episode as proof that the leadership did not want them in the front and would prefer to sacrifice nationalism for their own interests and power (Markakis 1987:126–27). Numerous fighters—especially the younger, educated radicals, many of whom were Christian—broke with the ELF altogether. Some abandoned the movement completely, while others regrouped in different regions. Among the latter was Isayas Afwerki, later the secretary general of the EPLF and the current president of independent Eritrea.

Other developments in 1970 helped fuel nationalist sentiment and move it further from its lowland, Islamic roots, including some important ELF victories, the imposition of Ethiopian martial law throughout Eritrea, and increasing violence against civilian populations. Indeed, "since the ELF was a front, not a political party, it was open presumably to all groups subscribing to its goal of independence for Eritrea" (Markakis 1987:128). At the same time, however, the pluralism of the front made it difficult to create a unifying nationalist framework even as it provided an "early testing ground for various ideological approaches to building a unified nationalist movement" (Killion 1998:186). This proved decisive for dissident groups seeking to create a different kind of movement altogether, despite numerous attempts to refashion the ELF in structure and ideology.

Despite these difficulties, the ELF fostered a genuine nationalist identity among its fighters and members. While portrayals of the Eritrean liberation struggle tend to focus almost exclusively on the EPLF following its emergence during the 1970–73 period, the ELF continued to recruit fighters from all regions and backgrounds up until its dissolution and exile into Sudan in 1981–82. The front continued to grow in numbers and strength even as it fought against both the EPLF and the Ethiopian regime. While the front's nationalist framework lacked clarity, and its structure was wracked by the internal sectarianisms born of its deep roots in preexisting sociocultural patterns, the men and women who became Eritrean in the context of the ELF remain very cognizant today of the front's role in their consciousness and experience, as I discuss more thoroughly in the latter sections of this chapter.

Pluralist Nationalism

Because it lacked clarity, consistency, and firm institutional mechanisms, the nationalism that the ELF inculcated in its members retained a fluidity and flexibility capable of accommodating multiple identities and backgrounds. In better moments, this flexibility allowed for healthy dissent among members; a range of political currents and ideas; tolerance for loyalties such as ethnicity, religion, and kinship; and the continuing recruitment of new fighters of all backgrounds. At worse moments, continuities between the ELF's nationalism and preexisting social patterns devolved into rigid sectarianisms, narrow power struggles between individuals and collectivities, a lack of coordination and discipline, and military vulnerability.

In her exploration of competing nationalist projects in Belize, in which unity and difference are coconstructed in efforts to define the nation, Laurie Medina (1997) applies the notion of pluralist, synthetic, and hegemonic nationalisms. Each one of these nationalisms participates in the overall construction of Belizean nationhood, respectively embracing ethnic and racial differences, homogenizing them, or identifying the nation with a single dominant population. Pluralist nationalism is characterized by the way such differences are rendered highly visible and also legitimized through their coexistence and persistence within a larger, unifying national identity. The nationalism constructed by the ELF represents such a formulation, in which differences based on religion, region, kinship, and class not only continued to matter but also formed part of the structural logic of the front itself.

Ultimately, the ELF's pluralist nationalism failed due to the front's internal political fragmentation and pressures applied by the EPLF and the Ethiopian regime. At the heart of contemporary critiques leveled at the EPLF and the postindependence regime by former ELF members, however, lies the flexibility of this pluralist nationalism and its ongoing competition with the EPLF's synthetic nationalism (explored later). In the words of one longtime exile and EPLF activist, "The people who were in Jebha [ELF] were more democratic as a result of the demise of ELF. It's because it was more open—you did not have that strict mental discipline, and that's one reason leading to its demise. Because they were more open, more democratic, because the structure was not that rigid, the people from Jebha are more open-minded, in fact." This contrasts with the rigors of both the EPLF and the postindependence government, as I discuss later. It has also borne lasting consequences for contemporary transnational politics.

Nationalism and the Homogenization of Identities: The Eritrean Peoples Liberation Front

Origins and Structure

The Eritrean Peoples Liberation Front, or EPLF, formed from a coalition of two groups that abandoned both the ELF and other competing factions around 1970 to create a new front altogether.[5] Not yet adopting a name for itself, the leaders of this movement—which included Isayas Afwerki and Ramadan Mohammed Nur—penned a highly influential statement titled "Our Struggle and Its Goals" (NeHnan Ela'man).[6] The document, which revealed a sensitive, nuanced perception of the ELF's emergence among lowland Muslim communities, became the basis for the EPLF's ideological and nationalist program. It also anticipated the kinds of critiques and questions that would be leveled at it by the ELF and other competing forces, including the Ethiopian regime.

The authors of "Our Struggle," reportedly Isayas and Ramadan themselves,[7] admitted up front, "It is true that almost all of us or a majority of us are Christians by birth, cultural and historical background."[8] Following a detailed history of Eritrean claims to nationhood and an analysis of the emergence and development of the ELF, the authors stated:

We wish to make it clear that we separated from the fascist administration of "Jebha" and not from fellow freedom fighters. It is a big shame that there should exist religious, ethnic, and other divisions within the Eritrean liberation struggle. As freedom fighters, our role should be to eradicate this and other ills of Eritrean society; and in no way should we create a situation wherein such ills could be accentuated. . . . The nature of our separation might give the impression that we gathered on the basis of religion. But what alternative did we have? In fact, what saddens us is not the fact that we have gathered together and separated, but the harsh causes that forced us to do so, for we uphold the primacy of our country and our people over religion. We are freedom fighters and not preachers of the gospel. What led us to take the stand we have taken is revolutionary conviction and not spiritual preaching. We consider what we have done to be induced by revolutionary courage, honesty, and love of our country. . . . Whether it be amongst our people or within our armed struggle, the opportunist bosses of "Jebha" have, in the pursuit of their selfish interests, found it expedient to promote ethnic and sectarian antagonism and managed to create and sustain numerous divisive factions among the Eritrean people and fighters.[9]

The document went on to list the objectives of the new front. Among them were "to create a society where no economic exploitation or political oppression of man by man exists," and "to establish a National United Front with no distinction as to religion, ethnic affiliation, or sex."[10] Indeed, the founders of what would soon become the EPLF, or Sha'bia, meaning "popular," managed to lay out in this single document a more defined ideological and nationalist framework than the ELF had done in its first decade, in part because its authors had once been part of the ELF. "Our Struggle and Its Goals" rapidly made its way throughout international Eritrean networks and galvanized scores of people either disenchanted with the ELF or not yet converted to the nationalist movement. At the same time, however, it entrenched the image of the ELF as Islamic separatist and politically vacuous and the emergent EPLF as Christian-led and ideologically sophisticated.

Justifying Synthetic Nationalism

The image of the ELF as reactionary, sectarian, and Islamist was actively constructed in the Ethiopian propaganda of the period. But it was also entrenched by the highland Christian background of many of the EPLF's founders and the front's subsequent self-presentation strategies. Since the earliest days of the liberation struggle, Ethiopia cast the Eritrean movement in terms guaranteed to frighten and alienate highland Christians, upon whom its power base depended. Deploying its own hegemonic nationalism (Medina 1997), which constructed Ethiopian national identity in terms of the dominant *kebessa*, or highland history, culture, language, and Orthodox Christian religion, the Ethiopian regime denied the legitimacy of Eritrean nationalism in part by casting the ELF as Muslim, peripheral, dangerous, and Other. Such an approach highlighted and exploited the differences between Eritrean Christians and Muslims by obscuring their common qualities, experiences, and relationships.

Ethiopia capitalized on the negative experiences of early Christian recruits to the ELF and propagated the idea that the front was fighting to create an Islamic state. Referring to the original ELF leadership's ties to Arab governments and movements, Ethiopian discourse framed the nationalist movement as secessionist rather than anticolonial. It also sought to stem the spread of nationalism among highland Christians by denying Italian colonialism as a basis for nationhood and therefore undermining Eritrean claims to uniqueness. After the formation of the EPLF and a massive increase in Christian participation, however, the nationalist movement could no longer sustain even an epithetic description as Islamic. Thereafter, Ethiopian tactics focused on sowing religious and political discord between the two fronts and undermining the basis of nationalist claims by trivializing Eritrea's colonial past and denying Ethiopia's imperial occupation.[11]

Among the EPLF's early tasks was a twofold ideological effort. First, the front countered Ethiopian claims by emphasizing the legacy of Italian colonialism and British occupation. At the same time, it discredited the ELF and its nationalism by highlighting the latter's sectarian tendencies. The EPLF sought to distance itself, and the definition of the nation, from pan-Arabism and Islam and from the actually existing ethnic, regional, and kin-based divisions in both Eritrean society and the ELF. To that end, it situated Eritrea squarely within the African colonial context and drew upon class-based ideologies of Maoism and Marxism-Leninism to justify its approach. Adopting the language of Third World nationalism and pitting its left-wing revolutionary socialism against the Cold War hegemony of the United States, the EPLF presented itself as a secular, African, anticolonial, class-based movement with rural roots that opposed all imperialisms and sectarianisms. Moreover, it sought to transform Eritrean society during the course of struggle into a progressive, egalitarian, and radical democratic environment. It emphasized the ELF's Islamic origins and its ethno-regional and kin-based dimensions in order to bolster its own legitimacy and appeal, even as its propaganda colluded with Ethiopia's to entrench the idea that the ELF represented Muslim interests while the EPLF represented Christian ones. Using the ELF as a foil in nearly every conceivable way, often manipulating Ethiopian propaganda to its own advantage, the EPLF sought to break the association between nationalism and Islam, sever the pro-independence movement's deep roots in lowland sociocultural patterns, and develop a more rigorous ideological and military structure that would support its immediate and long-term objectives.

One of the EPLF's major successes over time was the continuity between its organizational structure and nationalist ideology. The relationship between these features of the front stemmed from its adoption of democratic centralism as the turbine of power and authority, a mass-based organizational strategy that drew fighters and civilians into a pragmatic process of political education and social change, and a strong analytical focus on "nationality" and class as the major cleavages in Eritrean society. However, the emergence of this highly disciplined military front with statelike administrative characteristics (Pool 2001) transpired over nearly a decade, and not without some violence and repression. The rise of the EPLF took place in the context of near constant attacks by Ethiopia and civil war with the ELF. As such, it was both fitful in its development and extremely powerful for those who entered its ranks.

Beginning in 1973, then, the EPLF leadership, with Ramadan Mohammed Nur and Isayas Afwerki at the helm, took major steps to subvert the logic of the ELF's zonal system and thus eradicate the sectarianisms it fostered. In an effort to thwart ethnic and religious tensions before they began, the leadership deliberately refused to adopt either Tigrinya or Arabic as official languages and forbade associations of any kind to form on the basis of ethnicity, region, or religion. It also chose to mix up individual fighters of different backgrounds rather than zoning them according to linguistic, religious, ethno-regional, or kin affiliation as the ELF had done (Pool 2001:75). With democratic centralism at its authoritative core, the front developed strict procedures for ensuring obedience to the political line (with severe punishment for dissidence or recalcitrance) and created extensive programs for political education, literacy, and military training.[12] These early initiatives contrasted with the ELF's more relaxed approach, in which "things seemed to happen more by chance than design, discipline was loose, and the guerrillas within the ELF appeared to have more diversity of outlook than those in the EPLF" (Connell 1997:75).

Also beginning in 1973, however, the EPLF experienced a major internal spasm that solidified its commitment to democratic centralism and revealed a serious intolerance for dissident politics in its ranks. The Menk'a movement, as it was called, involved a relatively small group of fighters, most of them former students in Asmara or at Addis Ababa University, who criticized Isayas Afwerki in particular for centralizing control over the front. They called for both more democratic decision making and the implementation of Marxist-oriented social programs. After lengthy debates and a trial, five of the leaders of Menk'a were executed by the EPLF leadership and the "ultra-leftist" dissident movement was crushed (Killion 1998:309). The EPLF further centralized its control and devised severe punishments for dissidence (Pool 1998:25). Several years later, in 1976, another internal movement known as Yamin, or rightist, also emerged. Little seems to be known about this movement except for its relationship to Tigrinya regionalist highland identities rooted in Akele Guzai and Hamasien provinces. Its members criticized the EPLF leadership for neglecting their own home regions and recruiting for the EPLF in ways that would ensure broad representation (a process that often required targeting particular populations). Like

Menk'a, the Yamin movement was rapidly crushed and its perpetrators executed in 1980.

Through structure, authority, and discipline, the EPLF constructed an institutionalized framework for synthetic nationalism. In addition to intolerance for political dissent, this synthetic nationalism aimed to "create a shared national culture by mixing and combining practices and values associated with constituent ethnic cultures" (Medina 1997:760). After its first congress in 1977, the front's reorganized central committee and political bureau fully represented Eritrea's diverse social, political, educational, religious, and cultural composition. Through implementing rigorous political education training for fighters, mandatory literacy campaigns, and the Maoist practice of criticism and self-criticism, the EPLF leadership propagated its analysis of Eritrean society as cleaved by class and ethnic divisions and justified nationhood on the basis of successive colonialisms, of which Ethiopia was the latest example.

Drawing upon arguments first made in "Our Struggle and Its Goals" and elaborating on them in its 1977 *National Democratic Programme*, the EPLF incorporated into its educational programs a strong focus on Eritrea as a multiethnic nation. The front emphasized that Eritrea's nine different "nationalities," with unique linguistic and cultural attributes to be preserved and celebrated, each possessed a fundamental equality of rights vis-à-vis one another. Religious beliefs should be the private province of individuals and should not have any bearing on politics. Women had to be mobilized and the fetters of traditional patriarchy smashed. And finally, the front argued, secular socialism based on class alliances between workers, peasants, and revolutionary intellectuals would drive the revolution and propel Eritreans into a new kind of society altogether, protected and guaranteed by an independent state under the EPLF's control (EPLF 1977). However, for such a project to succeed, existing subnational differences needed to be synthesized and homogenized to create a new kind of subject who identified first and foremost as Eritrean.

The multiethnic vision of national unity that the EPLF espoused, together with its pragmatic and disciplined ethic, composed what Matsuoka and Sorenson (2001) refer to as the EPLF's "moral economy." This moral economy remained as strong among individuals as it did collectively and expanded well beyond the realm of fighters in the field to include civilians and exiles as well. As Connell (2001:28) wrote, "The notion that each fighter had to model EPLF's politics was embedded in the structure of the organization, which set out to re-mold its members in order to transform the society at large." As heroes and guardians of that new society, fighters provided a role model for all other Eritreans who invested in the cause. The *tegadelti*, or fighters, literally embodied the new nationalist subject and their discipline and actions expressed the "essential" qualities of Eritrean people: humble, courageous, honest, loyal, compassionate, and fiercely self-determined.

At the same time, the necessary submission of all identities beneath the primacy of nationalism became what Pool (2001:89) refers to as a "form of social control, through the provision of a shared vision of the past based on a set of ideological precepts that demonized religion and tribe." This demonization of religion and "tribe" clearly stemmed from the EPLF's efforts to distance itself from the ELF as a movement, and in many ways, from preexisting social patterns themselves. Whereas the ELF remained embedded in the sociocultural patterns from whence it emerged and wanted to defer broad social change until after the struggle was over, the EPLF consciously removed itself from these preexisting patterns and created alternative social relations associated with nationalism itself, made possible through the institutional and ideological mechanisms of the front itself (Pool 2001).

This fact has led Pool (2001) to characterize the EPLF as "autonomous" from Eritrean society and impermeable to its traditional cleavages. I would argue, however, that the EPLF was no more autonomous from Eritrean society than was the ELF. Rather, it merely configured itself differently vis-à-vis that society, seeking to change existing social relations rather than uncritically reproduce them. Its position cannot be understood without constant reference to the kinds of sociocultural and political patterns it sought to alter. One of the most powerful ways in which it tried to accomplish such change was through the breaking of all former identities and allegiances among its recruits and resocializing them as members of the front. It also connected its class and nationality-based analyses to the everyday life of Eritrean civilians under its administration, teaching about exploitation and the possibility of change through local, naturally occurring, context-specific scenarios.

But it would be misleading to argue that the EPLF eradicated distinctions based on class, ethnicity, region, religion, gender, or generation, or that its nationalism remained impervious to them. By remaking selves within the life of the front and carefully synthesizing and homogenizing competing identities into a common nationalism, the EPLF created a new national terrain as well as a particular political identity. But that process, from its inception until the present, has been neither smooth nor complete. Contemporary Eritrean political culture and ongoing transnational debates about power, identity, democracy, and the constitution of society illustrate that nationalism is a continuous struggle, in which pluralist and synthetic models continue to compete for the definition of the nation and control of the state (see Medina 1997; see also Williams 1991).

Expanding Synthetic Nationalism: Organizing the Masses

Broader Eritrean society also participated in and contributed to the EPLF's moral economy, and it is partly in the relationship of the front to the broader population that the synthetic, yet inchoate, quality of the EPLF's nationalism became most evident. The incorporation of women after 1973 and the reconfiguration of gender, family, and sexual/marital relations within EPLF structure and nationalism were also central in this regard (see Bernal 2000; Connell 1997, 2001; Müller 2004; Pool 2001; Silkin 1989; Wilson 1991).

One of the EPLF's greatest avenues for social change proved to be the mass organizations it developed during the late 1970s. While the ELF actually created the first mass organizations of students, workers, and women in the late 1960s and early 1970s, observers have referred to them and to the ELF's social programs largely as "form over substance" (Connell 1997:87). Whether or not this is accurate is difficult to say, given the lack of available information about the ELF's mass organizations versus that of the EPLF, which have been hailed by many researchers as the key to the front's success and popularity during the liberation war. It is important to address here how the EPLF structured and mobilized Eritrean civilians in its mass organizations, as these became key purveyors of nationalist and political identity and the major avenues by which the EPLF created and sustained a transnationalist social field beneath its administrative control.

The push to organize and mobilize the "broad masses" (*Hafash*) locally and in exile occurred at a time when the EPLF was both maturing as a military and political front and also intensely engaged with fighting Ethiopia and the ELF. At the same time, the EPLF was absorbing large numbers of new recruits fleeing Ethiopian occupation and the internal fragmentation of the ELF. After Osman Saleh Sabbe—the master fundraiser for both the ELF and EPLF at different times—absconded in 1975, the EPLF was severed from the funds, supplies, and Arab allies Sabbe had cultivated and thus largely isolated from external support. During this period the leadership devised its hallmark strategy of "self-reliance" as a coping mechanism that incorporated by design (and necessity) the direct participation of Eritrean civilians. Modeled on Maoism and inspired by other nationalist movements in North Africa and the Middle East (see Pratt 2006), the EPLF's self-reliance and mass organizing strategies were closely linked together. Both consisted of fostering strong and positive relations with farmers, workers, women, and youth, as well as with exiles abroad who could help with money and supplies. Self-reliance also included capturing and rehabilitating any and all munitions and equipment from the Ethiopian troops. As Connell observed firsthand (1997:40), EPLF fighters were consummate pragmatists who "did more with less, treating everything that fell into their hands as a potential resource."

Creating and sustaining self-reliance required the coordination and cooperation of vast numbers of people, not all of them members of the fighting forces. By establishing mass organizations among segments of the population, the EPLF sought to utilize the potential of Eritrean civilians while also inculcating them with its particular political and nationalist consciousness. Ideally, under the EPLF's administration, everyday Eritrean men and women would experience the effects of the front's policies and praxis as they implemented them in their daily lives, guided by the fighters themselves. Within the context of the mass organizations, Eritreans would live under the EPLF's statelike administration while the front experimented with governance methods, political ideologies, and development strategies that could best suit diverse local conditions. The mass organizations were also intended to help neutralize the potentially fractious ethnic, regional, religious, and kin identities that had bedeviled early nationalism and the ELF by bringing diverse groups together for the first time. At the same time, they were slated to implement important social changes on the basis of other class, gender, occupational, and generational inequalities. In return for their participation and mobilization, the EPLF promised to provide the population with educational, health, veterinary, and practical services and skills, as well as military protection from the Ethiopian forces.[13] In this they typically succeeded, to an impressive extent.

As important components of the EPLF's statelike capacity, mass organizations were overseen by the front's leadership structure, which included a top-tier political bureau (or Politbureau) and a larger, second-tier central committee. The Politbureau supervised a number of administrative bodies, including committees for military and political affairs and departments of economics, health services, social welfare, and mass administration. The Department of Mass Administration, Kifli Hizbi, was responsible for the development and activity of all EPLF mass organizations, including those in exile. As Pool (2001:85) points out, the mass administration was a crucial instrument in the front's expansion, organization, and control over Eritrean society in the liberated, semiliberated, and occupied areas. Similarly, Connell (1997:5) sees the EPLF's main achievement reflected in these mass organizations, as they enabled "the direct engagement of much of the Eritrean civilian population in the process of social change and nation-building

. . . with broad social equality and popular participation across clan, ethnic, religious, gender, and class lines." He describes in detail how fighters used everyday scenarios, such as disputes over land, interethnic or interreligious hostility, spousal abuse, forced marriage, or health and hygiene problems, to educate people and create targeted projects for mass organizations.

The mass organizations, which grouped women, workers, youth, and peasants into their own "democratically functioning" associations, thus provided an important meeting ground for EPLF fighters and civilians as well as a kind of laboratory in which to test the EPLF's proposed reforms. Mass organizations were vehicles for imparting political education, historical and nationalist consciousness, basic literacy and hygiene skills, and new social and economic arrangements. They were also supposed to be small-scale social experiments in grassroots democracy and empowerment, giving local people an unprecedented chance to debate the structural conditions shaping their lives. Recognizing that categories of people were also internally differentiated on the basis of class and therefore uneven in their revolutionary consciousness, however, the EPLF subdivided the mass organizations and tailored its education and training for each constituency. Thus wealthy peasants were educated somewhat differently from poor ones, to help eradicate "bourgeois" tendencies and to elevate the self and public image of the poor and oppressed. In the case of youth, the front created separate divisions for older adolescents, called the Vanguards, and young children, the Red Flowers. While adolescents learned skills that prepared them to become fighters later, young children performed nationalist songs and dances. Women and children also frequently acted as lookouts or spies for the fighters.

Each mass organization's activities and training differed according to preexisting patterns of social differentiation and offered unique opportunities to participate directly in the revolution itself. As Connell observed, "Political activity became in many respects the national sport, with so many levels and points of entry that nearly everyone could play" (1997:102). Another aspect of setting up mass organizations entailed the breaking of traditional administrative systems that maintained links between Eritrean communities and the Ethiopian state and replacing them with EPLF structures. Land tenure reform proved to be an important method of intervention that simultaneously weakened the Orthodox's Church's power (and thus the linkage to the Ethiopian state) and altered class, kin, and gender privileges (see Tronvoll 1998a, 1998b). Under the EPLF, women and unmarried men could inherit land for the first time. Moreover, allowing representatives to be elected from each mass organization in a given area (workers, peasants, women, and youth) to broader people's assemblies (*baito*) provided another way of challenging traditional "feudal" power structures in which class, gender, age, and kinship determined authority and privilege (Pool 2001:119). While these processes varied across urban and rural locations and in different regional areas, the end result was the EPLF's ascendancy to the primary administrative force with broad support among the general population.

The Locations of National and Political Identity

Among Eritreans today, and especially those in exile, former affiliations with either the EPLF or the ELF endure as a primary basis for identification, shaping both exile communities and transnational exchanges with the Eritrean state and society. Despite the liquidation of the ELF from the field in 1981–82, the achievement of independence in 1991–93, and the emergence of the PFDJ government, political identities embedded in either the ELF or the EPLF powerfully endure in the imaginations and actions of Eritrean people. These identities frequently underpin fragmentation in exile communities, complicating the Eritrean party-state's transnational authority and representing a threat to its power and nationalist hegemony. Former factions of the ELF and newly created coalitions represent a very real opposition to the PFDJ regime and one of the primary forces behind calls for democracy, even as their activities are largely confined to exile locations. Moreover, the opposition continues to draw upon the ideological and cultural differences between the ELF and EPLF in the 1970s to stake their contemporary claims, while the ruling regime manipulates past grievances to reassert its own legitimacy.

But as much as political identities divide them, Eritreans also insist that a broader national unity exists above and beyond these narrower distinctions. Thus while nationalism unites in general, it also divides in particular: differences in political identity frequently indicate differences in ideas about national identity and nation building, internally cleaving people even as it brings them together through common historical experience. But how and why have political identities remained so important to so many Eritreans, even long after independence? Why do Eritreans wrestle so fiercely with one another over these distinctions, and what does it mean for the transnational project? Addressing these issues begins with acknowledging first and foremost that for those who lived through and participated in the struggle, becoming Eritrean took place in the context of becoming—or refusing to become—members of the ELF or the EPLF, revealing "a tendency . . . to merge national identity with political affiliations" (Matsuoka and Sorenson 2001:49).

Here, I lay a foundation for understanding the paroxysms of unity and disunity among Eritreans today by examining the relationship between nationalism, political identity, and other subnational identities. In particular I explore how the breaking and remaking of selves into new national subjects replaced traditional allegiances with loyalty to the ELF or the EPLF. How did the adoption of nationalism through the institutional mechanisms and ideologies of either the ELF or the EPLF alter other ways of knowing oneself and one's compatriots, and with what consequences? What common grounds did nationalism establish in spite of its internal divisions? What compelled people toward either the ELF or the EPLF in the first place? Why does that identification continue to carry so much weight for so many? The answers to these questions help us grasp the depths that politics plumb in the individual and collective lives of Eritrean people. They also point us toward further answers about ongoing clashes within the nation-building project and the centrality of exile as a locus for new ideas and practices of selfhood, citizenship, belonging, and state-civic relationships in transnational contexts.

Birthing the Eritrean Family: The Implications and Uses of Kinship

Throughout this chapter, I have shown how the EPLF's particular synthetic nationalism stemmed from its reaction to both the ELF and the prenationalist patterns, identities, and power relations expressed and entrenched by it. In the rest of the chapter, I further explore the interrelationship between political identity, nationalism, and kinship in particular. While identities such as gender, generation, religion, and region also remain important factors, kinship often mediates these by encompassing them within a larger and emotionally durable social map that nationalism then seeks to mimic, co-opt, or even eclipse. That is, in traditional Eritrean society, membership in a kin group also frequently delineates membership in other identity groups while proscribing important associated roles. Nationalism, for its part, adopts the language and logic of blood-kin connections but reorients them toward the national "family," disrupting the links between kinship and other categorical identities and replacing the former's affective power with its own (see Glick-Schiller and Fouron 1999). In this way, nationalism takes on a seemingly natural, or "primordial," quality for those who embrace it, while obscuring its ideologically based, "invented" nature (Calhoun 1997:33; see also Chatterjee 1986; Gellner 1983; Hobsbawm and Ranger 1983).

One reason why the EPLF was able to successfully reconfigure traditional sociocultural patterns and identities was its administrative, state-like capacity. Perhaps nowhere was this as evident as in the case of gender and sexuality. But changes in gender roles, marriage laws, and sexual relations are first and foremost changes to the family itself and the role of kinship norms in upholding certain traditional patterns. An analysis of the EPLF's approach to gender and marriage thus reveals key elements about the significance of kinship and family to the EPLF's nationalist project as well as the ways in which the front's administrative capacities complemented its ideological objectives.

In addition to mobilizing civilian women in mass organizations and raising consciousness about their specific social issues, both male and female EPLF fighters set powerful examples for female emancipation and potential by demonstrating the social constructedness of gender roles. To begin with, tasks formerly associated with either males or females became the equal responsibility of both, introducing a very radical notion of egalitarianism for traditional-minded villagers. After 1973, the EPLF began incorporating large numbers of women into its ranks and providing specialized training for their participation in all realms of the front. By 1977, fully 30 percent of the EPLF's forces consisted of women in various roles, from barefoot doctors, teachers, and veterinarians to engineers, mechanics, and platoon commanders.

The experience of women in the EPLF has attracted much attention from researchers as they have probed the extent to which the front reconstructed ideas about masculinity and femininity, and the relationship of these to the practical nationalist project (Barth 2001; Bernal 2000; Connell 2001; Hodgin 1997; Mama 1992; Müller 2004; Selassie 1992; Silkin 1989; Wilson 1991). Indeed, gender permeated most aspects of the EPLF's social reforms, enabling women to inherit land or initiate divorce, discouraging child marriage and female genital cutting, and providing women with novel opportunities to control their own lives in a patriarchal society. For female fighters, however, the changes proved even more far reaching. In 1977, the front cast many of these reforms into law, formally banning child betrothal, forced marriage, bride price, and dowry, and regulating sexual and marital relations among fighters. The front's policies attracted numerous young female recruits, who joined the front as fighters to escape the burden of domestic work, unwanted marriage, or other forms of oppression rooted in traditional patterns of gender and family (Tronvoll 1998a).

While the front's policies and praxis targeted traditional ideas about gender and sexuality, it neither drew upon feminism nor critically interrogated essentialist ideas and practices about female nature and roles. The EPLF's ideological orientation certainly recognized gender as a key location for oppression and exploitation, but condemned such oppression only insofar as it hobbled nationalist goals. Articulating its policies squarely in terms of nationalism only, the EPLF did not encourage women to develop emancipatory agendas exclusively on the basis of gender unless it served broader nationalist interests. In part this stemmed from the EPLF's overwhelming pragmatism: for a small society waging war against a much larger and stronger one, the front simply could not afford to exclude half the population. At the same time, such an approach exhibited its own internal contradictions. Bernal (2000) examines how women's incorporation into the EPLF and the front's practices of gender equality entailed the "defeminization" of women, who became physically and emotionally divorced from their former roles as domestic producers and reproducers. This "repression of the domestic" and "erasure of the feminine" throughout the liberation struggle itself, Bernal contends, helps explain the regression of women's gains after liberation.

In these ways, the reconfiguration of gender and marriage undercut traditionally complicit kinship systems by replacing their former structural authority with that of EPLF. Pool (2001:97) cogently notes that "EPLF appropriated the roles which had been associated with fathers and male family members," thereby becoming a kind of paternal figure for Eritrean society. The birth of children to fighter couples, moreover, spawned the phenomenon of entire EPLF families, in which the front became the primary kinship referent as opposed to the traditional lineage. Of course, these changes did not take place without concomitant contradictions. While practices of collective childrearing, for example, cemented the front as a "family" and reoriented kinship patterns in relation to nationalism and the EPLF, it also colluded with traditional devaluations of motherhood and implied that women could not be powerful in such roles. For former women fighters in Eritrea today, a return to civilian life and its domestic demands has been extremely difficult, with much of society—including male ex-fighters—viewing them as insufficiently feminine according to traditional standards (Bernal 2000).

The idiomatic appropriation of kinship or patriarchy in the EPLF is not uncommon for nationalist movements. Nor is it alien to any number of possible imagined communities, as Herzfeld (1997:5) notes: "Perhaps people everywhere use the familiar building blocks of body, family, and kinship in order to make sense of larger entities." The EPLF's usage of family, kinship, and blood metaphors, however, carries additional significance when we recall how traditional kinship patterns were sources of division, fragmentation, and class inequality in prenationalist Eritrean society as well as in the early ELF. Similarly, the extent to which this transformation relied upon the EPLF as an authoritative body indicates that forming national or political allegiances may not take place simply, or even primarily, at a discursive level. The experiential realities of becoming a nationalist were clearly embedded in the structure and praxis of the front, helping establish what I have referred to as the primary bond between national and political identity, wherein nationalism itself was configured in relation to the organizational and ideological features of the fronts that ordered everyday life and oriented the nation in a particular direction.

The role of kinship in the EPLF's synthetic nationalist orientation becomes even more compelling when we examine the indoctrination process among EPLF adherents. In contrast to the early ELF, in which kinship remained a dominant recruitment strategy, especially among Muslim lowlanders, EPLF fighters frequently violated kinship bonds and obligations in their adoption of political identity. That is, individuals did not necessarily join the front because their family members had already done so; many appeared to have joined the EPLF (or the ELF) without regard to the wishes of their families, or in some cases to evade the exigencies of traditional kinship obligations (Tronvoll 1998a). Several observers of the EPLF in the 1970s noted that fighters frequently dropped their surnames, or even their given names, to indicate their primary commitment to the front and nation rather than their families (see, e.g., Connell 1997:70). In addition, fighters frequently found themselves facing off against their brothers, sisters, cousins, or even their own parents, during the years of strife between the ELF and the EPLF. That men and women willingly chose political affiliation over the bonds of kinship once again illustrates the extent to which national and political identity were coconstitutive and helps us make sense of the enduring connections people feel with the ELF or EPLF today. It also helps us see the ways that the EPLF as a statelike entity established an intimate presence in the private lives of citizens.

Patterns of Political Identity

Of course, not all Eritreans belonged to the ELF or the EPLF. Nor did all embrace nationalism and its goal of independence. Some Eritreans continued to identify with Ethiopia, especially those living there throughout the struggle, while others strategically adopted various political allegiances to maximize their chances of survival. Some joined the Ethiopian Derg regime or groups like the Ethiopian Peoples Revolutionary Party (EPRP). Men and women witnessing the violent civil war between the ELF and the EPLF often rejected both fronts as a matter of conscience, although they professed nationalism in general. Aware of the multiple sacrifices involved, still others could not bear to abandon their responsibilities to their families and communities to become fighters, but neither could they endure being drafted into the Ethiopian army or the Derg's national service programs (*zemecha*). Instead, many chose to become refugees. So while the ELF and EPLF may have dominated the Eritrean experience, the broader nationalist project faced further challenges stemming from instability of the region and its own internal contradictions, rendering it always inchoate, uneven, and problematic. The endeavor to complete nationalism's historical task continues today, ever vigilant of the many real and potential ruptures within.

The question of how and why certain individuals chose affiliations with the ELF or the EPLF is both more and less complicated than it appears. Based on our understanding of Eritrean political culture and identity since the 1940s and 1950s, it would not be unreasonable to expect that region, ethnicity, religion, or kinship influenced, or even determined, political identity. But this does not seem to be the case for the majority of people, even if it played a role for some, and certainly formed a pattern in the early ELF. Scholars who have addressed this issue at all have apparently been stumped by it. For example, David Pool notes the important distinction between ELF and EPLF political identities but tarries only briefly in his musings about how and why such identities formed and mattered. He writes in a footnote, "Over the years I have asked scores of Eritreans why they joined the ELF rather than EPLF. The answers provide no evidence for the view that the ELF was Muslim lowland and the EPLF Christian highland. Some gave personal reasons: a friend had contacts with the ELF and they went along with them. Others stated that they saw no significant difference; others that the ELF was the founder liberation movement; others that they had been in ELF secret cells" (Pool 2001:142).

Similarly, my own research revealed the often serendipitous nature of political affiliation. Based on the historical, sociocultural, and ethnographic evidence, it seems that historical contingency played perhaps the greatest role in determining Eritrean political identity. Interviews with men and women who became fighters with the ELF or the EPLF reveal that, more than any other factor, chance structured their decision to join the front. In fact, for many the choice revolved, not around which front to join, but rather whether to join the armed struggle at all, particularly in areas still controlled by the Ethiopian regime. Similarly, most civilians living in areas liberated by the fronts chose to affiliate with whichever one provided protection and administration at the time. Through indoctrination and the conditions of daily life, these populations often formed enduring loyalties to the fronts.

For the men and women who became fighters, several factors played a role in influencing political affiliation. Among these were the particular time period one joined, where one lived, whichever front happened to be closest or made first contact, or which front one's most trusted friends or relatives had joined. Only in the early ELF did religious, ethno-regional, or kin identities appear to predominate, and only in isolated instances did conscious evaluation of political differences between the fronts factor into one's decision. And while some Eritreans insist that people tended to choose the ELF or the EPLF if members of their family had already done so, as much or more evidence exists to show that families were often terribly divided by political affiliation. Later chapters offer further ethnographic evidence illustrating the impact of political identity in the lives of real men and women.

Whatever the reasons for joining the ELF or the EPLF, the origin of one's affiliation diminishes in importance compared to the consequences of it. More than a decade after independence, the nexus between political and national identity remains key to understanding the experiences and aspirations of Eritrean individuals, communities, and the transnational nation-state. One of the main factors contributing to the durability of political identity, however, is the ELF-EPLF civil war and the legacies it has left for Eritrea and exile.

The Eritrean Civil War: ELF versus EPLF

The ELF-EPLF civil war was fought intermittently from 1970 to 1982 and remains one of the most important, albeit least understood, moments in modern Eritrean history. Given the lack of reliable documentary evidence available and the fact that it evokes some of the most painful and difficult memories for those who observed or participated in it, the civil war has received disproportionately little attention compared to its real impact on Eritrean exile communities and the transnational nation-building project. For many former ELF affiliates and fighters who resettled in the United States as refugees, the civil war is the freshest memory of the independence struggle and the main reason they live in exile today. It is also a repository of grievances that continues to feed old grudges and feelings of mistrust, hostility, and betrayal. Contemporary calls for "reconciliation" attest to the continued presence of the civil war in peoples' individual and collective lives, as I discuss more thoroughly in chapters to come.

A War without Beginning or End

Despite the rather well-developed historical record of battles waged by the ELF and EPLF against the Ethiopian forces, much less has been written about those between the two fronts.[14] The details surrounding the civil war's inception and trajectory remain cloaked in rumors and propaganda, leading Pool (2001:71) to comment, "It is nigh impossible to disentangle what actually happened." In general, however, we can trace the origins of the ELF-EPLF civil war to the same time period when the splinter groups that eventually formed the EPLF broke away from the ELF as dissident factions, around 1970 (Killion 1998:138). At that point the ELF reportedly held an informal meeting in which Abdallah Idris and Osman Azaz decided to "liquidate" the emergent opposition (Al-Amin 1992, cited in Pool 2001:70).[15] The actual fighting did not commence until February 1972, however, when ELF units attacked and fought with two of the dissident factions in a sporadic series of battles that continued through 1974, until villagers in the highland town of Zagher intervened in the conflict and urged both sides to seek unity (see Connell 1997:48).

In 1977 further sustained fighting erupted between the fronts, until the Khartoum Agreement was signed between the leaderships in October of that year. However, 1977 also witnessed the alliance between the Soviet Union and the Ethiopian Derg regime and a series of devastating offensives against both the ELF and EPLF. These pressures resulted in the EPLF's 1978 strategic withdrawal from the liberated areas to the northern Sahel region (see Weldemichael 2009), a major decision that dramatically affected the mass movement among Eritreans in the United States, as I will discuss in Chapter 3. One EPLF fighter recalled in an interview with me how they passed through areas controlled by the ELF while retreating from the Ethiopian attacks and were denied respite because of the tension between the two fronts:

They [the ELF] refused to let EPLF bring the wounded and the refugees and the big cannons when Ethiopia came. The EPLF wanted to retain the weapons behind the liberated areas, which were in the desert towards the Sudan, and in the mountains. The EPLF base in the east was in under a big threat from Ethiopia, so they wanted to move everything behind the lines of the ELF. Then the ELF said, "well this is our liberated area so you will not bring them here." And you guys tell us you are Eritreans?! That was the final spark before we kicked them [out] in 1981.

Indeed, the events surrounding the EPLF's strategic withdrawal damaged the possibility for a lasting resolution between the ELF and the EPLF. Both fronts began holding secret negotiations with the Derg regarding an end to the war and the future of Eritrean independence, and in 1980, the ELF's additional negotiations with the Soviet Union created further friction with the EPLF. Similarly, the alliance between the EPLF and the northern Ethiopian Tigrayan Peoples Liberation Front (TPLF), vexed the ELF, not least of all because it affirmed the suspicion of cultural, religious, and ethnic affinity between highland Eritreans and Ethiopians long harbored by many Muslim Eritreans.[16] Amid all this tension, the Derg again launched a ferocious attack on Eritrea in July 1980. The ELF's lines could not withstand the offensive and their forces retreated, leaving the EPLF to shoulder alone yet another barrage later in August. Once again the civil war flared up between the fronts, this time initiated by the EPLF. Working with the TPLF, EPLF forces attacked the ELF in the east, driving them across the highlands and west toward Sudan. Two more peace agreements failed, and the EPLF at last succeeded in defeating the ELF. In September 1981, the last of the ELF fighters, their families, and members of mass organizations fled across the Sudanese border.

In retrospect, it appears that the ELF-EPLF civil war passed through two distinct phases of sustained fighting, from 1972 to 1974, and from 1978 to 1981, with the years in between punctuated by skirmishes and failed attempts at peace and unification (see Killion 1998:138–40). As Iyob notes (1995:120), both fronts had multiple opportunities during the years of the civil war to cooperate, interact, and work toward unification. All of these floundered on the hostility caused by personal rivalries, differences in political identity and nationalist orientation, and competition for control of the struggle as a whole. Within the ELF, moreover, pushes for internal reform continued to threaten the leadership and weaken the organization overall. While its composition was not altogether different from that of the EPLF in terms of religious and ethnoregional distribution by the time of its exile into Sudan (Killion 1998:140), the many competing political currents within it created problems for cohesion and cooperation. As a result, the EPLF firmly gained the upper hand in terms of both the civil war and the nationalist movement itself.

Although segments of the ELF remained active as an opposition movement in the years following exile, the organization continued to suffer violent internal paroxysms. Various factions sought to regroup in Sudan, trying to salvage the front and keep their perspective oriented toward the overall liberation of Eritrea. But the leadership of the ELF largely proved unwilling to relinquish any control despite the virtual implosion of the front. One dissident group, Saghem, favored joining the EPLF and continuing the struggle against Ethiopia. Many of its members reentered the field and joined the former rival front successfully; several of them now serve in high government posts today.[17] Others, however, were captured by either the ELF or EPLF leaderships and imprisoned or executed for dissidence. Still others gave up the struggle altogether and turned their attention toward building lives in Sudan or abroad.

All those who participated in or witnessed the civil war have contended with its caustic legacy. For some, the bitterness of Eritreans fighting one another prevented them from joining the struggle at all and encouraged them to leave the country as refugees. Naizghi was a teenager at the time and would have been a prime recruit for one of the fronts. Although he favored independence and supported the national-ist movement, he chose flight to Sudan over the torturous sacrifices required by the adoption of political identity. In an interview with me he recalled, "In 1979, when EPLF tried to capture Massawa, I was in Geleb with my mom, and my brother and my dad were in Massawa. So at that time, I mean you can see Jebha [ELF] here, and also EPLF, Sha'bia. But I didn't like it, you know, the way the movement was run-ning at the time. The civil war between the two. Especially—see, Geleb is a very small place, and the people were so divided. In a single family, one of them might be Jebha, the other Sha'bia, the father might be EPLF, and the wife might be ELF."

Others, like Tsehainesh, found themselves caught in the center of the maelstrom, leading them to renounce their membership in any political group. As a fighter for the ELF, Tsehainesh followed orders given to her, mostly performing medical tasks. When she became pregnant, the front sent her to care for fighters wounded and dying in the civil war. Her voice becomes barely a whisper as she remembers this time in her life, shortly before she went into exile in Sudan and registered to come to the United States with her husband, also a fighter in the ELF. Her expe-riences continue to color the way she views Eritrean political culture today, using the term *civil war* to reflect current tensions between those with opposing political identities:

I was in the civil war. I was a first-aid nurse, helping whoever was wounded or dying. . . . Before the war, I got married. But then when they [EPLF] pushed us [into Sudan], I was pregnant with my son. The only choice is, you have to go to EPLF or you have to go to Sudan. I couldn't go to EPLF because I was pregnant. And I was not happy also, with the civil war. So I went to Sudan. Today, the politi-cal issues . . . I don't care a lot about what politics is going to be, who is going to be President, I don't care. We pay a lot of people for that freedom. A lot of people died in the civil war. I don't want to see any civil wars again.

And Asgedom Abraham, who reaches back to this moment in particu-lar when seeking the source of fragmentation in his own life and that of the midwestern Eritrean community, recalls even more intensely the way in which he wrestled with exile in Sudan, imprisonment for belonging to the dissident faction Saghem, the power of his identification with the ELF, and his ultimate decision to resettle in the United States. His lin-gering disillusionment more than twenty years later illustrates the legacy of the civil war in the fragmented selves and communities that com-prise—and complicate—the Eritrean transnational state and society today.

This chapter has examined the emergence of the ELF and EPLF and their different relationships as nationalist liberation movements to pre-nationalist identities and patterns. I have shown how each front constructed nationalist forms that related differently to competing identities and sociocultural patterns, and how recruits to the fronts deeply internalized their respective political identities through the institutional and ideological mechanisms of the fronts, thus linking national identity to either ELF or EPLF identity. I have also examined the way in which the ELF-EPLF civil war affected ELF members in particular and shaped the conditions of exile, as so many of those Eritreans who became refugees and ultimately resettled in places like the United States were embroiled in that war.

For the EPLF, the social reforms, organizing strategies, and synthetic nationalism it deployed reconfigured traditional sociocultural patterns in such a way that formerly powerful links between individual and collective identities, such as kinship, ethnicity, region, or religion, were summarily broken and re-created vis-à-vis the front itself. For fighters especially, this process entailed a radical rupture with one's former self and a subsequent rebirth into the EPLF with the front as the primary collective referent. However, while the EPLF succeeded in reconstructing identities and shifting power relations, it did not eradicate the bases for differentiation themselves. As Pool (2001:196) notes, "Whereas the EPLF instilled nationalist sentiments and values in its members, unreconstructed sub-national loyalties lurked in the hearts of broader Eritrean society." The persistence of subnational identities and the incompleteness of the EPLF's nationalist project, as I discuss later, is reflected in Eritrean exile communities and their relationship with the Eritrean state and local society.

But it is the cleavages related to political identity that remain particularly acute in Eritrea and exile. Political identity generally can be theorized as the way in which nationalist identity became subjectively meaningful to people through their participation and socialization in institutions, organizations, and ideologies created by either the ELF or the EPLF, which (re)ordered their daily existence, and helped them envision an independent nation-state. Often subtle in its influences, at other times overt, the enduring relationship between nationalism and political identity continues to shape the way in which Eritreans of the revolutionary generation define the nation-state and the way in which the nation-state under EPLF/PFDJ defines Eritrea and Eritreans. We now turn to the story of Eritreans in exile.

Chapter 3
Transnational *Tegadelti*
Fighters and Exiles in the 1970s

> What a mockery, then, to live in exile when no one sent you there.
> Exile, moreover, from a place that does not exist.
> —Umberto Eco, *Foucault's Pendulum*

Seyoum

It was a rather bumpy ride from Asmara to the small village of Haddish 'Adi, off the main road that snakes a languid descent toward the city of Dekemhare, and beyond that, the smaller town of Segheneiti. The Land Rover lurched and whined against the grinding shift of its gears, each bump sending a puff of dust from the rear of the vehicle where five newly procured bags of wheat were stacked, their flimsy nylon exteriors stamped *USA*. White-shawled women appeared now and again in the distance, slight frames stooped with the weight of wood or babies upon their backs. Some prodded along wiry donkeys, others turned to demurely beg a ride as we flew past. I caught glimpses of brown faces as they approached and receded, a hand holding a bit of shawl over a mouth, eyes narrowed against the dust we churned, the bluish outline of a cross tattooed on a high, shining forehead. I wondered to what unseen village they traveled and for how long they had walked like that, along the edge of what seemed deceptively like nowhere.

I was riding with Seyoum Zerai and an old friend of his, a philosophy professor in the United States, to the former's natal village in the Akele Guzai *kebessa*. The two men hollered to each other and to me above the droning racket in a mix of English and Tigrinya. In the backseat I piled myself against the driver-side door, grounding my body against the motion of the vehicle and competing with the wind to project my voice into Seyoum's good left ear. An innocuously smooth scar etched a wide and shallow valley from his right ear across his cheek, reminding me that he couldn't hear on that side. It remained a grisly memento of his years as a fighter with the EPLF and the wound that could have left him a martyr in the fifth offensive.

I had called Seyoum that morning to request an interview about his experience as a cofounder of the student organization Eritreans for Liberation in North America (EFLNA) in New York City in 1970, three years before he repatriated to become a guerrilla fighter with the emergent EPLF. He was friendly, interested.

"What are you doing *right now?*" he asked. "We're on our way to the countryside. Why don't you come along? Tsehaye can drive and you and I can talk. At least you'll get a nice view along the way."

"I'd love to come," I said, trying to contain my excitement.

"Good. We'll pick you up in thirty minutes. Where do you live?"

Less than one hour later I found myself on a road trip to Seyoum's '*adi*, the village of his birth. He returned there frequently to pay respects at his parents' graves and check on the status of his home, bearing goods to distribute to relatives and friends. This time it was the wheat.

Both men had been activists in the early 1970s with EFLNA, the first nationalist organization created by Eritreans living and studying in the United States. Seyoum was one of the elite few to have returned to Eritrea and join the struggle as a guerrilla fighter with the EPLF. Tsehaye had taken the more typical path, remaining in exile in the United States, building a life and a family and a career there, supporting the EPLF from afar and dreaming of the time he would return to a free Eritrea. That time was now. Tsehaye was overcome with emotion, his eyes shining behind thick glasses.

"All these years and I cannot believe I have not been to my '*adi*," he said.

Tsehaye was what people called *wedi* Asmara, a son of the city, someone who had grown up in that unique cosmopolitan environment, far from the rigors and simplicities of the countryside. But like all Eritreans, his familial roots were lodged in the rural villages and dusty way-station towns. For Tsehaye, the road trip was also a homecoming of sorts.

We flew along the winding roads, asphalt ribbons draped on mountainsides. Seyoum had not yet relinquished the wheel. He drove fast and recklessly, his head bobbing back and forth as he strained to get his good left ear in the conversation and keep an eye on the road. Occasionally we had to swerve suddenly to avoid the oncoming traffic of diesel-puffing buses and slow-moving tractor trailers. Horns tooting and arms waving, it seemed Seyoum and Tsehaye knew personally not only the drivers but also the passengers and hitchhikers as well. Eritrea was like that—an intimate country where everyone in all places and at all times seemed to know everyone else. In its positive manifestations, this created intense feelings of warmth, belonging, and camaraderie. At other times, it made one feel smothered, stifled, surveilled.

"Terhas!" Seyoum shouted to me, over his shoulder. "Do you see what is there below?" he pointed to a craggy cluster of rocks beneath the sharp incline of the road. Visible against the desiccated camel-colored earth were the rusty remains of a Soviet tank. Wildflowers had rooted and bloomed in the metallic skeleton of the exhausted war machine.

"It's a bit like Eritrea, isn't it?" I wanted to shout, but it seemed trite to think, let alone say aloud, and already my companions were hollering about something else—the rebuilding of the train tracks that were initially constructed during the Italian colonial era.

Soon we came upon yet another powerful symbol of reconstruction in this postwar world: a cluster of a dozen or so young men and women on the roadside, none of them probably older than sixteen, clad in brightly colored T-shirts and tatty jeans, printed skirts and headscarves. They each carried a handmade pickaxe or shovel and were busily hacking away at the stony mountainside, widening the area in preparation for improved pavement. Small-scale development and infrastructural projects like these characterized independent Eritrea. The young people paused from their work as we slowed to pass by. Instinctively, I placed my palm flat against the window in a kind of greeting. No one waved back, but broad smiles of surprise greeted what must have seemed an out-of-place face. I recalled my own first experience in Eritrea, stationed in a semirural village to work in one of those summer programs, slinging a pickaxe in the morning and drinking tea with teenagers just like them in the afternoons.

"Do you know the *ma'etot?*" Tsehaye called out. "The summer reconstruction programs?"

"Yes," I shouted back. "I actually worked in one in 1995!"

"It's amazing to me," Tsehaye continued. "The youth give up their summer vacations to rebuild the country! Ha ha!" He laughed with sheer delight.

"Don't be fooled, man!" Seyoum growled. "They complain about it. They don't like to make the sacrifices we did!"

I didn't recall any of the kids complaining in 1995, at least not to me. Rather, I remember being deeply impressed with both their work ethic and their sense of national duty. But things had also changed since then. Compulsory summer work programs and National Service were beginning to lose their luster as more and more young people found their lives dictated by the government's demands for labor and defense as part of its self-reliant development strategy.

I thought back to a conversation I had had just a day or two before with my friend Belay's younger brother. We were sitting on the stoop outside the family's shop in downtown Asmara. The young man, Yemane, was testing out his English on me.

"Why did you interest on Eritrea?" he asked.

"Well," I said. "When I was in university, I was interested in the Caribbean and in Africa. I spent some time in Puerto Rico and Jamaica, and then I really wanted to go to Africa. I was trying to decide what I wanted to do with my life, you know, what kind of career to pursue. So I came here to Eritrea. It was such a great experience I chose to study anthropology. So now I'm here again."

Yemane was listening intently, nodding after every two or three words to show he understood. Then he gazed up at the cloudless sky and said, "I wonder on that. To make choice on your life. Here, they say 'you study this,' and 'now you work here.' Me, I will be a soldier anyway. Maybe the rest of my life." Yemane was matter-of-fact more than wistful. Then he asked, "Military service is required of all people in America?" I shook my head no. Yemane clicked his tongue in acknowledgment and chewed pensively on a stick.

The loud blowing of a horn jarred me from my reverie as we rounded a sharp curve and nearly slammed headlong into a truck. Tsehaye and I gasped in unison. Seyoum cursed and the Land Rover groaned. I decided it was time to broach my questions about EFLNA.

"So, Seyoum, I heard you were one of the original founding members of Enasa in 1970," I said. I used the more familiar name of the organization based on its Tigrinya acronym. "What can you tell me about that time?"

"Eh?" Seyoum replied.

I shouted the question again into his left ear.

"Oh," Seyoum shouted back. "I was actually in ESUNA at the time. That was the Ethiopian Students Union in North America. Eritreans used to belong to that one, up until we created Enasa. I remember being at a meeting when they were discussing the Eritrean question. They used to call it that back then, 'the Eritrean question.' A massacre had just taken place in Keren, all these peasants shot dead by the Ethiopian forces. Some of us wanted ESUNA to release a formal statement condemning the violence. But the leaders of ESUNA refused. That pissed me off. I walked out of the meeting, me and an Oromo guy named Yohannes."

"What was ESUNA's stand?" Tsehaye asked.

"Eh? Their stand? They denied the right of self-determination for nationalities. That's why the Oromo guy walked out with me too. After that, ESUNA split into two groups. The more radical group supported the self-determination issue. These were mostly guys who had just come from Addis Ababa. They were more radical, you know. They knew what was going on. The other group was made up of older guys who had been in the U.S. for awhile. And then there were the Eritreans. We broke away too, and formed Enasa. So if you count that, ESUNA actually split into three. But let me pull over now so Tsehaye can drive and Terhas and I can talk better."

He pulled into a turnout and the two men switched positions. When Tsehaye had finally mastered the gear shift, Seyoum turned his attention to me.

"I was at New York University in the late 1960s and early 1970s. EFLNA was just beginning as a result of this position ESUNA took. We met uptown, in the apartment of a guy named Mustafa Saleh. You know him? He died not long ago. But he was the first chairman of our group. We met in the International House on Claremont Avenue, in Harlem."

"I know it well," I smiled. "I used to live in an apartment building right next door." It was funny now to think of the hundreds of times I had walked by that building going to and from school at Columbia University, with not an inkling of its historical significance in the Eritrean transnational drama.

"Oh, so you know this part. Maybe you don't need me to tell you, then."

"No, no!" I protested. "I'm trying to reconstruct the history of EFLNA. I think it might have been more important to the independence struggle than anyone has realized yet."

"Important? Maybe. But all we had were ideas, you know. Ideas and ideologies, frameworks, plans. That's why I left and came back to the field. I was tired of all that philosophizing. I wanted to be part of the struggle in the field. The revolution was here, in Eritrea. Not in America."

Tsehaye tweaked his mouth into something between a grimace and a grin.

"*Mua!*" he uttered. It was a common expletive, used to indicate anything from intense agreement to frustration.

Seyoum's face grew mischievous.

"That's the trouble with you intellectuals," he added. "It's all form and no content."

"You don't think frameworks and ideas are important for social or political action?" I asked, sounding hopelessly intellectual myself.

"I just think all political or philosophical debates and arguments should be realistic, they should relate to people's lives and experiences, otherwise they are just useless talk. A waste of time and energy. Do you see that there?"

Seyoum pointed to a hamlet nestled in a valley below, camouflaged by the patchy, jagged landscape. It was barely detectable in the distance, save the church steeple and crescent-crowned minaret that jutted toward the heavens like divine sentinels.

"Why do those people build their church or mosque on the hill and their houses below? Look at that flat land over there. Why don't they build there? Because they know what they are doing, that's why. They build on the useless rocky land, and they save the good land for farming. Our people are not stupid. They have experience and live from experience. Progress is made through local knowledge, one step at a time, not from imported ideas."

Tsehaye was nodding, anxious to speak. "But there is no such thing as a single path to progress," he said emphatically. "Progress isn't inevitable or linear. There are always multiple possibilities at any time. This is what philosophy teaches us. . . ." He went on, in professorial mode now. He invoked grand ideas and distinguished names: Nietzsche, Marx, Hegel, Heidegger.

Seyoum craned his head to hear his friend with his uninjured ear.

"Eh? Eh?" he said gruffly. "All this comes from books. But what does it mean to people's lives? I have been in the field for the last thirty years. I have seen the misapplication of these philosophies, most of them based on something out of Western Europe. You can't live by a formula. It's not realistic." A querulous posture now dominated his affect.

"I'm not talking about formulas," Tsehaye argued. "I'm saying you can't insist there is one kind of inherent truth. There can be many different positions which are valid. . . ."

Seyoum dismissed such trifling nuances with a wave of his hand.

"Of course there are certain positions which are better than others! Of course there is a *truth!*" he insisted.

By now I had fallen silent again in the backseat, scrawling illegible notes. Later I would pin down Seyoum for a real interview, as we sat parked in the Land Rover while Tsehaye had coffee with relatives. At that moment I was more interested in their conversation.

The whole encounter was reminding me of the explosive debates in 1978 between the EFLNA activists who helped wage the war of independence from the urban United States, armed largely with their intellect and commitment, and the leadership of the EPLF in the field, who sought to build the revolution using both the local conditions and materials immediately surrounding them, as well as the support of Eritreans all over the world. Later, as Seyoum and the professor continued arguing over a lunch of *zilzil Tibs* at the humble Bana Hotel in Dekemhare, I couldn't help but comment aloud on how their conversation evoked those taking place in the 1970s between EFLNA and the EPLF, between theory and practice, between exile and Eritrea. The table fell silent. Seyoum flashed a kindly grin free of condescension, as if I were his own daughter suddenly waxing curious about her father's life.

"Forgive us," he said simply. "We are children of the 1970s."

I grinned back and mused my silent, serious response: *But this is also independent Eritrea, the Eritrea of the new millennium, when notions of progress (or development, as we call it now) are perhaps even more important than they were back then, when the conversations circulating among Eritreans at home and abroad have grown more intense and urgent.*

Are such debates about theory versus reality, truth versus perception, authenticity versus disingenuity, ever resolved or even resolvable? What else besides the obvious meanings do they indicate? From whence did the contours of this transnational debate emerge, and whither did they go? The road trip with Seyoum and Tsehaye saw only the beginning of my questions.

Coming to America: Ethiopian and Eritrean Students in the United States

As the nationalist movement mounted at home, and the trauma of the ELF-EPLF split and subsequent civil war were beginning to be felt throughout Eritrea, transnational developments were brewing in the urban United States.[1] This chapter draws our attention to the origins of transnational political struggle among Eritreans at home and in the urban United States by documenting the rise and fall of EFLNA, a small but potent organization formed by Eritrean university students and workers in 1970 to aid and participate in the Eritrean revolution.

With the efforts of perhaps only five hundred active members at its height, in less than a decade EFLNA evolved into one of the most powerful Eritrean nationalist organizations in the world aside from the EPLF and the ELF. EFLNA's codevelopment alongside the EPLF in Eritrea helped lay the foundation for the Eritrean transnational social field— that is, a set of practices and relationships designed to further nationalist goals by transnational means—which still conjoins Eritrea and its diasporas into a single, if not unified, entity. EFLNA therefore remains key to understanding many patterns underpinning contemporary North American diaspora life and the strategies of transnational integration and disintegration pursued by the Eritrean state under the PFDJ today.

The following is the first sustained account of this moment in Eritrean history. While Eritreans all over the world know about EFLNA, and many distinguished individuals belonged to it (including current government officials), only minor mentions of the organization dot a handful of sources. This chapter provides an original ethnographic history of EFLNA's mass movement in the United States and its relationship to the EPLF and represents the first comprehensive account of the sociopolitical identities and nationalist activism of the earliest Eritreans in the United States.[2] Through a detailed analysis of EFLNA's development and evolving relationship with EPLF, I show how together the two organizations mapped out a transnational movement that deliberately oriented exiles almost exclusively toward Eritrea, and toward the EPLF's nationalist project in particular. I also argue that the EPLF, consistent with its democratic centralist praxis and synthetic nationalism, came to dominate the transnational social field such that exile organizations like the ELFNA found their autonomy co-opted by the front's institutions, ideologies, and deterritorialized, statelike administrative power. A critical analysis of the relationship between EFLNA and the EPLF is therefore central to interpreting and explaining many contemporary features of Eritrean diaspora communities' internal organization and their relationship to the Eritrean nation-state and PFDJ government today.

After the Immigration Act of 1965 opened the United States to new immigrants from Africa, Asia, Latin America, and the Middle East (see Foner 1987; Portes and Rumbaut 1996), small numbers of young Ethiopians—Eritreans among them—began arriving largely for purposes of higher education (see Balsvik 1985). By 1970, a significant number had amassed in urban centers, and many of them had firsthand experience of the growing violence and repression associated with the failure of the Ethio-Eritrean Federation and the beginning of the Eritrean armed struggle.

Maintaining a strong interest in the political developments at home, most Ethiopian and Eritrean university students in the United States joined the Ethiopian Students Union in North America (ESUNA). The organization, which was founded in the early 1950s by a handful of elite pioneers, provided an early resource for newly arrived Eritreans and Ethiopians and a link to the mounting movements in Addis Ababa and Asmara. It was also a forum for the contestation of Eritrean nationalism, then called "the Eritrean question." Following the lead of the Addis Ababa–based National Union of Ethiopian University Students (NUEUS), which in 1967 passed a resolution condemning the Eritrean movement as "reactionary and sectarian," ESUNA adopted a similar anti-Eritrean position in 1969 (AESNA/AEWNA 1978:189; Balsvik 1985:383).[3]

ESUNA included many Eritrean members (some in executive leadership positions), and factions soon arose around the Eritrean question and other issues associated with class and ethnicity in Ethiopia.[4] The situation came to a head in late December 1970. On December 16 of that year, the Ethiopian army massacred more than one thousand peasants and workers near the Eritrean city of Keren as it attempted to subdue the ELF's "Arab-led insurgency" (Pateman 1998:120). The atrocities committed against the villagers in and around Keren, which included mass executions in churches and mosques, provoked a potent response from the small number of Eritrean students in the United States. When it became clear that ESUNA would not condemn the killings out of a reluctance to indirectly endorse the ELF or the Eritrean nationalist movement in general, Eritrean students all over the country began abandoning the organization. Adhanet Habte, who was one of fewer than a half-dozen Eritrean women studying in the United States in 1970, recalls her reaction—and that of her colleagues—following the massacres at Keren:

I called New York, and I asked them [ESUNA leaders] if we were going to have some kind of demonstration. . . . And they said no. And I said, but this is not a question of Eritrea or Ethiopia, it's a question about—I think it was 1,000 or 2,000 people being massacred. It's the massacre of innocent people, so something has to be done. But nobody wanted to do something in ESUNA. But all of a sudden, someone else by the name of Dawit Belay, who is now in New York, Dawit Belay and his group, Seyoum Zerai, and some other people, they called and said we are going to have a demonstration in New York, in light of this massacre that has taken place in Keren. So we agreed, and I went. All of a sudden, I never had any Eritrean feeling or anything, but the stand that [ESUNA] took, I didn't like it. That really offended me.

Thus EFLNA formed rather haphazardly in the days and weeks following the demonstration, which was held in front of the United Nations building in New York and was the first of its kind to occur in the United States. The EFLNA publication called *Harnet* or *Liberation,* later described the organization's formation as "a manifestation of emotional reaction by Eritreans in the United States to the barbaric massacre of Eritrean peasants and workers in Keren on December 16, 1970. Its formation was in no way the result of an organized and pre-planned effort by any coherent group or individual, as some have claimed, but a spontaneous manifestation of the general outrage of most Eritreans at that time."[5] However, it also reflected the social and political changes taking place in the Horn region as a whole, insofar as groups like ESUNA and EFLNA forged and retained important links to movements at home.

Following the demonstration, Eritrean activists sent a letter to U-Thant, then secretary general of the United Nations. Dated December 20, 1970, and signed "For Eritrean Students Abroad" with the fictitious name Fekri Selam, or "Love Peace," the letter was a petition of complaint about "the inhuman measures taken by the Ethiopian Government declaring a state of emergency and establishing a military administration over our country, Eritrea, on December 16, 1970." The students called for immediate UN intervention and demanded the withdrawal of the Ethiopian army, the release of Eritrean political prisoners, and the full implementation of self-determination on the basis of the UN charter.[6] While neither the letter nor the demonstration provoked much response from the United Nations, it did result in the formation of EFLNA, which over the following decade became perhaps the most powerful Eritrean nationalist organization in the world, aside from the ELF and EPLF. As a former leader of EFLNA's Chicago chapter, now a high-ranking government official in Eritrea, stated, "EFLNA's contribution to the armed struggle was explicitly recognized as one of the most important—or *the* most important mass organization—for the armed struggle, materially, publicity wise, and in the mobilization of Eritreans outside the country. The influence of EFLNA was not limited to North America. It was very influential in the rest of the world, including Western Europe, Australia, and some parts of Africa."

The Early Days: EFLNA, the ELF, and the EPLF

Following the December 1970 demonstration at the United Nations, a core group among the estimated seventy-five Eritreans who had attended it held an impromptu meeting in the late Mustafa Saleh's Harlem apartment to discuss the formation of the organization soon to be known as EFLNA. The attendees, some of whom came from Boston, Philadelphia, and Washington, D.C., decided to write letters to all Eritreans known to be living in the United States to inform them about the new "Eritrean movement" and invite them to the first meeting in New York on February 27, 1971.[7] At first calling themselves Eritrean Youth for Liberation (EYL), the nascent group went ahead and published one issue of a magazine called *The Eritrean.* Both were discontinued shortly thereafter when the group adopted the name Eritreans for Liberation in North America, often simply called "Efilna" for its English acronym, EFLNA, or "Enasa" for the acronym of its Tigrinya name (Ertrawiyen nNatsinet Semien Amerika). The new name reflected the students' desire to embrace the socialist ideals of the nationalist struggle and other anticolonial revolutionary movements to which they were exposed in the United States, including Black nationalist and Palestinian movements. As they increasingly cultivated an antibourgeois ideology and contended with American race and class hierarchies, many students adopted a working-class identity as well. The name Eritreans for Liberation in North America reflected their class consciousness and desire for national inclusiveness.

The first official EFLNA meeting in February 1971 again took place in Mustafa Saleh's apartment at the International House on Claremont Avenue, near 125th Street and Broadway in New York City. Members drew up a "working program" outlining their goals and proposed activities. These included efforts to bring all Eritreans in the United States into the organization, publicize the Eritrean cause as widely as possible, announce EFLNA's formation to Eritreans in other parts of the world, fund-raise for the struggle at home, build alliances with other progressive international movements, and, most important, establish direct contact with the fighters in the field. They set about pursuing these loosely defined goals in the months leading up to their first general congress, held in Washington, D.C., on June 18–20, 1971.[8] Some of EFLNA's founders and active members included those who later went on to occupy positions of power first in EPLF and, after independence, in the Eritrean government.[9]

EFLNA's first congress in Washington, D.C., brought together its nationwide membership for the first time. Discussions centered on the ELF, the nature of the struggle under its leadership, and the internal splits that preceded the formation of the EPLF.[10] Few people understood what was happening inside ELF and were not yet familiar with the emergent EPLF under Isayas Afwerki and Ramadan Mohammed Nur, but there was a sense of urgency about choosing one front or the other to support. Indeed, in later years, EFLNA confessed, "Even though hardly sufficient information was available on these conditions, there was a tremendous urge within the organization to affiliate itself directly with one group or another."[11] Some EFLNA members advocated remaining independent from either front, at least until the situation clarified. Others, among them classmates of Isayas Afwerki's in Asmara or Addis Ababa, felt an immediate connection to the EPLF. Confusion prevailed, and EFLNA nearly split into two camps over the issue. For Andom Berhe, the desire to remain unaffiliated, to watch and wait for awhile, stands out in his mind:

EFLNA had the first meeting, if you can call it that, to say what can we do, what should we do, how should we approach the situation. And then by that time, the EPLF was already a force. So the idea was, okay, we are for Eritrea, but are we going to get involved in this split ELF-EPLF thing? You know, nobody knew the differences with that, except the progressive ideas seemed to be coming from the EPLF side. There were really no messages from ELF, even though the ELF was more organizationally older, stable, it was writing books and all kinds of magazines. . . . At the time, the issue was that we, as Eritreans, have to organize ourselves in support of Eritrean independence, and we will see later how that support will be channeled, or will be structured, to link itself with what was actually happening in Eritrea.

Although EFLNA did make a tentative decision to provisionally support the EPLF, the debate over the split consumed the organization for the first three years of its life. In the meantime, the executive committee, with Tsegai "Dinesh" Tesfatsion acting as chairman, Mustafa Saleh as secretary, and Mogus Fasil as treasurer, sought to communicate with both the ELF and EPLF. "We sent letters, immediately," Adhanet Habte recalls. "Even before that, we started to communicate with both ELF and EPLF. The ELF never answered. But the EPLF, they sent us their goals and objectives, the one called *NeHnan 'Elaman,* 'Our Struggle and Its Goals.' It was translated by Alemseged Tesfai and Haile Menkerios." The response they received from the EPLF and the progressive nature of its statement, which was translated, reprinted, and widely distributed by EFLNA to Eritreans and non-Eritreans alike, captured EFLNA's imagination.

Despite its growing support for the EPLF, EFLNA wanted to understand more of the situation in the field for itself. To that end it sent a delegate to the ELF's 1971 General Congress in a liberated part of Eritrea. A University of California, Los Angeles, student named Berhane Andeberhan was chosen to make the journey, bearing messages and queries from EFLNA. He made it as far as Sudan, where he was detained by local authorities and ultimately returned to the United States. Haile Menkerios was more successful one year later, when he visited the field on a fact-finding mission. But the repeated failures to connect successfully with the ELF reportedly frustrated EFLNA members and pushed them closer to the EPLF.

In March 1973, EFLNA reprinted "Our Struggle and Its Goals" again in *Harnet* and prefaced it with an analysis of the split in the ELF that led to the formation of the EPLF.[12] The framing of the issues reflected the growing naturalization of the EPLF's position among EFLNA members that the class-based, religious, and regional fragmentations within the ELF were problems of the front's structure and ideology, and not necessarily tensions within the Eritrean nation. EFLNA highlighted the religious, regional, and class sectarianisms in ELF as an explanation for the otherwise vague ideological differences between the fronts. It associated the ELF in general and its leadership in particular with Islamic chauvinism, regional and kin-based patrimonialism, and petty-bourgeois class interests. Its ideology was described as "deficient, reactionary, and sectarian," and its ties with Arab countries vexed those who advocated a nationalism divorced from religious identity altogether. The ELF's ties with Arab states also led to charges of "narrow nationalism" and "Arabism." In contrast, EFLNA presented the EPLF much as the EPLF presented itself: as the antithesis of the ELF in its explicit multiculturalism, religious inclusivity, antiregionalism, and mass-based, progressive, democratic, and revolutionary character.

EFLNA's early analysis of the split between the ELF and the EPLF reproduced the discourse of the EPLF, although the organization continued to assert itself as autonomous and objective. But EFLNA had arrived at such a position only after much internal turmoil, partly related to the fact that many Eritreans arriving between 1971 and 1975 had developed strong sympathies with the ELF at home. For despite the EPLF's emergence in 1970–73, the ELF remained the dominant face of the liberation struggle. New arrivals to the United States were much less familiar with the EPLF, hostile toward the split and the ensuing civil war, and resistant to criticisms of the ELF. Gebrehiwet Kahsay, now a government official in Eritrea, remembers feeling offended by EFLNA's obvious goal of converting newly arrived Eritreans to the EPLF position. He recalls, "I was arguing, I was asking them why should EPLF be separated from ELF, why don't they fight inside the organization to change the situation? Even though I agreed there were a lot of things wrong inside ELF, why the split?" Similarly, Tedros Yemane had been a strong supporter of the ELF while at the University of Asmara. When he won a scholarship to Howard University and first met EFLNA activists in Washington, D.C., he became convinced of the EPLF's more progressive line. He notes that had he stayed in Eritrea, however, he may well have remained within the ELF. This dynamic repeated itself again and again as new waves of pro-ELF Eritreans arrived only to experience a conversion of political identity in the United States as they were socialized into the organizational and ideological framework of EFLNA.

In the ensuing years, as the ELF-EPLF split escalated into civil war and propaganda campaigns, EFLNA supported the EPLF but also tried to remain open to the ELF. Moreover, the distance between the EPLF in Eritrea and EFLNA in the United States meant that communication was spotty and months could pass with no word from the field. Tiny pieces of information—such as the successful theft of a few typewriters from a school by EPLF fighters—generated massive excitement. Letters sent by EFLNA to the EPLF frequently went unanswered. Kidane Gebrezghier remembers, "There was no frequency to the contact with EPLF. . . . We would get something from the field, any information, any, *any,* and it used to be a morale boost to the development of the organization. There was always encouragement, and I think the men [*sic*] in the field were getting encouragement from us as much as we were getting it from them. So it was very complementary. It was very genuine."

Then, in 1973, new confusion about EPLF arose. The front's harsh response to the dissident movement Menk'a, discussed in Chapter 2, astonished many EFLNA activists and raised questions about the EPLF's putatively democratic nature (see Iyob 1995:116–17; Killion 1998:309–10; Pool 2001:76–87). The Menk'a members who were later executed by the EPLF had many friends and former classmates within ELFNA, and the incident disillusioned more than a few. As it turned out, the EPLF's intolerance for different political currents would arise again and again throughout the front's lifetime, including after independence (see Pool 2001). Looking back now, some see the EPLF's intolerance for internal differences as a crucially underappreciated distinction between it and the ELF, expressed by this longtime EFLNA activist and EPLF supporter:

I think we lacked a lot of information about the ELF, because we didn't get it directly from the ELF. I think the problem with ELF was much more complex. There were different political currents in the ELF. To a certain extent I think the ELF was more tolerant of those different political currents as compared to EPLF. And that's why you see all those different ideas. But in a military confrontation of that intense situation, you always—all the political currents that were tolerated, they became more of a weakness. . . . [in] a fighting organization you need a military type of discipline, you have to have a command structure that is highly centralized and highly disciplined, and then you become very effective.

This trend toward the propagation of the EPLF's own brand of synthetic nationalism (which viewed the ELF in highly negative terms), its centralizing control and intolerance for dissent, and its deterritorialized administrative power all increased in the years to come. Not only did these trends constrain EFLNA's autonomy and ability to challenge EPLF, but they also laid durable foundations for the structure and character of the developing transnational social field, as well as the single-party regime's current authoritarian characteristics.

Small Axe: The Power and Autonomy of EFLNA, 1971–77

In 1971 the nationalist leaders Woldeab Woldemariam, Osman Saleh Sabbe, and Taha Mohamed Nur journeyed to New York in a delegation to the United Nations, their mission to petition for Eritrea's self-determination. There they met with the small but eager group of EFLNA activists, once again in Mustafa Saleh's apartment. Through intimate discussions with the three major figures, EFLNA gained a clearer understanding of the issues within ELF, the formation of the EPLF, and the way in which their organization could better support the independence movement as a whole.

Woldeab Woldemariam, the "father of Eritrean nationalism," as he is today called, had an important impact on the North American movement in particular. First, he urged the students to remain abroad rather than return to Eritrea to fight. Cognizant of the powerful location exile could be from his own years in Cairo (see Chapter 1), Woldeab told the activists that the revolution would benefit more if EFLNA stayed abroad and maintained autonomy from both the ELF and EPLF. He also gave important advice on EFLNA's structure and encouraged the students to create a full-time executive committee that could run the organization effectively. Tewelde Alem comments on the impact of the visit: "Woldeab and Sabbe in 1971 put a lot of things straight to us. We were very confused about what was happening, you know, what the situation in the field was . . . what the roles of certain individuals were, strange names from far away. And they explained quite a few things to us, and gave us a new perspective. . . . And from then afterwards things started to really begin to be clear, the muddled affairs of Eritrean politics, as it were."

EFLNA held its first elections in 1971 to form the *akayadit shumagalle*, or executive committee. A central office was set up in a small apartment on Manhattan's Upper West Side. By 1974, yearly elections were taking place in which members competed nationwide for executive positions, and some took up recruiting as almost a way of life. Stefanos Danyo, Yemane Gebreab, and several other members were jokingly dubbed "the Seattle Seven" after they acquired a battered Volkswagen and set about visiting universities all over the country where Eritrean students were known to be. In the East Coast cities of New York, Boston, Philadelphia, and Washington, D.C., independent EFLNA chapters also formed. Following the pattern spontaneously established by the first general meeting in June 1971, scheduled annual congresses began drawing members from all over the country to Washington, D.C., once a year, usually at the end of the summer. The annual "D.C. Festival" held every August, one of the largest Eritrean diaspora gatherings in the world, still remains patterned on EFLNA's congresses.

By its third congress in 1973, EFLNA established its *wushtawi andeHeki*, or internal constitution, specifying the structure of the organization. The United States was divided into four zones, and any city with two or more Eritreans could form a chapter, or *tchenfer,* whose leader communicated directly with the executive committee in New York. Elections for the executive committee took place at the annual congress, and officers relocated immediately to New York, laying aside their studies to run the organization full time. Quarterly meetings also convened in each of the four zones, with the most centrally located city as the designated meeting point. Other special events drew people together, such as demonstrations, cultural nights, or other progressive organizations' meetings where EFLNA activists might win non-Eritrean supporters. These included, among others, groups like the Palestinian Liberation Organization, the Black Panther Party, the Angolan National Liberation Movement (MPLA), and later the Central Organization of U.S. Marxists-Leninists.[13]

However, certain issues provoked repeated conflict in the organization's early years. One was the increasing class, gender, and political diversity of Eritreans entering the United States, while another was the worsening conflict between the ELF and the EPLF at home. Newcomers seemed to need constant reeducation to the "anti-bourgeois mentality" as well as conversion from ELF to EPLF political identities. At higher levels of the organization, some chapters nearly came apart due to personal and political conflicts. In December 1972 an emergency meeting of the entire membership was called in New York, and EFLNA stopped in its tracks to reevaluate itself and its goals, echoing the Maoist-inspired EPLF strategy of criticism and self-criticism. EFLNA's findings about the nature of its own organization were later published in the January 1973 issue of *Harnet*. Of particular concern were the different class sensibilities emerging among EFLNA's membership that seemed to impede the evolution of a firm organizational structure and unity of purpose. Some members seemed intent on using EFLNA merely as a social club, while others viewed it as a conduit for joining the armed struggle in Eritrea, or even as the intellectual "nerve center" of EPLF itself. Certain members were also criticized for their alleged efforts to manipulate connections to the struggle in the field for their own advantage, especially a group called *m'ezuzat*, "the obedients," a few individuals who intended to control EFLNA clandestinely by monopolizing inside connections to powerful cadres in Eritrea.[14]

Indeed, EFLNA was all of these things, and the crisis of 1972 witnessed important changes as a result. First, several leading members repatriated to Eritrea to become fighters, Seyoum Zerai among them. Second, significant augmentations to EFLNA's structure, ideology, and activities were instituted. These included the formation of various subcommittees slated for different tasks, such as publicity, which was responsible for creating and disseminating information about the Eritrean cause to non-Eritrean groups in particular; political education, which gathered reading materials from numerous sources, including classics of Marxism, Leninism, and Maoism, as well as writings produced by the ELF and EPLF;[15] and fund-raising, which organized things such as cultural nights and dinners, film screenings, and special public lectures to raise money for the EPLF. This committee also located material items to donate to the EPLF, the most substantial of which were thousands of field jackets for the fighters. In 1975, a fourth permanent education committee was formed, which conducted research on various topics relevant to Eritrea's revolution and the future independent state, as well as translated, published, and/or reprinted books and manuscripts for EPLF fighters and EFLNA members alike. One example of the latter was a booklet titled *Hassan Abdelkhader, Red Flower* [*Hassan Abdelkhader, Qeyih Embaba*], a culturally reworked version of a Chinese Maoist text detailing the dawning of revolutionary consciousness in the life of an everyday Eritrean. Another was a book of indigenous revolutionary songs collected by the New York chapter (*Bahelawi Derfetat'n Sewrawi Mezamurat'n*). Other materials included manuals written by Eritreans educated in the United States on how to design and construct latrines, clinics, and other practical structures.

Indeed, one of EFLNA's greatest legacies has been the amount of printed material it produced, translated, published, and distributed. Using but a single, small printing machine that members procured and learned to use by trial and error, EFLNA produced materials for EPLF fighters in the field as well as Eritreans in Europe, the Middle East, and other parts of northern and eastern Africa. In addition to its regular magazine *Harnet* and its Tigrinya-language political journal *N'QHat*, or *Consciousness*, EFLNA culled, translated, and reprinted selections from EPLF publications such as *Vanguard* [*Fitewerari*] and *Spark* [*MaHta*]. EFLNA authors composed original texts such as *Revolution in Eritrea* (1975), *In Defence of the Eritrean Revolution* (1978),[16] *The Role of Women in the National Democratic Revolution of Eritrea* [*Tera deqenstyo ab hagerawi demokraseyawi sewra Ertra*] (1977), *The Importance of Women's Participation in Revolution* [*Agedas'net tesatfo deqenstyo ab sewra*] (1978), and others. Beginning in 1977 EFLNA also began reprinting all EPLF materials ever published for redistribution in North America and Europe. They obtained copies of all texts used in the field, some of them originally written in Russian, Vietnamese, or Chinese, and reproduced and distributed abroad the Tigrinya translations done by the EPLF. EFLNA members also produced original studies about Eritrea's resources and economic potentials, many of them as doctoral dissertations, and constructed detailed lists of practical skills, training, and interests that EFLNA members could apply to the revolution and future state, which were submitted to the EPLF leadership.[17]

All of these written materials were integral parts of EFLNA's political education dimension, a rigorous program designed to alter historical and class consciousness and shape revolutionary nationalism. The EPLF used similar techniques, although given the high rates of illiteracy in Eritrea, only a select group of cadres—"organic intellectuals," as it were (Gramsci 1971)—received advanced training. They then transmitted their knowledge in ways the rank-and-file fighters and civilians could grasp and put into practice (see Pool 1998, 2001; Connell 1997). Written materials were therefore central to both the EPLF's and EFLNA's organizational strategies and thus important for the consolidation of nationalism through political identification with the front itself. Indeed, as Anderson's (1991) seminal work on the origins and spread of modern nationalism first pointed out, widely distributed written materials are a constitutive feature of real or putative nations. The simultaneous consumption of the same ideas in the lingua franca of a group of people generates a sense of common personhood and shared past among participants. Both the EPLF and EFLNA deployed this technique extensively within their ranks and via the transnational social field evolving between them. They often relied on each other for a steady stream of political writings and readings. Just as for the fighters in the field, political education sessions occupied a pivotal place in EFLNA's regular activities and its ideological connection with the EPLF.

In 1975 the link between EFLNA and EPLF strengthened considerably. The closer relationship developed partly due to increased visits by EFLNA delegates to the field, as well as Osman Saleh Sabbe's departure from the EPLF and alleged looting of the front's financial resources. At that point the EPLF made strong overtures to EFLNA, asking for financial assistance in particular. Already many EFLNA activists had quit school in order to work several jobs to raise money for EPLF. Often living eight or ten to a single apartment, members dedicated all of their time and the majority of their resources to support the struggle at home.

For the "workers" in EFLNA, earning money as members of the urban proletariat provided prestige and a competitive edge over the "bourgeois intellectuals" who concentrated on political philosophies and education. As EFLNA adopted more and more rigorous antibourgeois positions, it demanded that its members shed privilege from their lives and consciousness. On average, EFLNA raised more than two hundred thousand dollars per year and sent it directly to the EPLF.[18] With an active membership of perhaps five hundred people at its height, this averaged about four thousand dollars per person per year, raised exclusively for EPLF.

Within EFLNA, however, the pressures on individuals from different backgrounds intensified. EPLF's financial needs and growing anti-intellectualism shifted prestige onto workers. While students continued to produce literature and shoulder political education tasks, the revolutionary philosophies they learned and taught, which lionized the rural peasantry and working classes, contradicted their own position as elite intellectuals. As the structural and ideological bond with the EPLF intensified from 1975 to 1977, intense pressures within the organization mounted. Although EFLNA was not a formal mass organization of the EPLF, an emergent submissiveness to the front created tensions among different sectors of EFLNA. Many members clearly valued and guarded EFLNA's autonomy, fearing they would lose control of their own activities and their ability to question the EPLF leadership if they became too entangled with the front. Others, however, believed that joining the EPLF would enhance their participation in the revolution.

The advantages of autonomy were clear to many EFLNA activists. Remaining close but apart from the EPLF gave EFLNA the chance to debate and disagree with the front's leadership in a way that no other organization has since been able to do as effectively. Although there is a tendency today to view EFLNA as a handmaiden of the EPLF, for most of its life it retained an independent spirit and identity. Within its ranks flowed different political currents, class identities, gendered experiences, and ideas about how to define the nation and build toward a future state. In letters exchanged between the EFLNA and EPLF leaderships, usually via the front's offices in Khartoum and Aden, and later Rome, EFLNA often asked the EPLF to account for certain political positions it published in the pages of *Vanguard* or *Spark*, or to further clarify tactical strategies it adopted.[19] EFLNA did not blindly accept all that the EPLF did and said. As Tsegai Woldu remembers, "[EFLNA] hoped it would be the source of intellectual support for EPLF, and it had a lot of international support [too]. . . . Because of this EPLF looked to EFLNA as almost part of the leadership, a kind of partner. And this created the idea that we were equal to, if not better than, the EPLF."

However, the anti-intellectual current in EFLNA and internal pressures to reproduce EPLF's mass-based strategy and consciousness encouraged a backlash against EFLNA's origins among elite university students. The deployment of the EPLF's class analysis within EFLNA heightened anxieties and competitive tensions between activists, some of whom argued that class backgrounds determined revolutionary consciousness. Finally, disagreements arose regarding some members' engagement of internationalist philosophies and broader race and gender consciousness versus those who cultivated a narrower, nativist focus on the EPLF's synthesizing and homogenizing nationalism. As a result, the philosophical, heady aspects of EFLNA's relationship with EPLF and its ability to challenge the front's leadership and strategy began eroding. Internal pressures to conform to the EPLF's ideology and to live as much as possible like the fighters in the field intensified. As one member put it, "For those who didn't go to college, the most crucial thing was to work and collect all the money you have and send it to the field, but not to raise any kind of critical issues or question EPLF. . . . Your contribution, your participation, became evaluated through the money you donated, not through your critical thinking." Another member recalls how the adoption of EPLF's class analysis and nationalist orientation shaped EFLNA's internal relations and activities in the late 1970s: "And then the intelligentsia, the intellectuals as such, did not even come to the meetings, with the exception of a very few. Because we used to call them 'bourgeois nationalists' and all that shit. . . . So they didn't even come to the meetings at that time. So whoever was a member of *Enasa* [EFLNA] was by my definition a proletarian, you know, a worker, the masses. But there were also a few intellectuals, and their contribution was excellent."

The erosion of EFLNA's intellectual vitality corresponded to its enhanced role as a financial and ideological support system for the EPLF. It also coincided with the EPLF's increasing emphasis on self-reliance. As a necessary and pragmatic policy adopted to cope with the front's isolation, self-reliance included harnessing the resources of the national "selves" abroad. Indeed, Article 9 of the EPLF's 1977 *National Democratic Programme* stated the front's intention to "organize Eritreans residing abroad in the already formed mass organizations so they can participate in the patriotic anti-colonial struggle" (see also Compton 1998).[20] This participation, however, was predicated upon total compliance and obedience to the EPLF.

As EFLNA became more integral to the EPLF's strategy, conformist pressures mounted. Active members worked harder to prove their loyalty to the EPLF and to one another and demanded the same sacrifices of others irrespective of their individual experiences and goals. As a result of these pressures, existing differences among members' subjectivities once again became fault lines in the organization. Instead of addressing them openly, however, EFLNA glossed over these conflicts as relatively insignificant given the urgency of nationalist goals. Some Eritreans therefore experienced the EPLF's nationalism and EFLNA's adoption of it as stifling and limiting. For example, those who did not really want to participate in the movement felt they had no choice lest they get branded traitors, while women found that all gender issues, including inequities within EFLNA, simply could not be addressed beyond the focus on national liberation. One reluctant recruit, thinking he had left "politics" behind in Eritrea, recalls his shock at discovering its greater importance in the United States:

In your mind you say, "everything's behind me now . . . politics is behind me. That's all I need to do now, is think for myself, that's all I want to be, that's what my parents wished for me to be." So when I came here, my uncle said we have to go to a meeting on Sunday. I said, "What meeting?" He said, "The Eritrean meeting." I said, "Excuse me? I'm not going! I didn't come here for politics!" He said, "You cannot even say that! You are going to be really, really expelled from the society! Eritrea depends on us, and if you don't go to the meeting you are signing your life away from the society." I said, "What do you mean? Don't tell me that. I'm not going to any meetings of any politics." He said, "You better think about it, because you are going." I said, "Well, what am I going to do? I am here, I am Eritrean, but I know nothing. Okay let me go." So we go over there, and as I said, I never understood politics! They talk about politics, and it's in my language . . . [but] believe it or not, more than half of it I would not understand, the terms they use, the political slogans, those kind of things. There is a thing about criticism and self-criticism. Every time, my name and [my friend's] name comes up, because we don't answer, we don't participate. I was even suspended at one point. . . . Well, it was a good experience, but hell for us.

Some EFLNA women also felt frustrated by the perceived contradictions between the revolutionary ideal of women's liberation and the practices of EFLNA itself. While the organization did break the linkage between gender and certain role-related behaviors, encouraging men to take up domestic tasks and women to debate politics, power dynamics between men and women did not fundamentally change. Women's study groups within EFLNA emphasized the same political education as the rest of the organization and did not engage many broader feminist ideas, although EFLNA as a whole purportedly advocated women's emancipation. And while men took up cooking and cleaning when it came their turn to provide for the rest of the group, former female EFLNA activists noted that over time, even these duties devolved back to women.

Similarly, as EFLNA members married and started families, women's political participation became more difficult as their domestic burdens increased. In addition to minding children, women were also expected to help plan and manage events, cutting down on their ability to substantively participate in them. Moreover, women were largely excluded from positions of power in the organization. Throughout EFLNA's nine-year history, only one woman ever served on the executive committee. Commenting on male dominance generally, she noted, "Eritrean women, they entirely accept whatever men tell them to do. And let me assure you, men, regardless of their sensitivity to the gender issue, that male chauvinism, when it comes to the practical daily life, remains with them. And they enjoy that. It really affected us, even in the armed struggle."

EFLNA women also found it difficult to maintain control over their own activities and were discouraged by the male leadership from addressing gender oppression or patriarchy unless in the context of national liberation. As a result, Eritrean women made few, if any, practical or ideological connections with American feminist movements. As noted in Chapter 2, feminism had little or nothing to do with the EPLF's rhetoric of emancipation within nationalism, whose class-based logic purported to eliminate other forms of social inequality, including gender oppression (Bernal 2000). EFLNA adopted the same perspective, but raising gender consciousness in the organization proved difficult, in part because of class differences between women. One female member recalls how less-educated women resisted serious political discussion and rejected potentially useful aspects of Western analysis, partly due to the fact that Eritreans were an isolated, nationalist community increasingly hostile toward "bourgeois intellectualism": "The biggest problem that we had, we couldn't associate—you know, we didn't go deep into the culture of American society. It's very hard, you know. We didn't have the chance to really go into the culture of American society. . . . Most of our women, they didn't go to school. They came there from high school, and when they came there from high school they ended up working as waitresses, or cashiers, or things like that. So they only communicate within their own circuit, within the Eritrean circuit." Thus, it was within EFLNA that the inability of nationalism to adequately address women's oppression emerged more clearly and earlier than it did in Eritrea itself.

Yet, in spite of these contradictions, those who literally lived within EFLNA experienced the organization as an ethos and way of life as much as a political movement. In this way, it reflected and reproduced the EPLF's own synthetic nationalism and moral economy (Matsuoka and Sorenson 2001), which required the submission of all other interests, ambitions, and identities to that of nationalism. These experiences of surrender and selflessness, and the attainment of a kind of "communitas" (Turner 1969), are what predominate in so many former activists' memories of the EFLNA days. This is part of the process by which political identification with the EPLF and its associated organizations like EFLNA made nationalism subjectively meaningful to people's sense of both personal and collective identity, how it structured their daily lives, and oriented them toward the future.

A Double-Edged Sword: Transnationalism and Its Discontents

As the relationship between the EPLF and EFLNA intensified in the late 1970s, the transnational social field encompassing Eritrea and its American diaspora took more definitive shape. By 1977, a near constant circulation of men and women were moving between Eritrea and its numerous outposts abroad. Individuals representing different organized wings of the global movement traveled regularly to Eritrea as well as to Eritrean communities throughout the United States, England, Germany, and the Middle East. But the most important linkages were those made directly between the EPLF and its proliferating global organizations. Increasing tours by EPLF representatives to Eritrean communities and organizations around the world became characteristic of 1970s and 1980s Eritrean activism. Illustrative of what Smith and Guarnizo (1998) call "transnationalism from below," these direct contacts cemented relations between the front and the increasing number of its supporters held in exile by the war at home.

However, the transnationalization of the Eritrean revolution also introduced marked discontinuities. In some ways, these reflected unavoidable contradictions in the construction of the nation at home. In other ways, they represented new dynamics produced by the imperfect suturing of local and diasporic identities and goals. The direct contacts made between activists abroad and the EPLF leadership highlighted the dissonance caused by transnationalist constructions of politics and identity. The birth of a transnational social field via the liberation struggle carried with it multiple possibilities for ruptures at the places where "trans" and "national" converged in individual lives and collectivities. Today that process reiterates itself in the relationship between the Eritrean transnation and the PFDJ-led party-state, evidenced in rising debates about democracy, the government's transnational authority, and the lack of autonomy of diaspora organizations (see Woldemikael 2005; Hepner 2008, 2009). The seeds of this troubled bond were sown initially in the late 1970s through contact between the EPLF as an administrative body and diaspora-based organizations like EFLNA.

Approximately twice per year, small groups of EFLNA members, usually chosen from among the national or local leaderships, undertook an arduous and covert journey into Eritrea via Sudan. Funded by EFLNA and charged with recording every possible detail about life in the field, as well as obtaining responses for EFLNA's questions and concerns, those who visited the EPLF's Eritrea experienced a surge of nationalist commitment and allegiance to the front. They met with leaders and rank-and-file fighters alike and observed civilian life in liberated Eritrea, recording the details of each trip for the movement in the United States. Upon their return to the United States, the delegates prepared lengthy, detailed studies titled *tsebtsab meda*, "field conditions," which they distributed to members. The reports recorded their observations about all aspects of EPLF's functioning in the liberated areas.[21]

In many ways, these details were the most desired and coveted by EFLNA members in the United States. While some remained focused on political philosophy and ideology, the majority of the organization's members yearned simply to know what life in liberated Eritrea was like and how the EPLF was building a new society. By documenting every aspect of the EPLF's statelike structure, EFLNA members not only felt a sense of belonging to the nation but also solidified their commitment to ushering it into existence. In response, the EPLF leadership began specifying which needs to meet and when and returned reports to EFLNA explaining how the funds they raised were put to use. At other times, EFLNA initiated specific projects with the approval of the EPLF, such as "Radio Liberation," a plan to install a radio station in the liberated areas. "Radio Liberation" later became Dimtsi Hafash, "Voice of the Broad Masses," which today remains the most accessible source of government-produced information for Eritreans at home.[22]

In other ways, EFLNA's visits to the field caused more consternation than clarity. At these moments, the gaps between theory and practice, between exclusivist nationalism and the internationalist condition of exile, became obvious. Drawing upon their education and detailed study of leftist political philosophy, as well as their knowledge of international movements and struggles beyond Eritrea's, some EFLNA activists pressured the EPLF leadership to account for its approaches within those broader contexts. The discussions were often related to obscure matters within revolutionary politics, such as whether or not Hoxha's Albanian model applied to Eritrea, or whether the Soviet Union, then backing Ethiopia against Eritrea, exhibited "socialist revisionism." At these moments, EFLNA flexed its autonomy, intellectualism, and internationalism most clearly. At the same time, visits to the field changed the way EFLNA activists thought about the nationalist revolution. Gebrehiwet Kahsay remembers how his visits to the field shifted his consciousness from abstract notions to pragmatic ones:

I stayed [in the field] about six months. It was a very long stay, but by the time I went I had a really clear picture of what was going on here [in Eritrea], and with the commitment of what we have to do to help in the homeland. And maybe up to that time we were thinking of supporting, helping, in many ways, but for me personally that was a turning point, to be fully committed, and work full time. . . . But when you come with ideas, when you want to discuss what you think, you will find out that you didn't understand certain things, because when you meet and discuss you will really understand the situation. Like after my visit to the field, as I told you, with all kinds of debates and discussions, there was no difficulty for me to understand which idea was right, because I saw what was going on.

For many EFLNA activists who visited or returned permanently to Eritrea, alternative political lines or philosophies, subnational identities, and broader, internationalist concerns diminished in importance as they were resocialized through the EPLF's institutional and ideological mechanisms.

Ambivalence toward EFLNA was not limited to the EPLF leadership. Rank-and-file EPLF fighters also developed opinions about exile activists, and the most astute often seized on the perceived discontinuity between EFLNA's political ideas and the realities of the battlefield. Some fighters had only heard about "the petty-bourgeois students in America." Others recognized their participation by the field jackets some fighters wore and the written materials arriving from the United States. EPLF cadres who traveled to the United States and other locations abroad also reported to the rank-and-file fighters on the activities of Eritreans there, especially the amount of funds raised, to help boost morale. One EPLF fighter who resettled in the United States as a refugee in 1983 remembers his impressions of EFLNA in the 1970s as ambivalent at best:

Our perception of them was mixed. Okay, to some degree they are Eritreans and they are helping their front. To some degree, when they try to impose their theories, which don't work in the practical world, then they annoy us. . . . And we will say, "Oh, they're just saying that because they are educated and they are telling me over there," and we don't like that. So we know who they are, and the educated mentality, how to—we try hard to handle it. . . . Not to hurt their feelings, and at the same time to integrate them. Although they are educated academically, they don't know the practicality or the reality of the field. . . . I prefer one who is not educated, but who knows what he is doing in the field, rather than someone who thinks that things will go by formula, you know?

But while more than a few EFLNA members and EPLF fighters scoffed at heady political and philosophical matters, insisting on the superiority of praxis and pragmatism, these sorts of debates did not simply go away as a result of the increasingly grounded relationship between the EPLF and EFLNA. They arose again soon thereafter and remain an enduring and contentious feature of contemporary Eritrean transnationalism.

In sum, while the reality of exile was incorporated into the narrative of Eritrean history and nationalist identity alike, those who remained in Eritrea's embattled terrain frequently looked askance at their compatriots living or returning from abroad. For the development of nationalist identity among EFLNA activists in the United States was both linked to, and crucially separate from, the process at home. Locally, Eritreans acquired and practiced nationalist consciousness through committed participation in the ELF or the EPLF and its civilian mass organizations. Nationalism helped make sense of Ethiopian occupation and the violence being wrought upon Eritrea at the same time that it mobilized resistance and drove the revolution. While EFLNA members also shared in this history, their identities and goals also became shaped by exile and the international currents to which they were exposed. Life in the United States compelled EFLNA activists to think and act not simply as nationalists, but also as immigrants, blacks, Africans, leftists, and perhaps to a lesser degree, feminists, partly because building Eritrea's revolution in the United States required relating its condition and struggle to other international movements and radical ideologies. At the same time, race-class hierarchies in the United States prompted a tangible decline in status for many otherwise privileged Eritreans, who found themselves drawn into American post–civil rights debates. Gender roles shifted as women were exposed to American gender constructions and competed with men in their educational and/or earning potentials for the first time. These new exile subjectivities sometimes resulted in painful ruptures when they interacted with locally constructed nationalism. For EFLNA members who returned to Eritrea to fight, discontinuities in class, gender, and political subjectivities emerged powerfully as they were integrated into the EPLF's nationalism and subjected to its centralist authority.

Some ruptures, however, are more fatal than others. Clearly, the EPLF succeeded at producing and propagating its synthetic, homogenizing nationalism among Eritreans at home and abroad. As the EPLF gradually came to dominate and control the form and content of all transnational exchanges, including proper national identity itself, the power and autonomy of organizations like EFLNA evaporated. In the same way it helped initiate the transnational social field, EFLNA also became the first casualty of its repressive and limiting capacities.

The Demise of EFLNA, 1978–79

Most Eritrean mass organizations, either at home or abroad, were actively created by either the ELF or the EPLF. EFLNA's relative uniqueness was that it formed independently of any existing pro-independence movement in Eritrea and sought to retain a measure of autonomy throughout its life. The demise of EFLNA in 1979 illustrates the extent to which EPLF-dominated transnationalism successfully secured the front's deterritorialized hegemony over the identities and activities of Eritreans abroad. This hegemony entailed the ability to direct and coordinate flows of resources and information, as well as to limit or prevent them, a pattern that persists well into the present moment.

As much of the literature on the Eritrean struggle has shown, mass organizations were central to the success of the EPLF's nationalist project (e.g., Connell 1997; Iyob 1995; Leonard 1988; Pool 1998, 2001). They also played a practical role in forging the transnational social field. Once in place in Eritrea in the late 1970s, they brought all other nationalist associations around the globe under direct EPLF administration and control, connecting them simultaneously to the field and also to one another. Despite its autonomy, EFLNA felt the gravity of that pull, as one member notes:

Well, you can tell that the EPLF wanted the organization [EFLNA] to be a member of the mass organizations. . . . It was organizing the students, the workers, the farmers [peasants], the women, into their own organizations inside the field. And the EPLF may have rationalized that Eritreans abroad should also be part of the mass organizations inside Eritrea. If there is an association of Eritrean students inside the field, then an association of Eritreans outside the field should also be part of that, because it had become a worldwide movement.

Feeling pressure from the EPLF, EFLNA voted at its eighth congress in 1977 to transform itself into two mass organizations: the Association of Eritrean Students in North America (AESNA) and the Association of Eritrean Women in North America (AEWNA). The move placed the organization under the control of the EPLF and on an equal footing with all other mass associations around the world. Within EFLNA, the decision was marked with ambivalence, however. Not all members supported the shift to formal mass organization status. Since its inception in 1970, EFLNA had exercised and valued its autonomy and distance, even as it had aligned itself with the EPLF. But pressures to centralize and homogenize all wings of the nationalist movement eventually led to EFLNA's dissolution, as one member explains at length:

The people that said "let's keep our independence," it's because they saw the gains we can have by being independent. In other words, we can pass independent resolutions, we can think independently, and if we can think independently, then we can become more resourceful to the struggle. . . . The people who said "we can't remain independent" saw the independence as an alienation of our organization from the struggle at home. And they said, "No, Eritreans cannot be independent—this is our struggle." So, there was a very strong, a very strong debate on both sides of the issue, let's stay independent, and let's be part of the revolution. And when they said let's be part of the organization, they are saying Eritreans everywhere—whether we are in the field or outside—we should be one, we should go the same way, we should be organized in the same manner. And the ones that said, no, let's be independent, it's because they wanted—I believe they were thinking in terms of independent thinking without any guidelines or restrictions or affiliations to the political thinking of the leadership of the EPLF. Not the cause itself—the cause is the same to everyone. But as far as independence is concerned, if we stay independent, we can give more resources and help more . . . but if you are part of the organization you can't condemn the leadership, you are bound by the rules and regulations of the front, and you have to do whatever the front tells you to do, and in that way you can't go and have an independent view of yourself.

While the decision to become a mass organization did not happen easily for EFLNA, it was a natural result of both the evolution of its relationship with EPLF and the trajectory of the independence struggle under that front. The move was formally accepted at EFLNA's eighth congress in 1977, to which the EPLF sent an official envoy, Andemikael Kahsai, and the new acronyms AESNA and AEWNA were adopted.[23] For many, this was the first real *tegadelay* [fighter] to stand before them, sent by the EPLF to shepherd them fully into the fold of the front, and it greatly invigorated the movement among members.

EFLNA's leadership, however, was already well acquainted with Andemikael Kahsai. In 1976, they had engaged in transnational debate with Andemikael, who was stationed in the EPLF main foreign office in Rome, Italy, and coordinated the front's communication with Eritrean organizations in Europe and North America. EFLNA's leadership had been gravely concerned with the Soviet Union's backing of Ethiopia and the EPLF's reluctance to publicly condemn the socialist superpower. In one letter dated June 14, 1977, Andemikael deflected questions EFLNA posed regarding Eritrea's place in international socialist movements of the day, consistent with EPLF's practice of maintaining communication with its supporters abroad while discouraging them from questioning the front's authority.[24] At the time of these exchanges, EFLNA's chairman was a man named Mengisteab Yisaq, who is remembered today as an extraordinarily committed, articulate, and passionate leader possessed of singular intelligence and charismatic appeal. He was also known to be commanding, domineering, and even dictatorial. Under his leadership, EFLNA became more centralized and less democratic in its decision-making and internal policies. Mengisteab himself tended toward monopolization of communication with the EPLF leadership and, as some members recall, tended to present his own perspective as fact. He was also deeply interested in international socialist and communist movements and read widely in political philosophy. Isolated from direct communication with EPLF representatives, the general EFLNA membership looked toward Mengisteab as a knowledgeable and authoritative leader. Most members trusted him completely, if for no other reason than his plain commitment to the cause: "He was always in the office, and he was always reading. He was always very into it. He sometimes slept there on the couch—he was committed one hundred thousand percent. We said, 'this guy is going to die here!' Everybody used to say to him, 'Don't you ever go home? Don't you go outside?' He was—obsessed."

Indeed, Mengisteab became obsessed not just with the struggle itself but also with the refusal of the EPLF's leadership to condemn the Soviet Union for its support of Ethiopia. In early 1978, Mengisteab traveled to Eritrea for the third time, allegedly looking to discuss the issue with the EPLF leadership. Through his reading of leftist political philosophy and his fixation on the notion of "Soviet revisionism," Mengisteab became convinced that the EPLF was in danger of losing the revolution to a distorted Marxism-Leninism. But such issues at the time were largely dismissed by EPLF pragmatists as semantic, impractical, and irrelevant. Mengisteab's efforts to convince the EPLF that the revolution was in serious danger as a result of a deviant ideological line were failing. When

EFLNA became the mass organizations AESNA and AEWNA, moreover, EPLF's tolerance for such discussions ceased.

Then in mid-1978, under successive attacks by the Soviet-armed Ethiopian Derg regime, the EPLF withdrew from most of the territory it had liberated since 1975. In the space of six months, the EPLF went from controlling large regions of Eritrea to regrouping at its base. To Eritreans abroad, it appeared a horrifying and sudden defeat. At roughly the same time, both the ELF and the EPLF began engaging in underground dialogue with the Derg regarding an end to the war. The ELF had traveled to the Soviet Union for the talks while the EPLF met with the Ethiopian regime in Berlin. The talks were in many ways strategic for the Ethiopians, as they hoped to sow further mistrust and hostility between the ELF and the EPLF. In the midst of these developments, EFLNA activists felt confused, disoriented, and desperate about the unfolding situation. But the volatility of the political situation and the desperate circumstances in the field led the EPLF to heighten its control over information and maneuver with even greater secrecy than in years past. This included withholding information from mass organizations. The EPLF rebuffed or ignored EFLNA's lengthy, repeated inquiries and failed to send representatives, as requested, to clarify the developments.

By the time EFLNA's ninth congress convened in August 1978, Mengisteab Yisaq in particular, along with other members attuned to his position, had grown absolutely convinced that the EPLF leadership was betraying "the people's revolution." Reflecting now, other active members at the time believe that Mengisteab's perspective emerged not only from his opinions about orthodox Marxism but also from his deep inside connection to the EPLF leadership. As one former activist recalls, "Mengisteab, if you know anything about him, did seem to have some conviction that something was very wrong in EPLF." He had reportedly suffered especially bitter disagreements with Sebhat Ephrem, then the head of the EPLF's Department of Mass Administration, or Kifli Hizbi, the division responsible for coordinating and directing mass organizations around the globe. Working largely by himself, but beneath the AESNA and AEWNA organizational titles, Mengisteab penned the now infamous text *Eritrea: Revolution or Capitulation?* and self-published it in October 1978.

The text, whose distribution reached all exile organizations and fighters in the field itself, was banned and confiscated by the EPLF immediately. The text announced that EFLNA had broken with the EPLF leadership and mercilessly condemned it for violating EFLNA's democratic rights and "imposing its capitulationist view" on the organization.[25] The book charged that the EPLF had "in the most shameless manner betrayed the national struggle and have proclaimed themselves as apologists for Soviet-led revisionist aggression."[26] It also accused the EPLF of creating a monopoly on both information and decision making, a kind of centralism run amok. The booklet further announced that EFLNA was reclaiming its former autonomous name and status, dropping the names AESNA and AEWNA and rescinding itself as a mass organization of the EPLF.

The pages of *Revolution or Capitulation?* documented the growth and development of EFLNA and its relationship with the EPLF, noting that EFLNA "considered its active revolutionary work and, in particular, the adoption of a correct political line as the prime codnition [*sic*] for creating an organic link with the revolution at home and uniting the revolutionary forces."[27] Moreover, "EFLNA's support for EPLF emanated from our free will. . . . This was made clear long ago in our fifth congress when we stated that EFLNA . . . has not only the right but also the responsibility to express its views, commend or criticize, support or condemn, accept or reject, in regard to any issue pertaining to the Eritrean revolution. Exercizing [*sic*] this right we must strongly brace up ourselves so that we don't become passive followers or an instrument of opportunists."[28]

To that end, the booklet claimed that EFLNA had been trying to engage the EPLF leadership in a serious political debate for more than two years (and appended copies of letters sent to the EPLF by AESNA and AEWNA to prove it). Distressed by what it saw as a revisionist tendency in EPLF politics (e.g., a deviation from the original and "proper" revolutionary agenda) appearing in the pages of *Vanguard* and *Spark*, EFLNA had also tried to engage the front's leadership by publishing its own ostensibly more orthodox line in the political journal *Consciousness.* Later, the booklet charged, EFLNA discovered that the EPLF had banned the circulation of its writings both in the field and through its offices abroad.[29] The EPLF had muzzled and isolated EFLNA from rank-and-file fighters, civilians, and other mass organizations. It had preempted the organization's autonomy and deliberately obstructed its efforts to create transparent consensus about political matters of utmost importance to the revolution and future state.

Shortly before the booklet was released, Mengisteab floored the membership at EFLNA's ninth congress in 1978 (also called AESNA and AEWNA's second congress) by relating in detail the exchanges of the past two years and the EPLF leadership's betrayal of the revolution. The membership, already confused and demoralized by EPLF's strategic withdrawal, responded with frenzied denunciations and condemnations of the EPLF and resolved to rescue the revolution. It was within this climate that *Revolution or Capitulation?* made its appearance in Eritrean organizations around the world.

But even within the congress not everyone agreed that EFLNA should split from the EPLF and rescind its mass organization status. One vocal opponent was Gebremikael Lilo, then secretary of EFLNA under Mengisteab's chairmanship. A split therefore also occurred within the executive committee itself over the issue. Overshadowing whatever internal and personal disagreements may have existed among EFLNA leaders and between them and the EPLF, however, loomed the dramatic split between EFLNA as an organization and the EPLF leadership as the revolutionary vanguard. By the close of the congress, EFLNA vowed to rescue not only its former autonomy but also the Eritrean revolution itself from the misguided clutches of the EPLF.

But within days of the ninth congress, members began questioning what had happened there. As one former activist recalls, "People went home after the meeting and started to ask themselves, 'What did we do?! I mean, how did we come to that conclusion? Yesterday everything was possible with EPLF and today we are condemning EPLF!' People started asking questions, friends started talking—it was crazy!" Wondering if they had made a mistake, they began to discuss regrouping behind the EPLF. By October 1978, at which time *Revolution or Capitulation?* appeared, the chasm had widened further. A large core of EFLNA members under Mengisteab Yisaq's leadership continued to defend the split from the EPLF, but over half had abandoned it to start planning a new mass organization. The EPLF issued powerful condemnations of EFLNA's "traitorous leadership," which reverberated around the world through the publications and statements released by other mass organizations. In its magazine *Resistance*, the Association of Eritrean Students (AES), the Eritrea-based umbrella to which EFLNA/AESNA had belonged, filled its pages with anti-EFLNA propaganda.[30] Throughout the United States, former EFLNA chapters also circulated memos to one another and non-Eritrean supporters, decrying the EFLNA's leadership and reasserting loyalty to the EPLF.[31] The core of EFLNA members who maintained their position against EPLF tried equally hard to win support for their actions. In a counterbarrage of letters and "special writings," EFLNA tried again and again to convince its own members and other mass organizations, especially Eritreans for Liberation in Europe, to follow their lead.[32] But their efforts overwhelmingly failed.

After the split in 1978, the EPLF mandated Hagos "Kisha" Gebrehiwet and Gebremikael "Lilo" Mengistu to salvage the remains of the pro-EPLF movement, but many people had scattered, embittered and demoralized. Rather than a well-coordinated effort carried out smoothly by the former two executive officers of EFLNA, as the EPLF had hoped, new chapters arose haphazardly and with little connection to one another at first. Additional problems also arose when many members,

even the most active, realized the extent to which the executive committee under Mengisteab Yisaq had monopolized contact with the EPLF
and contained another, internal layer of personal problems between
individuals. They floundered for awhile, not knowing how to establish
communication with the front. Eventually the EPLF did send two cadres,
Andeberhan Woldegiorgis, a former EFLNA founding member, and
Andemikael Kahsai, who staffed the EPLF office in Rome. The reorganizing movement in New York, then calling themselves Democratic
Eritreans in North America (DENA), organized meetings at the New
School for Social Research, only to have them disrupted by anti-EPLF
activists in EFLNA. As the cadres traveled around the United States trying to carry out damage control, EFLNA released statements condemning those returning to the EPLF as "glorifying capitulation" and trying
to dissuade people from attending the meetings with the cadres.[33] Vituperative infighting between those who supported the reorganization
behind the EPLF and those who remained in EFLNA continued for
months, until the tenth congress was held by the reorganizers in 1979.
Under Lilo's leadership, DENA voted unanimously to revive an EPLF
mass organization, initiated a bilingual magazine *Eritrea in Struggle* [*Ertra
ab Qalsi*], and helped take up the propaganda war against the remnants
of EFLNA.[34] As Lilo stated in a speech delivered just after the tenth congress, "This historic congress was a negation of the shameful 9th congress. It passed several important resolutions, one of which was that our
organization [DENA] should become an EPLF mass organization—
AESNA. The congress also came out with a full understanding that the
group that still continues to parade under the name EFLNA, a name it
is not worthy of, does not represent the sentiments and aspirations of
Eritreans in North America or the revolution at home."[35]

No one bore the consequences harder than Mengisteab Yisaq. As the
movement fragmented and factionalized, he was personally blamed for
creating the crisis with the EPLF. Suffering a spiraling descent into
depression, Mengisteab became erratic, confused, and despondent.
Concerned for his well-being, the EFLNA members who remained loyal
to his position put him under twenty-four-hour watch in their Harlem
apartment. Then, one day as he sat watching television, the formerly
admired, charismatic leader suddenly leapt out an open window, falling
three stories, where he was impaled on a wrought-iron fence below.

Like countless others, Mengisteab perished for his belief that Eritrea
should be free. Though I cannot help but wonder: On June 20 every
year, Martyrs' Day, when Eritreans all over the world light candles in
honor of those who died for the cause, is there a candle for Mengisteab
Yisaq among those flickering flames? Is he remembered as a martyr? Vili-

fied for being a traitor? Or deliberately forgotten for being an exile, a
bourgeois intellectual full of foreign ideas and abstract agendas?

The Eritrean mass movement in the United States never fully recovered
from its critical injuries of 1978. The remaining shreds of EFLNA gradually disintegrated following Mengisteab Yisaq's death, and while AESNA
and AEWNA continued their mass organizational activities, vitality and
momentum waned. Many formerly dedicated activists turned away from
the movement, still supporting Eritrean independence but no longer
defining their lives by it. Students returned to their studies, men and
women focused on careers and families. Some despaired that independence would ever come to pass. Still others became absorbed in humanitarian efforts and directed their energies toward the EPLF's Eritrean
Relief Association (ERA), perceiving it to be somewhat less politicized
an endeavor.

The 1980s signaled a new decade of growth and change for Eritreans
in the United States. After the passage of the Refugee Resettlement Act
of 1980, Ethiopians and Eritreans streamed into the United States in
unprecedented numbers (Koehn 1991; Woldemikael 1998). Where
before a mass movement of dispersed students and workers existed, families now coalesced into communities across the country. The EPLF itself
opened an office in Washington, D.C., and small satellite chapters of the
front formed in major cities, comprised of many former EFLNA members. But while mass organizations in Eritrea and other parts of the
world continued to flourish, the American wing of the movement
remained but a shadow of its former self: subdued, muted, restrained.

Several patterns of the 1970s, however, formed the structural under-
pinnings for the ongoing relationship between Eritrea and exile. First
and foremost, transnationalism—in this case, nationalist projects accomplished by transnational means—defined the form of the revolution and
shaped the global scope of its embrace. EPLF itself developed contigu-
ously with organizations like EFLNA and depended on them for sustenance and legitimacy. The front's strength, and the power of the
nationalism it propagated, were forged together out of its own locally
defined practices and policies and the unanticipated potentials of its
scattered peoples.

Transnationalism is a dialectical process fraught with internal contradictions. It harbors two souls: nationalism's circumscribed attachment
to place and its homogenizing, "unifying" project, and the inherently
more internationalizing condition of exile and diaspora. The EPLF's
gradual assertion of control over the transnational movement heralded
the arrival of its hegemony over the nationalist revolution as a whole
and foreshadowed the character of the independent state. Through an

evolving drama in which its ideology, practice, and nationalist vision were both reproduced and challenged from within Eritrea as well as in exile, the EPLF managed to secure its administrative and discursive authority. It also increasingly secured a homology between political identity and nationalism, defining all of Eritrean identity more and more in terms of the EPLF's specific organizations, institutions, ideologies, and practices. Evidenced in the 1978 EFLNA-EPLF split, resisting the EPLF's dominance signified a betrayal of the nation as a whole. However, the greater autonomy afforded by exile, and the efforts of Eritreans in the United States to act as genuine citizens of Eritrea—including challenging the transnational party-state—remain contemporary features at least partially rooted in the 1970s.

Thus the linkage between EFLNA and EPLF is the setting in which transnationalism's possibilities, as well as its contradictory and even repressive potential, first became apparent. It is where the EPLF tested and honed its strategies for exerting authority and governance across great distances. It is the origin of practices and debates still unfolding today. It forms the foundation on which contemporary Eritrean community relations rest and that which feeds their enduring restlessness. It is the continuing conversation between a battle-scarred guerrilla fighter in Eritrea and a philosophy professor in the United States. And it is the words of a contemporary Eritrean American man, too young to know EFLNA as it once was, but old enough to recall Eritrea before independence: "I honestly don't believe the problem between the EPLF and EFLNA was about ideology. I think, like today, it was more about power and control. For better or worse, the EPLF wanted control over its own agenda without too much influence from its supporters in the U.S. To the EPLF leadership, its supporters were just an extension of its fighting machine. But the methods it used to achieve control were crude, and it cost the nation dearly."

Chapter 4
Eritrea in Exile
Refugees and Community Building in the United States

> "Community" is nowadays another name for paradise lost—but one to which we dearly hope to return, and so we feverishly seek the roads that may bring us there.
>
> —Zygmunt Bauman, *Community*

Almaz

When Almaz Tesfazghi first came to the midwestern United States, she arrived in a far northern town where the cold, flat landscape seemed the exclusive province of white men and women still reveling in—and reeling from—the transformations of the 1960s.

"It was 1968," she recalled. "This was right after Dr. King was assassinated. There was still brand-new anger—the civil rights movement was happening, and the Black Panthers were being formed at that time. But you know, everybody was white, everybody had straight hair, it was the hippie movement. Nothing black was going on! I got this feeling like I wanted to be with black people. All these different movements—it made you want to have a movement of your own!"

Almaz had come to America by way of Addis Ababa, Ethiopia, to join her fiancé, who was attending university in the Midwest. Raised in Asmara during the BMA years and then during the Ethio-Eritrean Federation, she went to Addis Ababa in the mid-1960s to finish her schooling.

As we sat together in her comfortable office almost forty years later, she boiled tea with cardamom and cloves and related the story of her radicalization as an Eritrean nationalist in America. She had a large frame, her scent warm and sweet with high-end perfume, and her personality expansive and vibrant.

"I was sent to Addis like many other kids," she explained, her ringed fingers brushing the air around her. "Our schools in Asmara were being closed. I remember vividly in 1962 when we refused to go to school. We couldn't even tell our parents we were striking. But something was happening to our country. We didn't know Ethiopia would be like a colonial power. We lost the sentimental things like our flag, our schools were being closed, and we had to speak Amharic instead of Tigrinya. So we were rebelling against those. Then I went to Addis. I was there six years before coming to the U.S."

"Addis Ababa was quite a radical environment in those days," I said. "I've read about the activism of Eritrean students at the university especially. Were you involved in any of those movements?"

"Oh, no, no, not at that time," she smiled.

Indeed, Almaz had remained an oblique observer during her stay in the Ethiopian capital. Her consciousness and understanding of the independence movement in Eritrea also remained muted. In those days, most women did not engage in risky underground politics. That was the business of restless young men. Of course, Almaz felt a deep emotional connection to what was happening in Eritrea. But still she remained most invested in her small church group of young Eritrean Protestants studying in Addis, who met on a daily basis to socialize, pray, read the Bible, and speak their mother tongue of Tigrinya.

But in 1968, suddenly plunged into the Heartland, surrounded by lingering civil rights movement activism and other contrasting elements of both American progressivism and ethnic homogeneity, Almaz began to feel a certain stirring inside.

"I came here very silent, but aware that I wanted to be free from Ethiopia. The minute I came here, I felt a feeling for—there is like—you want to be with somebody, you want to be with other black people. So we went to a meeting of Operation Breadbasket. Jesse Jackson was a young man at that time."

Her face grew animated as she recalled the intensity of her own political awakening.

"It was amazing, the transformation for us! Jesse Jackson—he was a young man, our age, at that time—and he had so much energy. And he came in, the house was full, the place was just full with people, and when he came in, everybody got up. And I was wondering, 'What is he going to say? How is he going to calm down this group?' Then his voice came up, and he was so loud, and he was so mannish in his voice, and he said, 'I AM!' And the people said, 'I AM! I AM SOMEBODY! I am black and I am somebody! I am black and I am beautiful!' Oh! My God! I found my niche! That was the day of my birth, of being aware of who you are. There was a political side in life!"

In the years that followed, Almaz was transformed into an ardent Eritrean nationalist, dedicating all of her time and much of her young family's resources to supporting the struggle in Eritrea. She traveled in crowded station wagons all over the United States to meet with her compatriots and comrades in the movement known as EFLNA, with whom she argued the intricacies of Marx and Lenin and Mao and how they were being applied by the EPLF in Eritrea. She resisted the temptation to buy even basic items like dishes for her home because, after all, they would only go to waste when she returned to Eritrea to join the struggle.

Not even the birth of her first daughter prevented her attendance at the First Congress of the Association of Eritrean Women in North America (AEWNA). Swaddling the six-week-old in blankets, she set off with her close friend Elsa to Washington, D.C., by car. For years she kept jars at work and at her home labeled *dirar tegadelay*, "dinner for a fighter." No matter who you were, when you visited Almaz you dropped some change into that jar and you learned something about Eritrea and the EPLF.

"You were looking at a completely changed people!" she said. "Devoted to our country, whether it is money, time, political studies, anything you ask we are ready. That's it! We lived for that!"

Naturally, when Eritrean refugees were being resettled in the Midwest the 1980s, Almaz was one of the first to get involved. She had blossomed into one of the most respected women leaders in both the small Eritrean community and the local business world. She had become almost an icon of sorts, an individual example of what might be possible for her country. In her considerable success as a black immigrant woman in the white male world of finances, stocks, and bonds, and in her unequivocal dedication to anticolonial nationalism, she made the many delicate balances and tensions between Africa and America, feminism and nationalism, radicalism and capitalism, Eritrea and exile, seem effortless.

When the refugees began arriving, Almaz spearheaded a women's group where she aimed at helping women learn basics like grocery shopping, hygiene, and child care in the United States. As an active member of AEWNA, and later the chairperson of the local chapter of the National Union of Eritrean Women (NUEW), she felt a keen obligation to help her sisters. But she was shocked to discover that most of the refugee women were associated with the ELF and that they interpreted virtually all of her actions through the lens of political identity. This included her egalitarian relationship with her husband, she said. Thus it was a mark of Almaz's personification of the ideal EPLF woman in America that the newly arrived women saw her as pushing the front's agenda.

"Believe me, all I knew was that people were coming as refugees. I didn't know they had a stand with ELF or EPLF," she recalled. "These were not individual people, individual fighters. These were whole families. In some of our meetings there used to be tension, like if some of the songs we sang were from EPLF and not ELF, there would be tension, like even screaming and hollering. At that time, I just didn't know, I didn't understand what was happening."

"What *was* happening, exactly?" I asked gently.

Almaz sighed and refilled my teacup, passing me the sugar bowl and spoon.

"Well, I think people sensed I was Hamadi'e, you know, a member of the National Union of Eritrean Women, which was under the EPLF. I remember one event we did. I was the chairperson of the local chapter of Hamadi'e, and so I gave a speech. I talked about how in the early days the capitalist mentality came, and women became submissive to men, because there was an ownership of men towards women. Men controlled women so they would pass their capital or property onto their own children. I learned this in the political studies we did in our North America group. It was a very successful night; we had good food, we had music, we had speakers, everybody had a good time. But the next day, when we all got together to eat the leftovers for lunch, the women were so mad at me! Instead of being thanked I was blamed. Why was the speech I gave like that? Why didn't I let them hear the speech before I read it? Why was my husband helping me to cook the food? I came back home really crying. Later on it was explained to me, that in our group there were people who came from ELF, and people from EPLF, and those ELF women resented that I took a Hamadi'e stand. It was like saying I was EPLF. But I didn't understand there was anything but EPLF. I mean, ELF was gone, and we were all Eritreans."

"So what kind of effect did that have on the women's group you had started, or on the chapter of NUEW here?" I asked.

"It stopped me from trying to continue with it." For a moment her face grew sad, then quickly brightened again.

"But then it came to me—even in the beginning I was more of a church person. There are a lot of things you can solve through church, you know. There are a lot of services you can give and get through church. Youth need to be mentored, all of that. There is always a place for you if you want to help."

I recalled the last time I had attended services with the small evangelical Christian fellowship Almaz attended. While the adults sang and danced and clapped and shouted in the main hall, I had been in Bible study with the young people, listening to them talk about the challenges of growing up Eritrean, Christian, and African American all at once. It was true, what Almaz said. People seemed to be getting more out of church than anywhere else in the community.

"Do you still belong to the women's group? To Hamadi'e?" I asked. I had been to several meetings but had never seen Almaz there.

"No. I have been invited to join them, but I still didn't forget what happened to me. I'm not going to put my neck out again. They are doing fine, they don't need me. I know some of them still maintain that feeling, the feeling they had before, even though they belong to Hamadi'e now."

A slight frown passed like a cloud across her luminous, burnished skin.

"Even now I want to tell them to their face, yes I am an EPLF supporter! Even now, I haven't seen anything that doesn't make me support my government!"

At the moment, I felt the palpable conviction of Almaz's stand. But her delicate balancing of charismatic religion and nationalism became much more complicated for me when I carried out research in Eritrea, and especially when I interviewed one of the head pastors of the Mulu Wongeel Biet Kristyan, or the Full Gospel Church, in Asmara. While certainly no less devoted in his evangelical faith than Almaz, and even sharing some similar experiences as a sojourner and nationalist in the United States, the pastor's perspective on politics nonetheless seemed nearly incompatible.

The pastor had gotten his start over a decade earlier by ministering to the small but growing group of evangelical Christian Eritreans in the same midwestern city where Almaz lived. She had been one of his parishioners until he returned to Eritrea just prior to independence. And the tension the pastor revealed to me between postindependence nationalism and religion was striking, especially because one of the most enthusiastic Eritrean Christians I knew, Almaz Tesfazghi, had never commented on it.

As we sat together in his office somewhere near the wealthier neighborhood of Tiravolo, I found Almaz's words intervening with the pastor's like an impetuous, clanging gong. For his part, the pastor spoke slowly and deliberately, unaware of the contradictions I was working out in my head. He was serious to the point of being grave.

"In the past, everything had to be put into this national struggle. Minds, lives, limbs. But it cannot be about nationalism forever. You have to think about deeper issues in life. You think about life after death, and is there a God. . . ."

His voice trailed off momentarily. I sensed that he was choosing his words carefully.

"Both religion and nationalism are very powerful, and they can be used to mislead people. You cannot be without them. Religion is for here and the life hereafter. Politics is for here, but there are very important issues not part of its dogma. Since politics is everywhere, many people, especially in Eritrea, think nationalism can be a like a god, with a small *g*. Unfortunately, both can be abused, even religion, if the leaders are corrupt. . . . Politics is the same. It's more shameful when it happens in religion. But politics? Politics is one of those things."

Despite the subversiveness of his comments (which I only later fully appreciated), his face relaxed and he smiled, revealing a row of large white teeth. A few days later, as I sweated in the spirit beneath the gigantic yellow-and-white striped tent with thousands of Eritreans, I contemplated the considerable differences between the pastor's demeanor during our interview and during worship. As he strode across the stage and led the shouting and singing, a kind of otherworldly joyfulness poured from his soul while the perspiration streamed down his skin.

Undoubtedly somewhere amid the congregants were Eritreans visiting from the United States, perhaps even some from the community I studied. The midwestern congregation maintained a loose connection with the Full Gospel Church in Asmara, and when people like Almaz went home to visit, they attended worship services there.

That is, until the PFDJ government began closing down churches like Mulu Wongeel in 2002 and imprisoning pastors and laypeople. According to the government, the closures and arrests were because these evangelical churches—most of them relatively new and considered "alien" to indigenous religious traditions—had either failed to comply with rigorous registration procedures or had engaged in illegal activities such as accepting funds from foreign sources. Among those arrested was the pastor I interviewed, who had helped found Almaz's congregation in the United States almost fifteen years before. Like other religious or political prisoners in Eritrea, he was never charged with a crime or provided access to legal counsel. Seven years later he still remains incommunicado. Many of his parishioners are confined in aluminum shipping containers and often tortured until they recant their evangelical faith and promise to return to authentic Orthodox practice.

The discordant clashing of Almaz's and the pastor's words continued to ring in my head, growing louder and more insistent as the government increasingly bore down on religious minorities in Eritrea. One afternoon, back in the United States, I decided to stop by Almaz's office unannounced. While I told myself it was merely a friendly and casual visit, a chance to drink tea and catch up, the truth was that I wanted to see if her politics had changed now that her church was shut down and the pastor of Mulu Wongeel imprisoned.

As usual, she was warm and welcoming.

"Terhasina!" she cried, when I walked through the door of her office. She rushed to wrap me in a loving, fragrant embrace. "*Kemey allekhi, me'arey?* How are you, honey?"

We sat and chatted easily, smiling and laughing together. She was as kind and motherly as always. I found that in the midst of the puzzles that Eritrea and Eritreans presented to me, many of them quite unsettling, my affection for Almaz had only grown. Finally, I broached the issue I wanted to address.

"Almaz, I want to ask you about what's going on with the churches back home. You know, the closures and the arrests. I'm sure you've heard that two pastors of Mulu Wongeel have been imprisoned. What do you think about it?"

"Ay, Terhasina," she answered immediately. "The government would not do something like that unless there was a very, very good reason for it. You want to think that church people are always good and honest, but they must have been doing something very wrong to deserve this. I don't know, but I trust the government to do the right thing."

Then she shook her head and waved her hand in front of her face, as if to clear away a foul odor in the air.

"But let's not talk about politics now! I am getting ready to go back home in a few weeks, and I want to show you pictures of our little vacation house in Massawa! You must come visit there one day!" Stifling pangs of an unidentified emotion, I smiled and moved my chair closer to hers, craning my neck to look at the stack of photographs she clasped tightly in her hands, photographs she had taken in free Eritrea.

Broken Ranks: The ELF and EFLNA in the United States

The 1970s had witnessed both the high point and the decline of two very different players on the Eritrean revolutionary scene: one was EFLNA's pro-EPLF movement in the United States and the other the armed forces of the ELF fighting in Eritrea. While the ELF had laid the foundations of the armed struggle inside Eritrea since the 1960s, EFLNA had helped forge the transnational social field with the EPLF in the 1970s. Both organizations were therefore pioneers in key aspects of the nationalist liberation struggle. Moreover, each had experienced growth and vitality in the earlier part of the decade, only to collapse at its close.

The mutual decline of EFLNA and the ELF from 1979 to 1981, coupled with the overwhelming crises of war and famine in the Horn, ultimately led the two disparate groups to one another. In the United States, former EFLNA members cast about at the turn of the decade, demoralized and disoriented by the dramatic break with the EPLF. At the same moment, in Eritrea, the ELF was imploding beneath the weight of civil war with the EPLF, the struggle with Ethiopia, and its own internal factionalization. From 1980 to 1981, thousands of ELF affiliates amassed in camps at the western border or in Sudan.

In the mid-1980s, many of these people began making their way to the United States as internationally recognized refugees. There they encountered their EFLNA compatriots, most of whom had spent the hardest years of the war mobilizing for the EPLF from the United States. By all accounts, the encounter between the two groups was traumatic. The influx of Eritreans with varied backgrounds and experiences complicated efforts to define and organize an Eritrean diaspora community in the broadest sense of the term. Whereas the earliest students and workers in the United States had come largely from highland, urban areas and from similar regional, religious, generational, and class backgrounds, the refugee resettlement process introduced a more diverse population. Extended families and former guerrilla fighters alike arrived in large numbers, many with little education and few employable skills. Moreover, the majority of them had been associated with the ELF and looked upon the students and workers who had built EFLNA as part of the rival EPLF. And while many people tried to put politics aside and reach out to one another as nationalists, the Eritrean diaspora was wracked by conflicts related to fractures in political identity and nationalism and the presence of the EPLF abroad.

This chapter examines efforts to build a diaspora community during the years leading up to Eritrean independence and those immediately following it.[1] During that time, the EPLF successfully gained control over the revolution in Eritrea and extended its transnational administrative reach throughout exile communities around the world. Examining the internal relationships of such diaspora communities—including the effort to define "community" itself—reveals much about the character of the Eritrean transnational social field and the consequences of patterns that originated in the 1970s. In particular, it demonstrates the contradictory nature of transnationalism as both an emancipating and repressive force. It suggests that transnational processes can enhance the power of a deterritorialized, authoritarian state while also preventing exile communities from achieving stability and resilience as immigrant populations, hence disempowering them in both their countries of settlement and in postindependence Eritrea. At the same time, it opens up crucial spaces for transnational political resistance against the state and alternative ways of being Eritrean.

Coming to America, Again: Refugee Resettlement

While the Immigration Act of 1965 enabled the first Eritrean students and workers to come to the United States, the Refugee Act of 1980 resulted in the largest mass resettlement of Africans to North America since the end of the Atlantic slave trade (see Woldemikael 1998:90; see also Kibreab 1985). Until a sharp drop-off in 1993–94, Ethiopians and Eritreans constituted 93 percent of all African refugees admitted to the United States between 1982 and 1991 (Woldemikael 1998:90). Statistical data for refugees entering the United States for the years 1988–92 show that 21,901 Ethiopians and Eritreans entered in that four-year period alone (USCR 2001). Drawing upon the United States Committee for Refugees (USCR) reports and other supplementary data, Woldemikael (1998:90–91) determines that a total of 33,195 individuals resettled in the United States between 1975 and 1994.

However, the existing data is problematic. First, it does not disaggregate Eritreans from Ethiopians; until formal Eritrean independence in 1993 the term *Eritrean* remained a self-identifier and not an officially recognized national designation. Discerning the actual number of Eritreans from Ethiopians requires a methodological approach not yet attempted by the few researchers who have studied Eritrean and Ethiopian refugee resettlement in the United States and elsewhere. Indeed, as Kibreab (2003) notes, it is almost impossible to determine the actual number of Eritrean refugees worldwide and their various destinations. Analytically if not quantitatively, Koehn (1991) separates Eritreans from Ethiopians to account for their distinct experiences within the wider Ethiopian context. Both he and Woldemikael (1998) include data from the years prior to the Refugee Act of 1980, when small numbers of Eritreans and Ethiopians were admitted to the United States as "seventh-preference" immigrants, to arrive at their overall estimates of the U.S. Ethiopian-Eritrean population (see Woldemikael 1998:90; Koehn 1991:151).

Both authors discuss two waves of resettlement, the first during the period immediately following the passage of the Refugee Act, and the second from 1982 to 1991, with the highest concentration of arrivals occurring in 1982–84 (see Koehn 1991:151). By 1993–94, as a result of the collapse of the Ethiopian Derg regime and the attainment of Eritrean independence, the number of incoming refugees from Ethiopia and Eritrea soon was dwarfed by the rapid climb among Somalis and Sudanese (see USCR 2001; Farah 2000; Holtzman 2000). Since 1993, the first-generation population of Eritreans and Ethiopians has continued to grow, however, through legal immigration (such as the diversity visa and Family Reunification Program), as well as the asylum process, which constitute perhaps a "third wave" of resettlement.

As of 1993, when Eritreans all over the world registered to vote in the national referendum on independence, the embassy of Eritrea in Washington, D.C., estimated between fifteen thousand and twenty thousand Eritrean adults living in the United States. However, the actual number of Eritreans in the United States was significantly higher, if one counts children then under eighteen, as well as people who did not participate in the referendum.[2] A decade later, in 2003, the embassy of Eritrea estimated thirty thousand to forty thousand Eritreans residing in the United States (Embassy of Eritrea, personal communication). Because this figure still does not include those under the age of eighteen, nor does it account for those who for various reasons wish to remain under the official radar of the Eritrean government, the actual number of individuals recognized as Eritrean according to the 1992 Proclamation on Citizenship may be as many as one hundred thousand.[3] Demographically, this number is minuscule. To provide some perspective, the Eritrean population nationwide roughly equals, and may in fact be smaller than, the number of East Asian Indians in the Chicago metropolitan area alone.

Despite their demographic insignificance on the American immigrant scene, however, Eritreans and Ethiopians remain important in other ways. As Woldemikael (1998) points out, they both formed the first substantial community of new African immigrants to the United States and were the first refugees to arrive in large numbers following the Refugee Act of 1980 (see also Arthur 2000; Portes and Rumbaut 1996). However, relative to the composition of their home societies, those resettling from Eritrea and Ethiopia are drawn from a very narrow segment of the total population and therefore are unrepresentative of the diversity in their countries of origin. Due mostly to the refugee resettlement screening process, which favored those "whom the U.S. government defined as able to integrate into the society faster and better" (Woldemikael 1998:96), the Eritrean and Ethiopian population admitted to the United States was heavily weighted toward males from highland, Christian, educated, urban, and socioeconomically advantaged backgrounds. Indeed, the rigorous screening process typically took one to five years from application to resettlement and was fraught with numerous bureaucratic hurdles (Compton 1998; Cooper 1992; Kibreab 2003; Koehn 1991; Woldemikael 1998). Thus, by virtue of their ethno-regional, religious, and socioeconomic characteristics as well as their success in the often harrowing resettlement process, Eritreans in the United States represent a privileged portion of their home society.

Compared with European countries participating in the United Nations High Commissioner for Refugees (UNHCR) resettlement program, which includes Australia, Canada, Denmark, Finland, the Netherlands, Norway, New Zealand, Sweden, and Switzerland, as well as those countries that admit refugees on an ad hoc basis such as Germany, France, and the United Kingdom, the United States was late to begin accepting African refugees. By the mid-1980s, when Eritreans and Ethiopians were coming to the United States in large numbers, sizable communities had already amassed elsewhere in the world. Some people utilized family connections or extrabureaucratic avenues to resettle in North Africa, the Middle East, and the former colonial metropole of Italy (see Andall 2002; Compton 1998; Kibreab 2003). While no formal data exists comparing the Eritrean populations in these countries and the policies governing their selection and resettlement, the Eritrean population in the United States appears less representative of Eritrean society as a whole than do those in other exile locations. In particular, the highland Christian bias in the United States selection process stands out dramatically against the pool of all potential or actual Eritrean refugees seeking third-country resettlement, more than half of whom were Muslim. A cursory glance at Eritrean diaspora communities throughout the world suggests that many more Muslims and people from less privileged backgrounds settled throughout Australia, North Africa, and the Middle East than in the United States or Western Europe.

At the same time, however, compared with the Eritrean students and workers who arrived in the United States during the late 1960s through the 1970s, the incoming refugees diversified dramatically the nascent diaspora community. For the first time, the sons and daughters of more privileged families, such as those who had formed EFLNA, encountered peers with radically different experiences. While many of the resettled refugees may have shared similar backgrounds with the earlier student-worker migrants, their lives had been shaped by the intervening realities of violence, war, displacement, and in many cases, life in the ELF or the EPLF. Many had sacrificed their educational or employment opportunities to join the armed struggle and had lived with great hardship. Moreover, they brought with them family members of different generations, some of whom were as yet illiterate and unskilled, and from regions outside the major urban hubs of Asmara or Addis Ababa. Despite the rigorous criteria imposed by U.S. resettlement policy and the relative homogeneity of the resettled refugees compared with Eritrea's population as a whole, among themselves Eritreans perceived important differences in ethno-regionalism, religion (mainly Protestant, Catholic, and Orthodox Christian), socioeconomic status, education, and perhaps most important, political identity. This dramatically impacted the encounter between the student-worker generation of the 1970s and the refugees of the 1980s. It also had profound effects within the developing transnational social field.

Encountering Political Identities: The ELF and the EPLF in Exile

The students and workers who participated in the transnational revolution through EFLNA and the EPLF's mass organizations during the 1970s felt themselves to be deeply integrated into the life of *meda*, the struggle in the field. As Chapter 3 explored, however, the construction of a transnational social field proved an uneven process, fraught with communication gaps and power plays both vertically within the movement as well as horizontally across space. Even as some EFLNA activists viewed themselves as *tegadelti* abroad—communicating extensively with the EPLF, contributing funds and materials, and sometimes repatriating to fight—the vast majority lacked crucial firsthand knowledge of the hazards of everyday life in a war zone and the concrete challenges of being a fighter. However, the perspectives they adopted firmly reflected those of the EPLF, including their analysis of the ELF. Perhaps nothing revealed these disjunctures as clearly as the encounter between the student-worker activists in EFLNA and the incoming refugees during the 1980s.

Although EFLNA itself dissolved following the 1979 split with the EPLF, its former members and other EPLF supporters, some of them newly resettled refugees themselves, began joining local chapters of the front in the United States. Creating such worldwide chapters was a much more direct way for the EPLF to garner support and maintain control. In addition, the AESNA, which was recognized as a member of the Eritrea-based National Union of Eritrean Students (NUES), also continued many of the same activities EFLNA had done, such as hosting Eritrean cultural nights, fund-raisers, and visits by EPLF cadres. The AEWNA, for its part, became incorporated into the NUEW, formed by the EPLF in Eritrea in 1979. Supporting the nationalist war of independence under the EPLF was the raison d'être of all of these. At the same time, however, Eritreans had created no other associations within American society that were independent from the EPLF and/or addressed their concerns or needs as immigrant residents of the United States. All of their energies and resources had been directed transnationally toward Eritrea, and exclusively for the EPLF.

EPLF activists and members of the 1970s student-worker generation thus found themselves unprepared for the encounter with the incoming refugees in several respects. At first, even locating the newcomers could be challenging, highlighting the way that transnational links to the EPLF had superseded internal diasporic ones. Andom Berhe recalls:

We were at a loss, most of us who were there in America. Even organizationally, we were at a loss to find out where people were going. They were being resettled to small towns we didn't know, and it took awhile for them to figure out how to get ahold of other Eritreans. They just went to the social services department in their area and . . . became accustomed to those little procedural things you have to do, like getting a house, getting a welfare check, having their children in school, getting oriented and learning cultural issues. It usually took a year before they were able to get out of those small towns and find Eritreans in the nearest big city, to sit down and discuss Eritrea, and to learn there was an organization of EPLF.

Among those EPLF activists who resided in cities with large incoming refugee populations, a concerted effort was made to reach out to the new arrivals. Stunned at first by the number of multigenerational families arriving together and unsure how to negotiate the differences between themselves and the refugees, the student-workers drew upon the skills they had honed throughout the previous decade working with EFLNA and the EPLF. But many were unaware of both the intensity of their own EPLF subjectivity as well as the ELF orientation of so many of the refugees. The assumption was that a common nationalist commitment to independence would "unify" all Eritreans. That nationalist identity itself had been configured differently through the institutional, ideological, and experiential dimensions of the fronts had not been explicitly recognized or anticipated.

Kidane, a longtime activist in EFLNA, reached out to newcomers in California and was taken aback when he discovered that his actions were filtered through the prism of political identity:

I was in Los Angeles at the time, and I received most of them, personally, myself. At the beginning we saw them just as Eritrean refugees. Most of them didn't speak English, they didn't speak anything other than Tigrinya. We saw them as displaced Eritreans, we didn't see them as ex-Jebha fighters. So we gathered and gave them our best—we collected money, we collected clothes, we rented them houses, we bought them mattresses, sheets, supplies. We gave them bus tickets. And while we were doing this, they always had something in their minds, which we didn't—"We are Jebha fighters and this EPLF guy is trying to lure me into being EPLF too." That was what was going in their heads, I later found out. But when we received them, we received them simply as Eritrean refugees who needed our help, and we did our best. Then, sometime after they got settled, got their houses, jobs, all that, then they started calling us Sha'bia, or *muwed-a'ata*, which means "reactionary," I think, in Arabic. And we started seeing them as Jebha.

The lack of any community institutions not directly affiliated with EPLF vexed newly arrived Eritreans, who resisted the front's political and administrative presence from back home. Some Eritreans gravitated to the more developed Ethiopian community. But as the refugees began reaching ever higher numbers, and as the liberation war dragged on, people from every background began recognizing the need for Eritrean diaspora community institutions to serve two main purposes. First, such institutions should support the independence and relief efforts at home, as the goal of national independence formed the common ground uniting Eritreans regardless of political or other identities. Second, community institutions were needed as a resource for Eritreans in the United States as they contended with language, housing, jobs, education, and cultural adaptation.

But within the existing transnational context, how should such community institutions arise, and how should they function? Who should lead them? For those people who had long been organized under EFLNA and the EPLF, their skills, experience, and ideological orientation suggested a particular course of action. Because the EPLF remained the sole force fighting for Eritrean independence, they believed, all efforts should remain beneath its direction and control. But for those who had been affiliated with the ELF, the idea of allowing the EPLF and its members to define and control all aspects of community life offended them deeply. At the time, few EPLF supporters seemed to understand this, even if the passage of time provides perspective today. Tsegai, formerly active with EFLNA and a very strong supporter of the EPLF at the time, remembers:

Later, in the 1980s, when more Eritreans started to come, most of them were ex-ELF combatants, ELF cadres, ELF members. We started to look inward, to the community. We said we have to organize our community, and probably that was a serious mistake we made. It was necessary to look into the community, but the way we approached it was wrong. Because what we tried to do was recruit them to be members of EPLF. You know, these are people who just came from a hot war, who are very angry at both ELF and EPLF. We made a lot of fights in the community.

The push to create secular, "nonpolitical" community associations that could simultaneously contribute to the overall goal of independence and yet also serve the needs and aspirations of an increasingly diverse and contentious exile population proved far more difficult than anyone anticipated. For those who had internalized the EPLF's peculiar nexus of synthetic nationalism, which emphasized submerging all other identities and loyalties to the nation and to EPLF's authority, it seemed fairly obvious that former ELF affiliates and all others should simply accept the terms of the existing EPLF-dominated transnational movement. Defining the community association as "nonpolitical" meant that anyone could belong, but clearly the EPLF would determine the parameters of participation. For former ELF affiliates and those who rejected the EPLF-ELF divide, however, no institutions created or controlled by the EPLF or its members could be "nonpolitical." Those who had come from the ELF especially held expectations that diverse viewpoints and loyalties should be retained within an overarching, pluralist nationalism. The contrasting subject positions of a population already shaped by more than twenty years of divergence and conflict in political and nationalist identity turned the efforts at community building into a battleground that reproduced the myriad tensions brought from home. Complicating the situation was the fact that so many EPLF supporters in the United States had never lived through either the war with Ethiopia or that between the ELF and the EPLF and simply could not understand the perspective of their newly arrived compatriots. Their own identities had been molded by the EPLF's transnational project and their extended sojourn in a foreign land.

Perhaps none recall that tension surrounding the formation of community associations as distinctly as the former ELF fighters who found themselves outnumbering EPLF members and yet somehow excluded from existing institutions and the definition of "proper" national identity. Many perceived the situation as insult added to injury: the EPLF had driven the ELF into exile, had taken control of the nationalist revolution, and now would direct the kinds of organizations and activities communities in exile would have. In order to participate in the nationalist movement for independence, EPLF supporters seemed to be telling the refugees that they must relinquish their distinct experiences and their political identification with the ELF in order to embrace the victorious front. Gebre, an ELF fighter, describes the hostility and tension he felt within the Philadelphia community's early organizational efforts:

The EPLF had to justify the civil war, why it decided to fight against ELF. And one of the reasons they used to justify [the civil war] was the failing of the ELF. So [the EPLF supporters in the United States] were entirely against any ELF member. For them, being ELF is worse than being Derg. So this is where we start clashing. If I tell them I was fighting the [Ethiopian] Derg, I was in the war, they wouldn't believe it! Because already in their minds the ELF was bad, a bunch of bandits, a bunch of crooks, people who go around and sabotage the villagers and the people. So it was really tough to deal with in the beginning. It took years for us to express ourselves.

In Gebre's opinion, part of the problem seemed to lie in the fact that so many EPLF supporters from Eritrea spent the critical years of the war in the United States: "When we came, it was like 'Here are the Jebha members coming.' . . . The civil war was fresh and EPLF did not do us any good, it was not right, but they felt like we were just running away. It was getting pretty confrontational. . . . You see, they do not understand the life of *meda*. They did not know what we were doing—they thought we were not fighting, that we were living a luxury life out there in *meda*, and that's why we got kicked [out] by EPLF."

As previously discussed, mass organizations in Eritrea and the United States were important contexts for the production of the EPLF's synthetic nationalism. The years preceding the arrival of the refugees had witnessed the conversion of virtually every Eritrean in the United States to an EPLF political identity. Former EFLNA members therefore tried reproducing the pattern of the 1970s, in which new arrivals whose prior affiliation had been with the ELF were recruited and converted to the EPLF. But many former ELF members continued to seek spaces for independent identity and organization.

The idea of diaspora community associations suggested one such potential space. For ELF-affiliated refugees and those who did not readily support the EPLF or "the politics" in general, the opportunity to take control of building such autonomous institutions was attractive. However, the problems of political identity and the EPLF's transnational presence were so pervasive that community organizing efforts afforded scant refuge. Asgedom remembers:

[In the early 1980s] there was no community as such, no association. There were people of Eritrean descent here, that individuals could connect with, and mass organizations of EPLF. But we wouldn't even attempt to join—I mean, you have to remember, we still had the animosity, the disconnectedness. [In 1985], many Eritreans were trying to organize an Eritrean community. Still the issue of ELF and EPLF was a dividing line for forming a community. . . . The only existing organization was the political one [the EPLF]. And we were saying, we have to stand on our own, create our own Eritrean identity here, in the U.S.

Even EPLF supporters recognized the desire among former ELF affiliates to stake a place for themselves within the Eritrean transnational sphere of activity. Tsegai recalls:

EPLF people had mass organizations. So [ELF people] had really become the ones spearheading the community organizations. But then they became targets. I remember in one church, we almost had a fist fight, throwing chairs, calling names. It was the first time I had seen something like this. I said to myself, "Why would it happen like this?" So we ended it, and the effort disintegrated, and we didn't raise the issue of a community organization for several months after that. But there were a lot of people who wanted a community to form, because they had social problems, cultural problems, economic problems. . . . So, really people could not see this community organization outside of their political feelings, and the hostility they have towards those who represent different politics from them. Because the situation with ELF members was that they felt the community organization was an extension of EPLF, which they hated much. . . . And from our point of view, this [community association] had nothing to do with EPLF, because EPLF had its mass organizations. But they said, "We know how EPLF operates, you are going to dominate this organization."

Countless other respondents in both Eritrea and the United States echoed this same point about "the politics" as a source of enduring tension and mistrust in the Eritrean diaspora. In several places, communities split into separate associations as a result of the political divisions. Andom explains,

There was one group that started a community center in San Francisco, way back in the 1970s. And we said, "Could it be ideal [for the community center] to be associated with the mass organizations?" And it was quite a division. We [EPLF members] wanted them to be associated with the mass organizations. But the people who set it up there felt like, no, this should just be Eritreans, with no politics. . . . The second [association] came in Washington, D.C., later on, with people who were predominantly non-EPLF. They may not have been ELF, but they were not affiliated with EPLF. . . . At times, there were two community centers in one place, one very much pro-EPLF, and the other non-EPLF. The very active ELF cadres who migrated to America, I saw them participate in such community groups as leaders.

But the viewpoint of many EPLF supporters was that their non-EPLF compatriots were simply misguided and would eventually come around to accepting the front's leadership in diaspora. One government official, a former chairman of the EPLF in the United States, recalls the same time period, although from a perspective embedded within that of the EPLF leadership:

Politically, at that stage, it was difficult. The ELF members and fighters were bitter, you know, saying "EPLF abused us, because of the civil war we are out of our country and we ended up here, and not only this, but EPLF did it by joining with TPLF [in Ethiopia]." So it was really a time when we had to explain what happened. . . . It was time to start these communities, and we thought the political issue can be handled separately. Being a member of EPLF or not is one thing, but to be organized as Eritreans, to work for the community for the good of it and to help the country in general . . . If you are going to have a community, you have to recognize that there is no ELF, no EPLF, identify the issues and work for them. But they [former ELF members] wanted to politicize it. In some cases they wanted to use it [the community association] to condemn EPLF. So a conflict was coming.[4]

It is important to see how this perspective reveals the hegemony, or naturalness, of EPLF identity as one and the same with "proper" nationalist identity. This official betrays the assumption that creating community institutions according to EPLF's programmatic guidelines was not politicized, while the critique of such an arrangement by former ELF members was clearly politically motivated. He implies that the task for EPLF in facilitating community building in exile was to help "convert" former ELF members to these definitions and practices by asserting their essential Eritreanness rather than their political specificity.

To a significant degree, the EPLF proved successful. Despite the explosive early encounters and ongoing tension between EPLF supporters in the United States and the incoming ELF-affiliated refugees, the latter remained as committed to Eritrean independence as their EPLF counterparts. And even while EPLF/ELF political identities continue to matter in the present—perhaps even more so as the PFDJ government has grown increasingly authoritarian—it would be misleading to argue that they have endured unchanged. Over time, a great many ELF affiliates developed sympathies with the EPLF as the champion of the independence movement even if they did not formally join mass organizations or the front's chapters. Some eventually renounced their former ELF affiliations entirely to join the EPLF in the United States, or the PFDJ after independence. Still others became increasingly active in humanitarian relief work under the ERA chapters in the diaspora, which helped coordinate international food and medical assistance from hundreds of NGOs and channel it through the EPLF's main branch of ERA in Khartoum (see Killion 1998:205–7). Others retained their commitment to ELF and contributed to keeping the organization alive as an alternative to EPLF/PFDJ, albeit always in exile and not without persistent factionalization.

As Eritrea came ever closer to independence, more and more people rallied beneath a single nationalist banner identified with the EPLF. Within exile communities, however, many conflicts endured regarding the community associations, their leadership, definition, and roles. Actors on each side of the divide began recognizing the need to remove politics as much as possible from associational life in diaspora. As Fitsum, a resettled refugee who had participated in EPLF mass organizations as a youth in Eritrea, explained, "When we say 'Jebha,' not all who were part of Jebha remained Jebha. . . . There were a number of them who even though they didn't join EPLF, they were sympathizers. Not all Jebhas are against EPLF."

At the same time, Fitsum also acknowledges that people have not yet been able to overcome differences in political identity in their associational life: "We blame them and they blame us. This is our weakness. We should sit down and talk about it and forget ELF and EPLF. Here, we have the same goal. This community is for nothing else than to help Eritreans. What does community mean? Community means finding your lost brother or sister, helping people, building together for the sake of culture and language. It is our mistake on both sides."

As I discuss later, however, not everyone in the Eritrean transnational social field shared Fitsum's ideal definition of community or the sense that the political divide should be addressed openly. This included the EPLF/PFDJ leadership. Yet, increasingly aware of the tendency for diaspora communities to polarize between EPLF mass organizations and independent associations initiated by those not affiliated with the EPLF, the leadership in the field chose a somewhat radical course of action: to dissolve its historic mass organizations altogether and set guidelines for the structuring of "nonpolitical" *maHber koms.*[5] In its decision to assert transnational authority over community associations in diaspora, however, the EPLF leadership did not succeed in laying political identity to rest. Rather, it conjured specters that have never ceased haunting the living.

Ertra Kom: Defining and Constructing Community in Exile

The Dissolution of EPLF Mass Organizations and the Push for Community

Despite the suspicions of many ELF-affiliated refugees throughout the 1980s, the EPLF did not (yet) control the nascent community associations Eritreans were trying to form in diaspora. While many ELF members had interpreted the efforts of the front's supporters to establish the terms of those associations as the EPLF's own, the leadership in the field did not begin actively organizing such associations until just prior to the achievement of independence. As the EPLF prepared throughout 1989 to invade Ethiopian-held Massawa, on the Red Sea coast, money poured in from exiles all over the world who recognized this as perhaps the final decisive moment in the thirty-year liberation war. Their response seems to have alerted the EPLF to two dynamics: the massive potential of the diaspora for helping support Eritrea economically—far greater than in earlier periods of the struggle—and the possibility that former ELF members could effectively rally behind the EPLF on behalf of the independence cause. As Gebre put it: "If it comes to the overall national interest, then Eritreans have always been behind EPLF, even with our reservations and political differences. So at the time, supporting the liberation of Massawa was very important. And the EPLF started understanding, started realizing, that the bigger the number of Eritreans in the diaspora, the bigger the pool of resources for EPLF. So EPLF started exploiting it."

Indeed, 1989–90 marked a turning point in the Eritrean transnational movement. For the EPLF, victory over the dramatically weakened Ethiopian Derg regime seemed inevitable. As part of the front's final push to liberate Eritrea, the leadership issued a directive "dissolving" the worldwide mass organizations that had coordinated the efforts of Eritreans worldwide. Instead of working within their discrete associations of women, workers, students, and youth, Eritreans across the globe were asked to collectively refocus all their energies and resources on the EPLF's major push for liberation, including by returning to Eritrea.

Although information about the directive is spotty, and even current government officials could (or would) say little to me about what actually happened, its objective appeared to be twofold. On the one hand, the EPLF was encouraging its most active supporters to return to Eritrea and physically contribute to the momentum they expected would lead to liberation. On the other hand, the leadership was aware of the conflicts of political identity plaguing so many diaspora communities and needed to find new ways to consolidate national unity. In effectively abandoning the historic institutions that fostered a particular EPLF identity, which had at least partially influenced the structural divide between EPLF mass organizations and ELF-dominated, nonpartisan community associations, the EPLF hoped to ride the wave of sympathy that former ELF affiliates felt toward the front by placing them on an equal national footing with longtime EPLF supporters.

Respondents in the Eritrean government as well as those who live in exile reported that the dissolution of the mass organizations produced shock waves throughout the diaspora. In 1990, the Department of Mass Administration, or Kifli Hizbi, sent two officials from the EPLF leadership to issue and explain the directive. Mahmoud Sherifo, then an administrator within Kifli Hizbi, addressed thousands of Eritreans at the annual Eritrean Festival held in Washington, D.C. The directive outraged loyal and longtime supporters of the EPLF, who had dedicated years of their lives and most of their resources to supporting the front through its mass organizations. Whether Sherifo adequately delivered the message and articulated the front's decision remains a subject of some debate. One government official explains at length:

There were these yearly festivals, or yearly congresses, where somebody is coming from the field to address [everyone]. So [Sherifo] came then, and he said, "From now on there are no [mass organization] members, nothing like that, it's for everybody, this country." What he was trying to say was, people should not look into narrow membership of EPLF and all that, but the way he said it was— wrong. Very wrong. And it pissed off a lot of our members. . . . They were saying, "How after all these years that we worked, could you just say it like that? If there are things that have to change, then discuss those things." But the way [Sherifo] said it was not right, even though that's not what he was trying to put across in the message. The message was to say, now everybody is supporting EPLF, it's not like before, so we should broaden our view, we should include everybody, this should not be just a few members of EPLF saying, "We are members." Now almost everybody is a member because they are supporting EPLF, you know, taking EPLF as the only organization. So this is the message he should have said, that's what he meant, but he said, "You can't have small groups anymore, there is no need for that." This is the way he said it. So we kept explaining that's not what he said, or what he means, but it really made a mess.[6]

Regardless of Sherifo's handling of the situation, the response among EPLF supporters in the United States was overwhelmingly negative. As this man points out, and as numerous others I interviewed also noted, those who had been active in mass organizations suddenly felt as though their efforts were no longer valued. With one simple directive, the EPLF had placed them alongside former ELF members who had, in their view, opposed and even fought actively against the front, whose national identities were distorted by their membership in the ELF. In their anticipation of an independent state, the EPLF clearly wanted to help neutralize the bitter conflicts between its supporters and those who had belonged to the ELF or other political organizations in Ethiopia. In the place of mass organizations, the front promoted the community organizations, or *maHber koms*, as preferred locations in which to build unity and coordinate transnational participation. Their efforts created more problems than solutions: many formerly dedicated members of the EPLF turned bitter toward the front's leadership, and those who remained distrustful felt that the front now encroached directly upon what little autonomous spaces they had tried to carve out abroad. After liberation in 1991, further questions arose about the way in which diaspora Eritreans, and EPLF supporters in particular, should continue participating in the new nation-state. Although he had already returned permanently to Eritrea by that time, one former EPLF activist remembers how he felt when EPLF issued the directive:

We weren't really mass organization members; in reality, we were really partners in the construction of the country. Many things could have been done not to let [the organizations] go. . . . But I think the main setback might have been the idea that such organizations are no more needed in independence. My viewpoint at that time was, why not transform them into real associations? They could be career associations, they could be—those who are trying to support the school systems, or health systems, in Eritrea. There are many ways, because these people are committed. You know, but to simply cut it, and then to say, "Well, everybody's an Eritrean national now," or that kind of feeling—people said, "But what is our role? Where do we go?"

This man's comments suggest that had the EPLF desired it, its mass organizations could have been transformed from civilian wings of the front into civil society institutions for the independent state. But the directive instead alienated many former supporters and even discouraged some from returning to Eritrea after independence. His comments also reveal the extent to which Eritrean lives, collectively and individually, had been so dramatically shaped by the structure, ideology, and praxis of the front, that many felt cut off without its constant administrative presence.

Gebre, on a visit to Eritrea during the summer of 2001, explained to me over tea one afternoon in an Asmara café—owned by a repatriated former refugee of ELF background—how the dissolution of the mass organizations had affected certain individuals in the midwestern community. He told me that rather than receiving recognition or perhaps rewards for all the sacrifices they had made, EPLF supporters were "put in the same category as people who had done nothing at all, or people who had belonged to ELF." Many who had not actively supported independence, or had been ELF fighters, returned to Eritrea to invest or start businesses, Gebre said, gesturing around the café in which we sat as a case in point. But those who had supported the EPLF all along had little to invest because they had sent everything to the front during the struggle. More than a few had not been to Eritrea since childhood. "They felt left behind in the independent state," Gebre said. Another government official corroborated how the issue continued to plague the EPLF's relationship with its former mass organization members. "For many years," he said, "it would come up in every meeting that we do. You know, you go to raise something, an issue, and they say, 'Why do you need us now? This is what you said [in 1989].' So it came off totally wrong."

Thus the EPLF's efforts to redirect the energies of their former mass constituents into "nonpartisan" community associations faced difficulties at the outset. While the expansion of the EPLF's transnational control into this area of diaspora life sought to take advantage of the greater support it enjoyed among many former ELF affiliates the closer it brought Eritrea toward independence, it did not resolve existing political tensions within exile communities. Those who continued to resent the presence and power of the EPLF in the diaspora kept pursuing more autonomous institutions and actively resisted the EPLF's transnational agenda. In the following pages, I address the ongoing debate about the meaning and constitution of "community" and how it continues to shape, and be shaped by, both the EPLF's transnational project and the conditions of everyday life in the midwestern community I studied.

Community Associations and the EPLF's Transnational Power

With the dissolution of the mass organizations, the task of defining and organizing the *maHber koms*, or community associations, came to dominate the EPLF's agenda for the diaspora. Two patterns in particular emerge when we examine the front's justifications and guidelines for community associations in exile. First, the notion of the *maHber kom* was constructed as an essential cultural feature across Eritrean society and therefore a natural mechanism for the production and maintenance of a common national identity in diaspora. Second, virtually no overt discussion of the enduring tensions between ELF and EPLF political identities as key problems within actual or putative community associations took place. Rather, in accordance with the EPLF's synthetic orientation, these differences and their associated grievances were glossed over and denied within the parameters of official nationalist discourse.

In the late 1980s and early 1990s, regular articles about the importance of community associations in exile started appearing in the front's Tigrinya-language magazines such as the biannual *Hagerey*, or "Motherland." Throughout the late 1970s and much of the 1980s, the EPLF's numerous publications had regularly reported on the activities of its mass organizations around the world, including the amount of money and other material resources they had contributed to the struggle in the field. Around the time of the 1989 directive that dissolved the mass organizations, however, the EPLF's Department of Mass Administration (Kifli Hizbi) began reporting on the conditions of Eritreans in exile more generally and, within that, promoting community associations as necessary for building unity and maintaining national identity in diaspora. These kinds of writings aimed at contextualizing the Eritrean experience within that of expanding refugee and immigrant populations in the twentieth century to argue that such associations were key to social and cultural survival. The EPLF also pointed out that they could be important sources of power and legitimacy for the emergent Eritrean state vis-à-vis the various nations in which Eritreans had settled.

One June 1989 article in *Hagerey* titled "Eritrean Exiles and Their Community Experience" claimed to draw upon the sociological literature on civic associations to make a case for why Eritreans should develop similar institutions to those of other immigrant and refugee groups in the West.[7] Citing the efforts of Jews, Greeks, Italians, Vietnamese, Chinese, Koreans, Indians, and Arabs, the unnamed author of the article defined the goal of such institutions in the following terms:

Civic associations, by bringing people together under the lowest common denominator, provide a conducive environment for development. More than what divides them, what unifies the members of the community is usually greater. Communities create the right atmosphere for the development of a single unified goal based on common interests and pursuits. Additionally, by respecting individual interests and feelings, communities advance the common good. In short, by virtue of its utility in allowing for participation, a community unifies the interests, preferences, wishes and feelings of all its members and provides a very important service.[8]

The objectives of these associations, the article stated, are to support the political, technological, and economic development of the country of origin, as well as assist exiles with education and skills. They should also provide moral and social support for people struggling within racially and socioeconomically stratified host societies. For Eritreans in diaspora, the author asserted, the realities of racial discrimination and economic disadvantage had been particularly acute. Moreover, the needs of Eritreans in exile could not be met by informal mutual help between friends and family. Rather, organizations were needed to help create systematic solutions to the typical problems Eritreans faced and to channel the aspirations they harbored for Eritrea itself. But the creation of such associations was hampered by certain trends:

[Few] or no studies were done about how to set up these communities. Impatience and competition has lead to the creation of more than one community under the banner of "cooperatives" and "social clubs" in some cities of North America and Europe. While a limited number of Eritreans participated in both, others who tried to merge them proved unsuccessful. The wish of the Eritrean exiles was to create a unified community, but this was frustrated by competition and personal clashes. But in some cases, organizations with broad public support were created.[9]

The article went on to name several ways in which Eritreans had achieved success in exile, among them advances in the education and socialization of children born abroad, the increasing frequency of sports events and holiday celebrations, and most important, the achievement of "consensus" and "greater unity" as well as an increase in "anticolonial activity," or support for the nationalist revolution. At the same time, the article stated that "notwithstanding these positive developments, Eritrean communities fall short of what was expected and hoped for."

Outlining the kinds of ameliorating measures that should be taken, the author revealed an approach deeply embedded in EPLF ideology and praxis. Among the recommendations offered were that "those [communities] with experienced fighters, education, skills must come together for a common interest of their people and work together" and that "[those] who disrupt harmony and understanding in the community must be invited to correct their ways or must be criticized." Both of these recommendations were consistent with the leadership-by-example organizing strategies and Maoist-inspired practices of criticism and self-criticism long utilized within the EPLF.

Similarly, an article in the January 1990 edition of *Hagerey* titled "Eritrean Community Development: By What Means?" emphasized the importance of "community institutions" in traditional Eritrean society.[10] While such institutions undoubtedly varied greatly across ethno-regional groups, the article treated Eritrean culture and society as relatively homogenous and offered only vague examples of traditional community institutions. Other than an imprecise cultural justification for the notion of "community," the examples provided little that was translatable to the refugee experience in the West. Moreover, the only ethnic group specifically mentioned, the minority Nara, seemed a carefully chosen example intended largely to illustrate the multiethnic inclusiveness of the EPLF's approach rather than the specific benefits of existing community institutions:

For instance, early leaders of the Nara ethnic group were practicing democratic methods to govern themselves. To defend themselves from their enemies and to preserve their social and cultural way of life, they built fortifications and their houses on higher ground. At night they would stand guard by taking turns and during the day they would descend to the plains below to cultivate their farms. Today there are numerous community structures (in the villages) that can be cited as examples. Residents of villages and hamlets live in close proximity to each other and solve mutual problems through collective efforts.[11]

According to this formulation, local community institutions had constituted a bedrock on which contemporary Eritrean society, despite massive political upheavals and great internal diversity, continued to rest. A common Eritrean national identity was cast as emerging organically from the "democratic" and egalitarian practices found throughout Eritrean "traditional" communities, long upheld by the EPLF as the seat of authentic culture, providing a compelling reason for their continuation as primary organizing principles throughout Eritrea and its exile communities. Moving from the example of traditional rural communities, the author noted that

Eritrean identity, dignity and unity have been maintained and solidified at a national level. At this moment, when the number of the liberated towns and villages is growing, our people are unified under one vision and are assuming a role in governing themselves. And a new chapter is emerging in the cultural and political life of the people. The Eritrean communities that are sprouting in exile are expected to renew, revitalize and broaden the rich cultural legacy. Wherever they are, Eritreans must build "Little Eritreas."[12]

Like its 1989 counterpart, this article also outlined once again the kinds of problems Eritreans faced as they struggled to create sustainable associations in exile. Glossing over the exact nature of the difficulties, the author noted that "disagreements and internal conflicts end up negatively affecting the unity of the members," and perhaps more specifically, "some members or non-members, because of their misunderstanding regarding the community and thinking of it as if it is without benefits or utility, or that it only benefits one side at the expense of others, view the community as if it is backward, useless, or a place of rancor."[13] At the same time, the author asserted that these issues should indeed be resolvable over time, "since all the misunderstanding that is claimed to be present is very minor and secondary to the desired development of the community."[14] Nowhere did the author discuss the actual conflicts, however, reflecting the EPLF's general unwillingness to recognize the problem of political identity by naming it directly. As I discuss later, a similar dynamic occurs today when supporters of the PFDJ government address the kinds of criticisms and potential platforms offered by those critical of the regime.

The EPLF's decision to dissolve its mass organizations and tout community associations as the preferred method of both diasporic and transnational engagement thus accomplished two tasks: it subverted the efforts of non-EPLF members and those opposing the front to create autonomous spaces in diaspora, and it provided a new arena for propagating the EPLF's nationalist orientation. Community associations were intended to become a vehicle for the neutralization of fractured political identities by subtly dismissing those differences and recasting the Eritrean nation as organically founded upon the same kinds of "traditional community institutions" the EPLF sought to create in exile. Thus the front at once incorporated these associations into its transnational sphere of influence at the same time that it appeared to remove distinctions based on political identity by abolishing its own mass organizations and discursively constructing the nation as though it ultimately transcended the narrower political identities of the ELF and EPLF. Again, this approach was continuous with the way in which the EPLF's synthetic nationalism had absorbed and homogenized the prenationalist cleavages of religion, ethno-regionalism, and even kinship.

But perhaps most interesting in the EPLF's approach to the community associations in exile was the way in which Eritreans were encouraged to participate in the civil societies of their countries of settlement and to strive for internal unity through "democratic" methods and practices. The 1989 *Hagerey* article opened with the assertion that "it is not possible for those living in exile to attain political power in a foreign political system" and went on to suggest that "instead, it is important to create community for the exiled population" as a way for immigrant and minority groups to gain the support and attention of the host country government both for themselves and for their country of origin.[15] Perhaps recognizing the power of certain ethnic lobbies in countries like the United States, such as Jewish support for the state of Israel or the success of many first-wave immigrants in gaining political power (and thus the United States' attention for their homelands), the EPLF encouraged Eritreans to utilize the resources and various constitutional freedoms of the United States and European nations by organizing themselves into powerful enclaves.

The strategy echoed that of the early mass organizations such as EFLNA, whose major task, in addition to supporting the revolution at home, was earning support for it among foreign constituents. The EPLF emphasized the significant role that community associations could play abroad and on behalf of Eritrea if they drew upon both their internal democratic tendencies (glossed as essential features of Eritrean traditional society) and the democratic practices available to them in the West. I will return to the uses, meanings, and conflicts over democracy and civil society in the Eritrean transnational project in the final chapter. For the moment it is important to note that these were important elements in the EPLF's justification for building community associations in exile.

From Independence to the Ethio-Eritrean Border War

Eritrea Is Free: Whither the Community?

Clearly, the events most powerfully shaping Eritrean exile communities and their institutions have been those happening in Eritrea itself. The long struggle for independence had dominated the hearts, minds, and daily lives of exiles for many years. It also established a foundation to guide their activities and goals, despite certain tensions relating to political identities and the EPLF's transnational administrative control. The attainment of independence in 1991–93 changed the situation yet again and opened a new chapter in the efforts to build communities in diaspora. With Eritrea's freedom secured, those living abroad could now turn more attention to their diaspora communities and the increasing need for sustained institutions, especially those that could benefit children. Many people hoped and expected that bitter political divisions would cease to matter now that the one common goal shared by the EPLF and ELF had finally been achieved. For a brief period anyway, it seemed they were right. The grievances between the former fronts washed away in the euphoria following independence.

But as the EPLF began transforming itself into a government, and as the front's headquarters in Washington, D.C., metamorphosed into an embassy, the state's role in connecting diaspora communities back to itself also matured. A more concerted attempt to coordinate diaspora associations as part of the Eritrean nation-state began to take shape. As a religious leader in Eritrea who ministered to Eritreans in America at the time of independence explained to me:

After independence, the Eritrean government tried to really enforce those Eritrean communities, in different towns and cities in the States. And what happened was, there was an Eritrean community already. And many of the people, especially those who belonged to ELF, wanted it to remain an Eritrean community, embracing all Eritreans. With the new pressure of Hegdef [PFDJ] trying to organize the communities, it brought more division. It was a problem in all the communities, all over the country. I got more involved in 1997, because we wanted to see the benefit for all Eritreans, not just those who belonged to Hegdef [PFDJ].

One of the main ways the Eritrean government tried to involve itself directly in community efforts was through sending officials from the embassy around the United States to hold meetings and educational sessions on how to organize and mobilize such associations. Moreover, EPLF chapters, now chapters of the PFDJ Party, were encouraged to play leadership roles and help facilitate individuals' relationships with the state by mediating official embassy business, planning events for national holidays, and distributing videos, tapes, and CDs that proved immensely popular as well as profitable. In the midwestern community, the PFDJ's newly invigorated attempts to assert control over community organizations upset many longtime leaders who had not been affiliated with the EPLF. After noting that the first year or two of independence witnessed a dramatic mellowing of tensions related to political identities, Asgedom explained to me how the PFDJ's plan to organize communities reopened all of those wounds. It also personally affronted him as a community leader:

The good relations didn't last long, till 1992, or 1993, when someone came from Washington, D.C., and said he wanted to form an Eritrean community. Many Eritreans here told him, "We will form our own, you cannot form it for us." The embassy was doing that at the time—for whatever purpose, they were trying to create some sort of community organizations that would support their own base. But here, everyone was very, very keen on now thinking that if we are going to be independent, our association has to be formally independent. . . . The PFDJ is a political institution. Sometimes they sent instructions through the embassy to the community organizations, and there were times I said to them, "The embassy doesn't instruct me. You can take your letter back. We are an independent community organization."

Thus, even after Eritrea became the newest nation-state in Africa, the "freedom" of its diaspora communities became even less certain than before. Many of the internal issues that had developed throughout the 1980s endured unresolved well into the 1990s. These continued until the border war with Ethiopia broke out in 1998, at which time Eritreans turned all of their attention again to Eritrea, temporarily suspending the more specific concerns of exile to protect what they believed was the sovereignty of the state itself.

But however powerful Eritrea and its state apparatus have been in shaping Eritrean diaspora communities, other factors specific to American society have also played a role. On the one hand, characteristics common to American society as a whole affect Eritreans as a collective, national population. On the other hand, the local spaces that Eritrean communities occupy also contribute to the particularities of their internal relations and orientation toward Eritrea. Because this study is not a comparative one, it is not possible to address here the variations across Eritrean communities in different U.S. cities. Nor can we ascertain why vibrant, healthy institutions prevail in some locations, while others remain forever dogged by internal fragmentation and malaise.

Yet because of the discernible, patterned strategies that the EPLF pursued in shaping a transnational social field to serve the liberation struggle and independent state, it is possible to examine the impacts and consequences of these on specific diaspora communities as part of a more general phenomenon. Moreover, because the phenomenon of "diaspora" itself is characterized by connections between communities abroad as much as by engagement with the real or imagined homeland (Hall 1990), most Eritreans living abroad have significant knowledge or experience of other Eritrean communities within their own country of residence as well as in other countries.

Throughout the course of fieldwork in both the United States and Eritrea, I encountered numerous individuals who had spent extended periods of time in different parts of the world, drawn together by bonds of kin, friendship, and political affiliation. They were able to—and often did—comment on trends they observed across Eritrean communities. Several times, a brief conversation with a stranger on an Asmara street corner or in a café evolved into an extended discussion, in which the dynamics of my interlocutor's particular community abroad, as well as his or her reflections on Eritrea itself, revealed much about the global contours of the Eritrean transnational social field and its variations across space. And while these variations may be very important in their own right, two patterns were overwhelmingly consistent: the tense encounter between EPLF and ELF political identities and the way in which Eritreans were acutely aware of the party-state's presence within diasporic spaces. Repeatedly throughout the course of my research, Eritreans—both those living in exile and those who stayed home—revealed an understanding of the worldwide diaspora, and the Eritrean state's transnational project, as part of a complex, differentiated, and not unproblematic whole that comprises what we know, and map, as the Eritrean nation-state. In the remainder of this chapter, I more closely assess the midwestern community as one node within that elaborate web.

At Home Abroad? Defining and Practicing "Community" in Exile

There can be no denying that the midwestern Eritrean community I studied has seen its share of troubles, both internally and as an "ethnic" population in the urban United States (see also Teklemariam 2002). Repeatedly in the course of my research, leaders expressed the need for intensive "soul searching" about the community's difficulties. Their threefold objectives—still elusive after nearly eighteen years of concerted effort—were to sustain a working community association that could effectively coordinate all the smaller groups beneath it to participate in the transnational nation-state in ways everyone felt comfortable with and to secure much needed resources for local members (Hepner 2003). Several ongoing efforts were made to formulate a kind of "workshop" where the community could hash out, once and for all, their various tensions and the reasons their attempts to sustain a secular, nonpartisan community association had floundered. Often, my presence was treated as part of this overall process, and I felt myself at times becoming a therapeutic figure for those who shared things with me that they confessed were extremely difficult to say to other Eritreans.

Indeed, the weight of the transnational project and the demands placed upon the community by the PFDJ party-state (or by the EPLF) since the 1970s, as well as individuals' own deep and sincere commitments to their nation and families, have dramatically weakened the community's ability to form stable diaspora institutions that serve the very specific needs of the U.S.-resident population (Hepner 2003). We have seen throughout the earlier part of this chapter how attempts to form the community association were affected by struggles over nationalism, political identity, and the EPLF's attempts to define and control associational life in exile. In addition, as Chapter 5 will address in more detail, the financial burden of paying taxes to the Eritrean government, sending remittances to family members, and participating in other special fund-raising events, have siphoned off the scarce resources of a population whose major forms of employment cluster in the lower-wage service sector (cab drivers, hotel staff, child care providers, and parking attendants, for example; see Teklemariam 2002), leaving little left over for projects in the United States. The very presence of the PFDJ in diaspora, in the form of local chapters and even the embassy itself, is a controversial subject and one factor contributing to the paralysis of community associations and other groups that have tried to form and function independently.

In addition, the process of defining both a community and its objectives has been extremely unclear. Much of this murkiness stems from the semantic confusion and perceived antagonism between organized and unorganized forms of community life. The definition of "community" that Eritreans seem to uphold as most legitimate is that of the *maHber*, the formal, organized association, or gesellschaft, that is goal-oriented, ostensibly democratic, and squarely in line with the overall goals of the

Eritrean nation-building process (however that might be defined). The notion of a more loosely defined population with important shared characteristics, who provide mutual support, friendship, and a sense of belonging, or gemeinschaft, is generally not considered "community." This very crucial difference first became clear to me when I found myself constantly clarifying with my interlocutors that I meant "community" in the most general sense, *Hibrete-seb*, while for them the word seemed consistently evocative of the formal association, the *maHber kom*. It became even more important as time and again people expressed feelings like the following, shared by a very active, dedicated woman who served on both the community association board and in the leadership of NUEW: "Even though we don't have a community, the Eritrean people get together when somebody dies, when there is a wedding, when there is a christening—whenever something happens to someone, everyone comes and contributes, participates. So even though we don't have an Eritrean community, we still get together, especially for our country. That is our priority." This tension has been a major feature and repeated stumbling block for the midwestern community as it seeks to achieve balance between its simultaneous roles in Eritrea and exile. And this obstacle seems to emerge directly from the historical manner in which the EPLF defined modernist mechanisms for expressing and practicing national identity.

Indeed, in 2001, the local *maHber kom* ceased functioning altogether (again). At its annual congress in June, which unexpectedly became its last, the association finally imploded beneath the weight of internal conflicts and intense ambivalence toward the institution itself. The main item on the meeting's agenda was to elect a new nine-person executive committee to replace the outgoing members. Tired and exasperated, most of the board members could not wait to leave their posts. "Today I will become a free man," the community association president told me as we chatted in the minutes before he called the group to order. But the meeting turned up few who were willing to take over. Only the usual forty to fifty people showed up at all, many of whom had already dedicated their time and energy to leading the association in the past. A commotion arose as people cursed each other for unwanted nominations and argued that they were already serving posts in existing groups such as the PFDJ or the churches. The outgoing president, an intense and volatile man named Kifle, rapidly took a different tack and began hand-selecting successors who he said showed the commitment necessary to lead the community.

A cacophony of voices protested Kifle's unilateral action. Amid the confusion, malaise, and frustration, one man called out, "What about the *baito* [traditional people's assembly]? Where is the democracy in this?" Meanwhile, Henok, an outgoing board member, seemed to choke back tears as he lamented to no one in particular, "Where is the appreciation? I have worked so hard the last year—we need a workshop to address all of this anger." Asgedom jumped to his feet, drowning out the fracas to make a passionate speech on behalf of the workshop plan, as others called out their support or rolled their eyes in exasperation. Kifle, his temper aflame, cursed in English and sputtered, "We don't have *nothing*, man, okay? We are totally fucked up! No workshop will ever help us! We are never going to solve this Eritrean problem!" As I glanced around the room, taking in the scene, my gaze fell on Tsegai Woldu, a powerhouse activist in EFLNA in the 1970s. He had nodded off to sleep.

Community Institutions and the Search for Unity

Despite the dilemmas faced by the community association for more than eighteen years, including its cycles of coalescence and disintegration, other organized associations within the Eritrean community functioned more smoothly. The three religious congregations—Orthodox, Catholic, and Protestant—each held weekly services (bimonthly in the case of Catholics) and oftentimes Bible study, prayer meetings, or social events during the week. Similarly, the local chapter of the NUEW was meeting approximately every six to eight weeks during the time I conducted field research, while the PFDJ political party held regular meetings and political education sessions. Sports teams also proved very popular, with men and boys playing soccer several times a week in the warm months, and women and girls playing volleyball. In addition to these organized activities, informal gatherings and special events filled in the downtime.

However, the relationships between these organized groups, their individual mandates, and the interests of those who belonged to them were not always compatible with one another or with hegemonic, EPLF-inspired definitions of Eritrean national identity. For example, many people reported how, on several occasions, both the PFDJ and the former community association planned events on the same day or in close proximity, either due to a lack of communication or for deliberately antagonistic reasons. Other groups had developed a particularly strong identity that others viewed as threatening to the primacy of nationalism; for example, Protestant Pentecostal Christians who eschewed participation in many activities and discourses that, in their view, only served to sustain political fragmentation and conflict. While they remained self-defined nationalists and often contributed large amounts of money to supporting the Eritrean nation-state, most Pentecostals were very critical of existing distinctions between the EPLF and the ELF, and even between Eritreans and Ethiopians (see Hepner 2003). Moreover, Pentecostals tended to organize their social lives primarily around their faith, spending the bulk of their free time in church and Bible study with their coreligionists. Others in the community expressed concern that Pentecostal beliefs, practices, and identities were insufficiently Eritrean and were critical of their disinterest in other aspects of community life, such as cultural dancing at parties known as *gwylas* (Hepner 2003).[16] Similarly, members of the PFDJ Party usually held meetings on Sunday mornings, creating problems for those who wished to attend church services at overlapping times. Even unorganized groups, such as the men who gathered in local coffee shops and diners to discuss politics, often from an oppositional perspective, created discomfort among committed PFDJ members, who viewed their "teahouse talk" as undisciplined, irresponsible, and potentially threatening to national unity in the diaspora and in Eritrea as a whole.

In addition, other would-be organized groups that tried to fill a niche in the community met with resistance from existing organizations who guarded their turf warily and fretted over further atomization. Efforts to form a viable youth association to represent first- or second-generation young people were especially difficult. During the Ethio-Eritrean border war, a concerted effort was made to form a chapter of the Eritrea-based mass organization, the National Union of Eritrean Youth and Students (NUEYS). T-shirts were even printed with the NUEYS logo on the front. However, this effort floundered as well, likely due to the fact that NUEYS is officially an EPLF/PFDJ mass organization and therefore represented another (unwelcome) avenue for the party-state's administrative presence. It is not clear that Daniel, one of the erstwhile organizers, even understood that this was probably the issue. His explanation emphasizes instead the unfulfilled needs of Eritrean American youth:

We had a couple of meetings, just as individuals, there were like fourteen of us, in their mid-twenties, most of them. It was a positive thing, but some of the community [board] members didn't like it. They thought we were courting against them. And we had to explain, "This is what the youth association is, you guys do whatever you do, we will still support you, but we have to have a youth association. It's nothing against you, it's working for the youth." Young Eritreans who live in America, there is a whole lot of things happening. Especially the teenagers who are growing up here, who were born in Eritrea or here in America, they are being excluded from the community, because there is no big community where they can go and get information and help. So we tried to do a lot of things. We even rented an office . . . we paid from our pockets a couple months' rent. . . . So it was very costly for us, as individuals, and you can't ask young Eritreans to contribute a whole lot of money. Everybody was busy sending money for the country, for relatives, for families. You are stretched to the maximum level. So there was no point—I mean, unless you have the resources to do it, build a youth association, there is nothing.

To a large extent, the problematic relations between organized groups have emerged out of the structural tension between the transnational project encouraged by the party-state and the desire and need for autonomous organizations that can address the local diasporic realities. But these structural tensions also derive their meaning from the real or perceived conflict between official nationalism and competing identities as Eritreans continue to seek a definition of Eritreanness not dictated wholly by the revolutionary legacy and single-party state. The diaspora community and its various attendant groups, both organized and informal, constitute a kind of laboratory for testing out new ways of being Eritrean that do not always square with the definitions produced by the EPLF/PFDJ and as a result frequently appear antagonistic toward the state itself and its transnational agenda for diaspora organizations.

Interestingly, people of every background and persuasion, regardless of their former political affiliations or feelings about the current government, share a great deal of anxiety about a lack of coordination in community life and the emergence of "small islands" that express and reinforce existing and troublesome differences between Eritreans. For example, Asgedom, one of the most outspoken critics of the state's transnational presence abroad, nonetheless spoke very passionately about the need for coordination and unity. When I asked him why unity was important, he responded, "If we are to share this city, we need to be united as Eritreans." He continued, "There is so much at stake for being fragmented and disunited. . . . In the final analysis, if there is no framework of oneness, then unnecessary competition creates unnecessary friction all of the time . . . .There is also the fact that we are Eritreans, and have a long way to go as one people, we have so much at stake, and we have so much people around us that really want us to be divided and disintegrated. Our survival, the survival of those small organizations, also depends upon us having this sense of oneness."

Asgedom's statement illustrates how the structural and institutional features of the diaspora community are understood to be primarily shaped according to the EPLF/PFDJ's synthetic nationalism and how many Eritreans continue to search for broader definitions that can accommodate a wider range of political persuasions and subnational identities while still remaining legitimately Eritrean. Despite his former affiliation with the ELF and his critical stance toward the party-state's transnationalist presence, Asgedom remained deeply committed to Eritrean national unity both at home and abroad. And as the following chapters discuss, working out positive, productive relationships between different interest groups and subnational identities in diaspora communities is viewed by many people as a prerequisite to creating a more inclusive and democratic state and society in Eritrea itself.

While the concerns that these midwestern Eritreans shared about the polarization of the community into small groups may have a great deal to do with anxieties about nationalism and unity more generally, they also stemmed from very real shortages of resources and dedicated volunteers. In a small community whose time and assets were already spread thinly between life in a costly American city and obligations to the Eritrean state and family members at home, little was left for further projects. This became especially clear when the community association spearheaded efforts to purchase "a house" to use as a community center. Conflicts between the community association and the PFDJ chapter were especially acute, expressing the tension between the local realities of the diaspora (represented by the community association) and the state-sponsored transnational agenda (represented by the PFDJ chapter).

At the time the community association announced its objective to collect money for purchasing a building, the border war between Eritrea and Ethiopia was raging full force in the Horn of Africa. In addition to enhanced remittances that individuals and families sent to relatives and friends, a major fund-raising campaign in the diaspora was initiated by the Eritrean state as well as by Eritreans all over the world.[17] Once again, prior political affiliation or opposition to the PFDJ did not deter Eritreans from rallying to the country's defense. The Eritrean Development Foundation, the Washington, D.C.- and Asmara-based NGO that arose from the ashes of the ERA, coordinated its chapters all over the globe to carry out walkathons on Martyrs' Day (June 20), the proceeds of which were intended to support Eritreans displaced by the war. The midwestern city I studied emerged exemplary, raising $45,000 in one day. Similarly, at fund-raisers organized by the ad-hoc Eritrean Defense Committee, individuals and families harked back to the days of EFLNA as they pledged huge sums of money. Within several weeks, the community raised more than $850,000 to support the Eritrean government in its fight against Ethiopia. In addition, people purchased government bonds to prop up the wartime economy. Indeed, as the attainment of independence had done in 1991–93, the border war temporarily drowned out all of the internal conflicts.

The community association's focus on buying "the house" during a time when the emphasis and resources were all directed to Eritrea proved fatal. While many people initially supported the idea of buying a community building and contributed money generously, the plan eventually came under attack by those who felt that every available resource should be directed toward Eritrea as long as it was in crisis. By the time the community association had amassed $35,000 in donations, barely enough to put a down payment on a property, they had hit a roadblock.

The financial reserves of the community, already stressed with contributions for the war at home, had been tapped out. As the association continued to prod, people who formerly supported the plan to buy a building became very upset. The motives of the community association came under fire, and some people began suggesting that the association was trying to undermine the PFDJ and, ultimately, Eritrean sovereignty, by redirecting money and attention that should be spent on Eritrea. Tsehainesh, active in NUEW and a former ELF fighter, recounted why she thought the idea to buy a house was poorly timed and highly suspect:

> You have to know your people first, what kinds of needs they have. At that time, there was war in my country! I would prefer to give $500 to the people who were suffering and dying, who don't have even a tent to live in! They were everywhere in the mountains, just displaced. Why did they [the community association] raise the issue at that time? Because they were against EPLF! That's why I don't support it at the time. I don't want to pay $500 to put it in a bank and buy a building for the community at a time when the country needs help! It's bad that they raised the issue at that time. *You can't support the community and your country at one time.* Once there is peace, nobody asks you for help, and it's okay to do it for your community. But at that time the situation in my country was very bad, and the government was asking for a lot of money. They [the community association leaders] were going from home to home, asking for $500. I don't know, I would like to have a building or a place for the Eritrean community. But not at that time. . . . *When you ask for money for the community it means you are in competition with the government.* [Emphasis added]

Past or present political affiliation or group membership appeared to have little to do with whether people supported the community association's efforts to buy the building or whether they vocally opposed it. In fact, many people who articulated viewpoints critical of the PFDJ and its presence in the diaspora nonetheless saw enough of a distinction between the party and the state to warrant supporting the government in time of war. Others who fully supported the PFDJ and actively contributed to the war effort saw the community center as yet another way to consolidate Eritrean unity at a particularly important time in the country's history. And still others, perhaps no more than a handful, did indeed appear to be using the community center as a way to divert resources away from the government for reasons related to political opposition.

The crucial pattern that emerged, however, had to do with the way in which many active PFDJ members and supporters continued to see the community association as part and parcel of the party-state's mandate to build unity in the diaspora, and ultimately to control it, whereas others in the association's leadership viewed the purchase of a building as essential to the community's autonomy from the Eritrean state's transnational agenda. In addition, more than a few shared Tsehainesh's feeling that diasporic concerns and transnational commitments to Eritrea were mutually exclusive. The result was a bewildering conglomeration of motives, agendas, viewpoints, and politicized goals that eventually contributed to the association's demise. The struggle that had waged throughout the 1980s and 1990s over the community association's role as an autonomous, diasporic institution versus its potential as a key element in the EPLF/PFDJ's reproduction of nationalist identity and state power appeared to have come full circle again. Witness two diametrically opposed visions of the community association's role, both articulated in 2001: the first, aired by Habtu, captures the way in which the EPLF/PFDJ and its members abroad continue to view organizations as primary locations for the production of unified transnational subjects and hence a unified nation:

Hegdef [PFDJ] is a political organization, Sha'bia [EPLF]. So Hegdef supports the government. Hegdef's teaching, Hegdef's organization, is to support this government. What they do is organize the people. So we support Hegdef, and we support the community [association] very much. Whether they like it or not, when people organize in one association, it helps the government. That's why we fight for the community [association] to grow and be organized. . . . The community [association] has its own agenda, and they talk about that agenda, not Hegdef's agenda. But if the community [association] is united it helps Eritrea, the people, and the government. That's our theory.

The second perspective, posted on an Eritrean Web site known for its anti-EPLF/PFDJ bent, reveals how those critical of the EPLF/PFDJ's presence in the diaspora resent the appropriation of community organizations they believe should provide services in host countries:

No one can deny the role the "community centers" played in the mobilization of resources during the liberation struggle. That has greatly contributed to the weakening of the occupational regimes that led to the independence of the Eritrean land. However, the intolerant culture that prevailed during the years of the struggle was perpetuated in those centers. They remained partisan bastions intimidating anyone who moved an inch outside the PFDJ-drawn line of discipline. . . . These organizations, many of them enjoying tax exempt status (e.g. 501 c-3 in the USA), do very little of what convention [sic] community centers do. You won't find them counseling the youth; you won't find them assisting with gang problems, alcoholism, drug addiction, divorce and separation, refugee resettlement, assimilation into host countries, job training, job services, etc. . . . Politically, their function is not to reconcile old wounds but to pour salt over them.[18]

The tension between Eritrea and exile, between the Horn of Africa and the United States, between the diverse interests of exiles and the state's transnational agenda, are not the only contradictions Eritreans live with and among. A decidedly acute tension also characterizes the relationship between organized and unorganized forms of social life, which leads many people to assert the failure, nonexistence, or impossibility of attaining "real" community. An ethnographic investigation of Eritreans in diaspora, however, reveals that community, in some sense at least, does exist. One young woman, born in a Sudanese refugee camp to ELF-affiliated parents, expressed it in these terms:

The organization hasn't been able to get going. It seems like they're kind of organized without being organized. It's hard to describe it, like it's there, but once you try to put it into words or try to structure it, it becomes hard because you find out all of the divisions that are in it maybe. Yeah, so it's there, but you can't put it under one umbrella, in a sense. What unites them is that they're Eritreans and everybody cares about each other, but when you try to put politics or something in it, it gets hard. I mean if it's just a get together just to raise money for Eritrea, everyone will show up, but if it's going to be an organization, people get suspicious. You know, "Who's in it?" You know, sometimes that determines—even if it's neutral, if they know that person's political view, they don't want to be part of it, so it becomes hard when you try to make it into an organization. But, it's there as far as Eritreans just caring about each other.

As we have seen to this point, the historical and sociopolitical realities of Eritrea and exile account for at least some aspects of the troubled relationship between diaspora Eritreans as an "ethnic" population sharing important bonds of kinship, national origin, language, culture, and historical experience and their attempts to create stable institutions. In other ways, however, the tension between organized institutions and the informal, face-to-face qualities of community also relates to the efforts of the EPLF, and the Eritrean revolution as a whole, to carry the small and largely traditional Horn of African country into the modern world order.

Indeed, an important goal of revolutionary nationalist movements, especially those in the developing world, has been to bring about a new reckoning between patterns of traditional society and those that enable the formulation of a modern nation-state capable of negotiating both legitimacy and a place in the global political economy (see Donham 1999b). As Malkki (1995b) has pointed out, the nation-state form remains the dominant geopolitical and sociocultural configuration around the world today, leading both real and putative states to struggle tirelessly for their place in the "national order of things." Even in the age of globalization, which includes features such as increased international migration, refugee flows, transnational identities and processes, new technologies of travel and communication, and multinational capital and post-Fordist "flexible accumulation" (Harvey 1996; Jameson 1984), the nation-state has retained its significance as a central feature of human organization and social life, if not necessarily sovereign administration (see Ferguson 2006; Glick-Schiller and Fouron 2001; Hansen and Stepputat 2001, 2005).

For new, marginalized, and poor nation-states like Eritrea, the goals of "development" and the meaning of sovereignty under globalizing conditions are especially acute and preoccupying (O'Kane and Hepner 2009). Nationalism plays an important role in relationship to these goals and dilemmas, as one of the central promises nationalist leaders impart to their populations is a new era of social and economic development for the sovereign state (Chatterjee 1993). However, negotiating both economic development and internal sociopolitical stability in a country with historic tendencies toward fragmentation, sectarianism, and ecological disaster is no small task, and Eritrea is by no means alone in this struggle. Throughout the postcolonial African continent, the quest for the nation-state has been "flawed at the outset" (Laakso and Olukoshi 1996:11) due to the contradiction between the idea of the state as comprised of a unified national culture and the actually existing diversity of those who would be incorporated into the nation-state. In this regard, the efforts of Eritreans to forge "unity" are by no means unique.

At the same time, however, the historic dilemmas facing all African nation-states have been made all the more complex for Eritrea because they have taken place largely in the era of globalization, the conditions of which have included the out-migration of 25 to 30 percent of the country's total population. The Eritrean party-state led by the PFDJ (and the EPLF as a statelike body before independence) has sought to adapt itself to these conditions by utilizing transnational processes to the advantage of the revolution and now the postindependence nation- and state-building project. But the reproduction of the form of nationalism underpinning this project has been at serious odds with the actual experiences and interests of dispersed, diverse Eritreans. In addition to the historic differences explored in previous chapters, the realities of exile have introduced even greater complexity. As the state under the EPLF/PFDJ struggles to administer its unwieldy transnation according to the same patterns created during the revolution, the exclusivist claims of an already contested nationalism collide with the realities and exploded identities of those for whom nationalism has ceased, or failed, to meet real needs and supply compelling meanings. The crisis I discovered in the midwestern community is thus evidence of modernist nationalism's failure to cope with its own territorial and ideological projects according to the conditions wrought by globalization. While the Eritrean revolution was shaped from its inception by the movement of its supporters abroad and drew upon technologies and practices associated with transnationalism to facilitate its nationalist goals, conditions specific to the revolution have complicated the postindependence situation. Namely, the differences among Eritreans in exile, especially those related to political identity, have rendered state nationalism a disunifying force when deployed transnationally.

Although the EPLF attempted to extend its homogenizing, synthetic orientation by replacing its mass organizations abroad with broader and "inclusive" community associations that would discourage subnational or oppositional political loyalties, this approach has only kept alive grievances associated with the past and prevented stable diasporic communities from forming. As a result, the midwestern Eritrean community remains disempowered as an immigrant community in the United States, demonstrating how transnationalism can be limiting, repressive, and disabling. This is especially true when transnational relations operate according to the needs and demands of a nationalist state whose administrative capacities may be deterritorialized, but its ideology and interests remain narrowly oriented toward its local terrain, its own needs, and the maintenance of power. From the vantage point of exile communities, the transnational citizenry is being shaped to benefit the state, while the state does comparatively little to accommodate the genuine realities and needs of its citizenry abroad.

All of these processes taken together thus help account for the kind of conflicts occurring within exile communities, where an ambivalent entanglement with the Eritrean state's transnational project and the form of nationalism it represents leads people to struggle with one another and the one-party state in their definitions and practices of community. The EPLF/PFDJ's unrelenting focus on organizations and formal associations as the most legitimate (and controllable) form of social life reveals both the party-state's modernist orientation and the intensity with which it pursues active interventions in the lifeworld of its people (Habermas 1981; see also Scott 1998). Moreover, this penetration into the everyday realities of Eritrean diaspora communities prevents them from fully reterritorializing (Louie 2000) in relation to American society.

This incomplete reterritorialization works in the interest of the Eritrean state by keeping Eritreans oriented toward the sending society and government. At the same time, it subverts the party-state's control and objectives by encompassing within its orbit—and thus making itself vulnerable to—diasporic citizens with proliferating ideas, identities, and goals for Eritrea. Thus, for many Eritreans, far from "an island of 'natural understanding,' a 'warm circle' where they can lay down their arms and stop fighting, the *really existing* community will feel like a besieged fortress being continually bombarded by (often invisible) enemies outside while time and again being torn apart by discord within: ramparts and turrets will be the places where the seekers of communal warmth, homeliness, and tranquility will have to spend most of their time" (Bauman 2001:14–15).

Chapter 5
Ties That Bind and Sometimes Choke
Transnational Dissonance in Eritrea and Exile

> Only in the state does man have a rational existence. . . . Man owes his entire existence to the state, and has his being within it alone. Whatever worth and spiritual reality he possesses are solely by virtue of the state.
> —G. W. F. Hegel, *Lectures on the Philosophy of World History*

Eden

I met Eden Yisaq over the dead body of a man I never knew.

Several days prior, I had received a call from Elilta Gebremichael, a prominent woman in the midwestern community whose family I had come to know well. Her voice was hoarse and nasal. "*Aboy* has passed," she sniffed. "We would like you to attend the funeral, if you can."

For weeks I had been following the ups and downs of Elilta's father's illness and hospitalization. I was well aware of the emotional stress she was carrying on top of her responsibilities as a mother, a business-woman, and a community advocate.

"Elilta, *z'Haftey*, I'm so very sorry. Of course I will be there."

I felt a personal obligation to attend this event that went beyond my role as a field researcher. And this expression of personal concern was not lost on Elilta herself. Almost two years later, she came to my home after I had emergency surgery and cooked me *ga'at*, a starchy porridge smothered in melted spiced butter and yogurt, typically offered to women after childbirth and others requiring rich sustenance.

But *Aboy* Gebremichael's funeral also allowed me to observe such a central life event as it was marked by the Eritrean exile community. It was the first among many that I would attend. As I came to understand later, funerals and wakes, known as *enda Hazen*, expressed important ties and tensions among community members as well as transnational ones with Eritrea.

Following a viewing and service at the local Orthodox church, *Aboy* Gebremichael's body would be prepared for its return to Eritrea for interment. It was the preferred practice and a goal that families were expected to meet for relatives who had the poor luck to die abroad. Returning mortal remains to mingle with the earth in a family's home village held great symbolic importance for the continuity of kinship, land, and nation. Considerable expenses were involved, and many community members made financial contributions according to the *equb*, or rotating collective credit system. It was one more sacrifice at a time when resources were stretched even thinner than usual due to the border war with Ethiopia. Moreover, the practice was complicated by the government's policy that the diaspora next of kin who were returning the body must be fully paid up on the 2 percent income tax for all years since independence.

And so it was that over the ashen face of *Aboy* Gebremichael lying peacefully in his casket that Eden Yisaq and I first exchanged glances.

"Hello," she barely whispered as we passed by one another. Later, when the service had ended and people were engaged in quiet conversation in groups both large and small, Eden emerged out of the milling crowd to stand beside me.

"I just wanted to introduce myself," she said, sticking a hand out confidently to grasp mine. "I'm Eden. I noticed how you seemed to know *Aboy* Gebremichael's family, and I'm just curious, you know, because it's usually only Eritreans at these things. So I was just interested in who you are. I hope that's not rude or anything."

She was a tall and stunning woman, about my age, with beautiful tawny skin and a cloud of curls that floated around her head like a halo. Not a trace of accent hung on her words. She spoke like a well-educated woman raised on the East Coast. I liked her instantly.

I told her my name and briefly explained why I had come. Only part of it was for anthropological research, I said. Mostly, it was because I was a friend of Elilta.

"I didn't actually know *Aboy* Gebremichael, though," I said. "Did you?"

"Um, I met him once or twice. But you know how Eritrean people are. We come out like this and get together to support each other in times of crisis. At least, that's what we're *supposed* to do." A certain inflection laced that final phrase, but its meaning escaped me.

Presently we were joined by several other young women who each greeted me warmly. Like Eden, they had all been raised in the United States and seemed to know each other well. For perhaps the first time in my fieldwork experience to date I was among genuine peers. I felt myself relaxing and falling into the kind of conversation that comes easily to those who share a common cultural background and set of experiences. Although there were crucial differences between me and all of these young women, we were all American enough. And I just happened to be an American who knew something about Eritrea.

"So, how long have you been in the U.S.?" I asked Eden.

"Since I was a kid," she replied. "I came here in the early 1980s with my mom and one of my brothers. We were resettled as refugees during the liberation struggle."

"And have you been in the Midwest all this time?"

"Oh, no. First we went to Alabama. God knows why, that's where we got sent. It was really horrible and difficult for us. There were hardly any Eritreans, and my mom didn't speak a lick of English. My older brother was here but he basically abandoned us to refugee world. So later we moved to Boston. I ended up going to school there, at Harvard. After I graduated I got a job here. I still haven't gotten to know all that many Eritreans yet. I kind of do my own thing with my own little circle of friends. Mainly, I just work a lot. I have to support myself, pay my loans and all that. I also send money back home to my other brother in Eritrea. I'm pretty much all he's got at this point. The rest of us are . . . gone, you could say."

She seemed sad, or resigned. I didn't know which.

We were interrupted by the exit of the deceased's family from the interior of the church to the courtyard where we stood. It was time to get in our cars and drive to Elilta's home for the *enda Hazen*, where we would share a home-cooked meal and continue chatting quietly with the family and their guests.

"Do you need a ride?" I asked Eden.

"No, I'm going to beg out of this one. But we should hang out sometime," she said. "It's not every day you meet Americans who know about Eritrea."

She handed me a business card, embossed with the logo of a high-powered firm.

"Yeah, I'd love to talk more. I'll give you a call in the next week or so."

Eden and I did get together soon thereafter, and I rapidly came to think of her as a genuine friend rather than solely as a research participant. It was a delicate balance to strike, especially when she agreed to a formal interview. I sensed she had things to get off her chest, and I found myself troubled by my own dual motivations. I wondered if it was possible to be both friend and researcher all at once. Eden, for her part, wondered how she could be any help to my work.

"I'm probably not the best person to ask about the community here, or about Eritrea. At least not right now," she said. "I've got issues."

I was used to the modest claim that people knew little or nothing when I asked to speak to them on the record. But that was not what Eden meant. Rather, she indicated that her thoughts and experiences were somehow unusual, perhaps even extreme. But I doubted that was the case. Where there is one story, there are many others like it. So I asked Eden to share hers, and she agreed, despite our mutual ambivalence and doubts.

When I arrived at her condo in a well-appointed high-rise, she was talking on the phone in rapid-fire Tigrinya. Out of respect, I deliberately tried not to understand.

"Make yourself at home," she whispered, covering the receiver. "I'll be off in a sec."

As I wandered around her apartment some photographs pinned to the wall drew my attention. I moved closer to inspect them. One was of Eden in her Harvard graduation regalia. She looked perhaps a decade younger. Her curls fell to the middle of her back, her face was brilliant and beaming and somehow more innocent. In her hand she clutched a rolled-up paper tied with a ribbon. Beside that picture was a grainy photo of indeterminate history and low-budget production quality. It was of an elderly woman wrapped in a white cotton *netsela*, on her knees in the dusty earth, her hands stretched above her, a look of either rapturous joy or inconceivable pain etched on her face. She appeared to be crying, or maybe laughing.

Eden appeared beside me. "Sorry about that," she said.

"No problem. I was just looking at these pictures. I'm curious about this one," I said, pointing to the grainy photo of the woman on her knees.

"That's my mother. It was taken at the airport in Asmara. She was on the first planeload of people to return to Eritrea right after liberation in 1991. She got down on her knees and kissed the earth. She was overjoyed to be home."

"Wow. Your mother must have been quite a supporter of the struggle."

"She was more than that. EPLF was her whole life. She gave everything to front, and I mean everything—her jewelry, all of her money, everything we had. When the Ethiopians came into our town, the EPLF fighters took us away with them to live in a liberated area. That's basically where I grew up, in *meda*, in the field. I went to Revolution School as a child. I didn't even know there was a war happening, really, until we came to the U.S. as refugees. And even after that, my mom kept supporting EPLF. She was one of the *adetat*, you know, The Mothers, who gave their children and everything else they had to the struggle."

Her face grew immeasurably sad. "Everybody loved my mother."

"Where is she now?"

"She's dead. She fell really ill and passed away suddenly. Ever since then my life has been different. Nothing looks the same. Nothing. It's changed everything about my relationships with . . . everyone and everything."

"What do you mean?" I asked as gently as I could.

"Well, in the obvious ways, but also the not so obvious. It's a really painful thing to lose someone like that. It would be for anyone. I mean, we survived a war, being refugees, all of this hardship—only for her to go back to the country she loved and to end up like that. Two of my other siblings were martyred in the struggle a long time ago—they were EPLF fighters. And my other brother who is still in Eritrea, well, you know how that is. It's a poor country and he's just trying to survive. He was a fighter too, though I think the whole political situation has really messed him up. So that leaves me. I've had to help take care of him and his family from here. I also had to make all the arrangements for the funeral in Eritrea, and handle the legal stuff associated with what was left of our family's property. All of that stuff you have to deal with when people die, you know."

"So you've had to go back and forth?"

"A couple of times, yeah. It was really hard. I won't ever go back now. I feel so horrible saying that, but I can't help it. I can't help how I feel. I don't ever want to go back to Eritrea again. Everyone has been so affected by this collective suffering. It's like our individual pain gets lost, or gets magnified, I don't know which."

At that moment, Eden's beautiful face seemed to collapse with the weight of trouble and responsibility. She looked older than her years, exhausted, emotionally drained. I glanced back at her graduation photo and for a moment could barely recognize her as the same person. I wanted to embrace her, but she seemed to cultivate a protective distance between herself and everything around her.

"Did the community here give you any support?"

Something between a bitter laugh and a choke of disgust escaped from her lips.

"Support me? Hell, no. After my mom died, there were all kinds of things I needed to do: money I had to raise, forms I needed to fill out and get approved, powers of attorney to arrange, and who knows what else. You know how the structure works. I had to go through the community association and the government representatives here, who were supposed to help me get the paperwork done through the embassy in D.C.

But it was during the border war when all this went down, and no one had time for my little problems. Even though my mom was devoted to EPLF and I had paid up all my taxes, there were all these problems and questions about what I had contributed, how much money I donated to the border war effort. I just wanted to bury my mother with the dignity she deserved, and help my brother back home to take care of our legal responsibilities and make sure he had some security. But some people here raised issues, like, who is this girl to ask for our help on these personal matters when the country is at war again? At first they said they would help but later they were totally unsympathetic. I was really hurt and offended. And when I went home, it wasn't much better. Everyone seemed so desperate to me. I mean, we all fought and suffered for this country, we all loved Eritrea so much, and I felt like everyone was just grasping at me for what I could do for them, because I live in America. And my brother seemed so broken too. I felt awful. I still do. It eats me up inside."

She glanced at me. "I told you I'm not a good source of information. I'll bet nobody tells you things like this."

"It's your experience, Eden, and I respect it for what it is. I'm so sorry for your losses and for all your pain. It must be very hard."

She sighed against tears she courageously repressed. "Yeah, well, I try not to be self-absorbed and remember that God wouldn't put anything in front of me that I'm not strong enough to handle."

I thought then that Eden Yisaq was one of the strongest people I had ever met.

Almost a year later her last remaining relative in Eritrea confirmed this to me. I had traveled far outside Asmara to find him. When I got off the bus at the central depot I weaved my way through the market stands to find a pay telephone. I rang the number Eden had given me when I left the United States for Eritrea. I greeted the male voice that answered in Tigrinya and explained who I was.

"I'm a friend of your sister Eden," I said. "I'm from America. I took a bus from Asmara. I'd like to meet you."

In less than ten minutes Eden's brother Tekle pulled up in a well-kept cruiser that would have earned classic status in the United States. He stepped out of the driver seat with a broad smile and embraced me as though we were old friends. His face looked almost exactly like Eden's, but he was much older, perhaps by twenty years. The stubble on his face was gray and he was very thin. Like Eden, his face betrayed depths of sadness and hardship I could only try to imagine.

Tekle was soft spoken, almost shy. But he was clearly delighted to have an unusual visitor and seemed eager to share things with me. He drove me around the sun-baked town, pointing out the businesses their father used to own and the small café he still tried to manage, though there was no working capital to serve much besides Melotti beer. We went inside and drank although it was still early in the afternoon. Tekle had three beers for each of my one. Then we walked to the home where Eden had been born and where Tekle still resided. It was in some disarray, but I snapped his photo standing in front of it.

"For Eden," I said to him, though I wasn't at all sure it would make her happy.

Later we sat down together to talk more formally. I asked him about his relationship with Eden and how they managed together through the upheavals of their country and their family.

"Eden?" he said. "The help she gives is—I can't even express it. I wish I were a rich person; if Eden asked me for money to go around the world I would give it to her. She was sending three hundred American dollars a month to my mother when she was still alive. She sends clothes and other things too. My brother in America doesn't have the mentality to send anything here, so Eden does everything. I wouldn't expect her to be the youngest. In a household, most of the time, the oldest is the life-blood of the house and is the one in charge of keeping things together. But in our case, it's different. My oldest brother who also lives in the U.S., I don't know what happened to him. He just changed. But Eden? She has taken his place. She is everything to me."

Months later, when Tekle tried to depart Eritrea and was detained in another country for illegal immigration, it was Eden who handled the complicated negotiations and raised funds to help him get back to Eritrea safely. It was Eden who denied her own needs repeatedly to put her family members—living and dead—first. And all the while, despite her sacrifices, the state that still claimed her as a citizen seemed to question her political loyalty through the many complications she encountered and the ways she always seemed to fall short of its demands.

Indeed, Eden Yisaq was one of the strongest—and saddest—people I had ever met.

Transnationalism, Centralization, and Dissonance

Perhaps like most places in the world, Eritrea has always been transnational. Although we may have historically and collectively come to think of cultures, societies, and nation-states as more or less self-contained, discrete units, this geography is at least as imagined as it is real (Gupta and Ferguson 1997; Malkki 1995b). No culture, society, or nation-state ever exists or knows itself in isolation from regional and global dynamics (Wolf 1982). Political and economic efforts to fix populations and borders, to name and define cultural or national essences, and to exclude or include certain categories, persons, and practices are central features of what we know as "modernity." However, this masks the crucial flip side of what makes such firm distinctions of self and other possible in the first place: the constant, multiple, and shifting influences of who and what lies, and intervenes, beyond constructed borders. Whether through conquest, colonialism, or contemporary globalization, the effort to make specific places is a project of power across multiple spaces.

Charting the transnational structure and institutionalization of the Eritrean nation-state as it evolved over time provides insight into how such processes can be instrumental in the consolidation of centralized state power and the development of a transnational civil society (Hepner 2008). This chapter explores how Eritrea-based institutions acted as both integrating and debilitating mechanisms among local and exile sectors of Eritrean society in the years following independence. Some features of the transnational social field were well-developed, such as the mass organizations that began as early as 1970 with the EFLNA-EPLF relationship, which became sites for long-distance nationalism and governance. Others were more incipient, such as religious bodies, whose connections across Eritrea and exile was improvisational, ad hoc, and largely grassroots (Hepner 2003). Further aspects of the transnational social field were even more grassroots and unregulated, such as kinship networks, or the development of online communities (Bernal 2005a, 2005b, 2006).

The transnational social field in the 1990s certainly enabled and accommodated the party-state's power from above, but it also created popular spaces for new ways of being Eritrean and participating in the nation-state. While all transnational practices were built on the foundations and relationships—however conflicted—that were forged in the 1970s and 1980s, the unevenness and spontaneous growth of transnational institutions following independence gave rise to new developments. And despite what appeared from the vantage point of exile to be the emergence of new transnational modes for citizenship, sociopolitical experimentation, and civic autonomy, within Eritrea the party-state was working to consolidate control. Even as people at home and abroad struggled to connect transnationally with one another, these institutions and their constituents had to remain attentive to the state's needs, policies, and parameters for acceptable civic activity. The latter were still largely determined by the same nationalist logic and political praxis that drove the revolution beneath the EPLF.

In what follows I analyze the different components of the Eritrean transnational nation-state and social field, including the PFDJ Party and its various roles and policies, the unions of women and youth, and churches, as well as the role of the Internet and informal kin-based linkages. These features of transnationalism, I argue, have been implicated in both the state's increasing centralization as well as the discord that has marked both diaspora community life and the relationship between Eritrea and exile. Just as in earlier decades, when EFLNA activists returned to Eritrea to join the struggle in the field, transnational exchanges and encounters postindependence were riddled with dissonance. Thus I show how transnational dissonance—or the way in which exile-constructed identities and institutions generate conflict and contradiction when met with locally constructed nationalist goals—is implicated in the ways that transnational practices, relationships, and institutions enable new forms of participation and citizenship, while at the same time repress certain identities, practices, interventions, and institutions.

Transnational dissonance is produced in large part by the Eritrean party-state's administrative interventions into most spheres of life and the aggressive propagation of its own nationalist agendas among its citizenry at home and abroad, which exacerbates long-standing conflicts and often creates new ones (as we have seen). It is also visible in the state's efforts to block particular kinds of social remittances (Levitt 2001) from entering local society while encouraging more agreeable forms of exile political-economic and cultural participation. It creates painful tensions in the identities and commitments of individuals and families. But most important, an analysis of the dual nature of transnationalism in the Eritrean context provides us with a foundation for understanding how and why ideas and practices associated with democracy, civil society, and rights have become important in recent years and how, through their own efforts to support and resist the state, Eritreans in exile have come to form a kind of transnational civil society. Finally, it helps us make sense of the increasingly authoritarian character of the party-state, which has resorted to alarming human rights violations to maintain its power. Clearly, independent Eritrea finds itself amid dramatic changes associated with its transnational realities, ones that make those of the liberation war appear almost simple by comparison.[1]

The Ties That Bind: From Unions and the State to Kinship and Cyberspace

Mass Organizations after Independence

The role of the mass organizations of students, women, workers, and youth/students in the Eritrean transnational revolution is already well known. NUEYS, created by the EPLF in 1978, and NUEW, created in

1979, endeavored to coordinate the activities and identities of their worldwide members on behalf of the revolution under the EPLF.[2] Following a period of transition that partly coincided with the controversial dissolution of all mass organizations in 1989–90 (see Chapter 4), both NUEYS and NUEW reemerged in the mid and late 1990s, respectively, with revised mandates. In the case of NUEW, the organization defined itself in the postindependence period as a "self-financing, autonomous social movement" (Connell 2001:116), while NUEYS asserted itself as "an independent, non-governmental youth and students' organization."[3] Both saw themselves as coordinating and integrating bodies between Eritrea and its worldwide diasporas.

In 2001, NUEYS had approximately 135,000 members in Eritrea and 15,000 members abroad, and NUEW claimed more than 200,000 members total. Both recognized their twin roots in Eritrea and exile. The roles associated with their local and diaspora constituencies, however, were no longer as easily reconciled as during the years of the revolution, when a single ultimate goal—that of independence from Ethiopia—helped unite the visions and objectives of a diverse and far-flung people. First and foremost, the relationship of NUEYS and NUEW to the party-state has continued to mirror the subservience of all mass organizations to the EPLF during the revolution (see Pool 2001:180). While both declared themselves independent NGOs, they have maintained very strong ties to, and receive direction from, the PFDJ. During my field research I repeatedly heard NUEYS privately described as "the pinkie finger of the government," while critics of NUEW and former disillusioned members complained that the women's association remained more accountable to the PFDJ Party than to its constituents (some of whom were not PFDJ members).

The unions' failure to become autonomous civil society organizations since independence has disappointed and alienated people in both Eritrea and exile. Connell (2001:117) notes that many women formerly active in NUEW abandoned it after independence because it seemed insufficiently empowered (or empowering) and insensitive toward differences among women. In particular, NUEW seemed hostile toward middle-class professional women while favoring poor and rural women, a factor that later discouraged many skilled women in the diaspora from working with the union on projects they wished to initiate. Moreover, it seemed overburdened by its mandate to confront every issue affecting women, from child care, literacy, and job training to income generation and health care (Connell 2001:117). Yet when other indigenous women's organizations attempted to form to help diversify efforts at advocacy and development, they soon were shut down by NUEW and the PFDJ (Connell 1997:300–302). Similarly, women active within trade unions and the National Confederation of Eritrean Workers (NCEW), also controlled by the government, met with resistance in 1996 when they formed a women's committee to work on issues such as child care in the factory workplace (Connell 2001:121).

While NUEYS was also restricted in the form and range of its advocacy, it nonetheless took up more sensitive issues than did NUEW, including female genital cutting and sex education for the prevention of unwanted pregnancy, sexually transmitted diseases, and HIV/AIDS (see Connell 1997, 2001). Many of its more politically savvy constituents nonetheless begrudged the role NUEYS played in supporting government policy, including its complicity with the increasingly unpopular but mandatory summer work programs, military training, and National Service.

Like NUEW, NUEYS and the PFDJ have aggressively thwarted independent organizing among students. In July 2001, for example, an independent student union at the University of Asmara crumbled after its president, an ex-EPLF fighter named Semere Kesete, publicly criticized the summer work programs. Semere was imprisoned, and hundreds of students were arrested when they gathered outside the courthouse in peaceful concern. Shortly thereafter, virtually all university students were ordered to gather in the stadium prior to being bused to work camps in the hot, lowland regions, where two of them subsequently died. Throughout the entire episode, which sent shock waves through Asmara and crippled the country's only institution of higher learning, NUEYS remained silent.

Despite the restricted agendas of NUEW and NUEYS, which have tended to operate more like "government-organized nongovernmental organizations" (GONGOs) than anything else, both continue to do important work on behalf of their constituents. In keeping with the EPLF's nationalist orientation, NUEW defined its mission as "emancipation through equal participation,"[4] while NUEYS included in its list of objectives and activities numerous and multi dimensional undertakings. These were "building the youth that safeguard the sovereignty of their nation, [and] retain their culture and identity; preparing the youth to retain the achievements of the martyrs and pass it along to the coming generations; supporting and promoting the rights and equality of women and fight[ing] against negative gender perceptions; lobbying for children's rights; the promotion of national unity, tolerance, and respect for principles of democracy and Human Rights; respect[ing] the law and order, and accept[ing] the principles of fairness, equality, and unity in everyday life," as well as providing recreational, educational, and vocational outlets and training for young men and women ages sixteen to thirty-five.[5] To a great extent, NUEW and NUEYS are discursively and practically maintaining the social philosophies and transformations instituted by the EPLF during the independence struggle itself. They have also worked to fashion among their constituents the right kinds of national subjects: women who are gender conscious (though not feminist), self-reliant (re)producers for reconstruction and nation building, and obedient youth whose love of work, discipline, and respect for authority will carry the tradition of the militant freedom fighters, and the glory of the martyrs, into the era of development.

NUEW and NUEYS as Transnational Bodies

In 2001, both NUEYS and NUEW were just beginning to craft their post independence roles in the Eritrean transnational social field. Although NUEYS underwent reorganization in 1994, the foreign relations department, responsible for all administrative issues and projects related to the diaspora, did not emerge until 1998. Staffed by three dedicated young adults, the NUEYS foreign relations department shouldered a daunting responsibility. In addition to communicating directly with NUEYS's many regional headquarters around the world to coordinate the activities of diaspora chapters, the foreign relations department also planned and executed projects that brought together local and diaspora youth during the May–September season in particular.[6] These included an array of projects that expressed NUEYS's simultaneous roles in local Eritrean society, in diaspora communities, and as a conduit of cultural, economic, and technological exchange within the parameters deemed desirable by the government.

One of NUEYS-Asmara's most visible accomplishments during the time I conducted research was coordinating the shipment of dozens of refurbished computers from the NUEYS-Boston chapter and securing several diaspora volunteers to help set up and train local technicians at the popular Shebab Internet Café, operated by NUEYS at its main compound. With the lowest rates for Internet use per hour and one of the most attractive atmospheres anywhere, Shebab allowed people to conduct research, communicate with friends and family around the world, access international news media, and become otherwise well versed in the technologies and cultural mélanges associated with globalization. On any given day, hundreds of mostly young people gathered to wait for a turn on a computer, sipping cappuccino or soft drinks and leafing through dictionaries, encyclopedias, or European fashion magazines while they waited, surrounded by original paintings depicting images of technology and globalization.

In addition, NUEYS public relations worked on outreach activities with regional offices in the diaspora on programs aimed at integrating visiting youth with their local peers. These included helping to initiate new chapters abroad, organizing workshops and panel discussions on national unity and cultural conflict among diaspora and local youth, conducting travel outings for young people to experience different regions of the country together, and coordinating the participation of diaspora youth in the *keremtawi ma'etot*, or student summer reconstruction projects. NUEYS also oversaw carefully controlled visits of diaspora youth to Sawa, the central military training facility where all Eritreans must go to complete military training in their final year of secondary school (Riggan 2009).

NUEYS foreign relations also played a central role in helping to attract skilled Eritreans living abroad and placing them with existing institutions, many of them government ministries. NUEYS had considerable difficulty filling the posts, which ranged from accountants and archivists to nurses and librarians, due to outreach techniques and a certain perception among exiles that Eritrea after the 1998–2000 border war was becoming increasingly intolerant. Nonetheless, NUEYS could boast rather high attendance at many of its planned events: 148 young people joined travel outings to different regions of the country in 2001, and almost as many attended a workshop in which four local panelists and four from diaspora regions conducted a discussion about negotiating cultural tensions among youth from different backgrounds. This is clearly consistent with the EPLF's synthetic nationalism, which sought to homogenize identities as it created and enforced a single unifying one.

Compared to the role of student organizations during the years of the revolution, NUEYS chapters were more attuned to diasporic realities, although still administered through the transnational structure of NUEYS in Eritrea and therefore dominated by state-sanctioned objectives. Similar to EFLNA during the 1970s, each diaspora region's headquarters was responsible for maintaining communication with the headquarters in Asmara, as well as facilitating the development of smaller chapters within regions. Thus all NUEYS chapters in the United States and Canada communicated directly with the regional North American headquarters in Washington, D.C., which acted as a liaison with the office in Asmara. The lack of direct communication with Asmara was often accompanied by a lack of clarity in terms of the role of NUEYS–North America (NUEYS-NA) as a diaspora organization or as a transnational, Eritrea-oriented institution. While foreign relations officers of NUEYS-Asmara repeatedly told me that they encouraged all the diaspora chapters to have their own bylaws and to work within their communities to become locally specific resources, it was also clear that they expected these diaspora chapters to play a role in Eritrea itself, to adhere to the larger goals of NUEYS-Asmara, and to remain supportive of the government.

According to an information pamphlet published by NUEYS-NA, local chapters in the United States and Canada organized annual workshops about the college application process and financial aid, created mentoring programs between college graduates and high school students, raised funds to help with social causes in Eritrea and in their local community, organized informational sessions about Eritrea, and planned special events such as candlelight vigils and demonstrations to raise consciousness about Eritrea in the United States. Also listed as a "long run" goal was "to explore ways whereby youths can participate in short and long-term projects in Eritrea."[7] Thus the apparent focus of NUEYS in North America appeared to be concerned mostly with diaspora realities. Its structure remained transnationally fixed by Eritrean realities, however, creating a sense of ambiguity among its diaspora participants in particular. As we have seen in discussions of community associations (Chapter 4), this is a common dilemma for institutional components of the Eritrean transnational social field.

Like NUEYS, NUEW also revealed ambiguity in terms of its simultaneous roles and its linkages with the PFDJ. Connell (1997:267) notes that despite its 1998 reorganization, NUEW did not find itself radically restructured. Rather, it remained focused largely on supporting women with marriage and land reforms, political participation, skills and job training, and literacy, which highlighted the tension between NUEW's dual capacities as a popular movement of the revolution and a service organization (Connell 1997:267). Moreover, according to the chairperson of NUEW in Asmara, the union was so overwhelmed by postindependence concerns within Eritrea that it could simply not accommodate the perspectives of Eritrean women abroad, many of whom had become interested in what social or legal advocacy role NUEW could possibly play for them in their countries of settlement. At NUEW's fifth congress in 1998, where the union officially underwent reorganization, the few diaspora representatives present pushed for their chapters and contributions to be placed on the agenda. They argued that any positive outcomes achieved for women in Eritrea would be related to the successes of Eritrean women abroad, who would continue to participate in Eritrean society whether they repatriated permanently or not and would continue to support NUEW financially and in other ways.

Thus, in 1998, chapters of NUEW in diaspora again began emerging, linked to the NUEW's headquarters in Asmara. The organization opened an office in Washington, D.C., with a permanent representative, and sent an organizer to the various locations where Eritrean women had requested support from NUEW-Asmara. The chairperson herself traveled to several countries in Europe and the Middle East, observing the conditions facing Eritrean women and speaking to them about the role of the union.

Some of the efforts to reorganize NUEW diaspora chapters related to the eruption of the border war in 1998 between Eritrea and Ethiopia. In the midwestern community I studied, this proved the major catalyst for the formation of the local NUEW chapter. Infused with the nationalist sentiment that surged among Eritreans of all backgrounds, some women in the community also saw this as a chance to begin healing old wounds based on ELF/EPLF political identities. The initiative started with a woman called Tereza, who had initially been with the ELF but whose political identity had shifted in the United States through her exposure to pro-EPLF activism by her husband. Tereza convinced others that creating a chapter of NUEW would benefit their own community as well as Eritrea. As another woman, Abrehet, explained to me: "We started this women's association just to get together and help our country and to avoid the segregation between ELF and EPLF. That's our belief—it has to be like Eritreans are one family. Especially after the Woyane problem [border war with Ethiopia], we started getting together and having a strong women's association that is joined by all ELF and EPLF." Many women, however, felt unsure of NUEW's mandates, given its history and close linkage with the EPLF/PFDJ.

Although it started with more than fifty women enlisting on paper, the local NUEW chapter dwindled within its first year to a core of about ten or twelve women, who met roughly every six weeks. During the meetings that I attended, I was struck by how much more attuned the women seemed to be to the issues facing their own community than within Eritrea itself, although developments "back home" remained a constant referent. While the woman chairing the meeting referred several times to the mandates of the organization in Asmara (perhaps for my benefit), the actual focus of discussion remained largely on things such as who would bring what dish for the upcoming party, what news about the war with Ethiopia had been reported, or who spoke with relatives in Eritrea most recently and what they said. Sipping tea and passing bread, informal chitchat, and good-natured teasing and laughing made NUEW meetings frequently feel more like social gatherings than business meetings. One woman who seemed to attend meetings faithfully later confessed to me in an interview that she was not really interested in NUEW or other "political organizations" but simply wanted an opportunity to relax among friends on her one day off from work.

While not within the mandate of the organization, these social dimensions played an important role in exile communities, however, allowing women to come together despite certain potential barriers. Indeed, one of the objectives of NUEW-Asmara for both local and diaspora women was to encourage them to share their personal problems and seek mutual support and solutions from one another. As Tereza and other NUEW members explained to me in interviews and in meetings, women should ideally discuss their work, home, child rearing, and health concerns with one another. "If someone knows what is cancer, or why a woman should have certain foods while she is pregnant, she should teach the rest of the women and help them understand," Tsehainesh told me. Similarly, NUEW-Asmara's instructions that diaspora women should focus on children's education and Eritrean cultural abilities led several women to begin providing Tigrinya language instruction during church Sunday school and holding ceremonies recognizing the achievements of youngsters from kindergarten through college. Most women continued to view NUEW's significance in terms of what it could accomplish for Eritrea, however.

The intention of NUEW in Asmara appeared to be harnessing the support of women abroad to work within their own communities and societies of settlement on projects planned by NUEW within Eritrea, for the benefit of Eritrea. One such way women in diaspora could become effective members of the union was to become more familiar and civically engaged with the surrounding American communities in which they lived, as well as helping to inculcate their children with values that both distinguished them as Eritrean and identified their cultural heritage to themselves and others as positive. This approach, like so many other features of transnational relationships, seemed imbued with a certain tension, one that simultaneously encouraged exiles to become more acculturated to their societies of settlement in ways that could benefit Eritrea, but at the same time to preserve and reproduce cultural and national identity in ways that would ensure continued allegiance to the home country. During an interview, the chairperson of NUEW-Asmara illustrated this tension in her explanation of the union's expectations for Eritrean women abroad:

Now we have to look at all the things we geared toward Eritrea, and how to gear them towards women in diaspora also. . . . Women did everything towards the resources for the front [the EPLF]. But do they know their environments? We could have a kind of "know your environment" program and arrange or organize a tour around a certain area—for example, those living in the southern part of America would take a tour in an organized manner. Or hold a celebration for their children who have finished their high school degree. . . . So, how could we benefit from the situation that exists, and the different opportunities that exist in our different surroundings. . . . The other thing is, how can we really relate to the youngsters, communicate with the children. So this has to be discussed openly in the chapters, because our tradition is very secretive. If anything happens to my daughter, I might not want to discuss it. So the [NUEW] meetings have this meaning also. We have a good culture here, like we have this *equb* [rotating mutual credit] and we need to have meetings to just raise up all of these issues, and then you are sane when you go back home. [Women in diaspora] should never consider that they are different from women in Eritrea. This is also a major objective we expect them to achieve.

In addition to NUEW advocating that women in diaspora know their surrounding communities for the benefit of Eritrea and especially Eritrean women, the union also made similar efforts for diaspora women when they visited Eritrea. Some of these efforts included "know your environment" tours, in which NUEW organized trips to various regions of the country, encouraging diaspora women to familiarize themselves with one another and with local women who were participating in NUEW's projects. In this way, NUEW hoped to generate more energy and funding for actual projects on the ground, which in turn would give diaspora members a chance to feel invested. However, just as NUEW has confronted some internal challenges from women who would like to initiate independent organizations or projects without necessarily going through NUEW, so too has the union faced competition from diaspora women who would like to work at a different pace and with greater independence than NUEW generally accommodates. To her credit, the chairperson seemed to understand this dilemma of transnational administration versus autonomy:

There are women who are saying they will organize themselves but will not be called after the NUEW chapters, but if we give them a project they will do it. So there is an NUEW chapter in Stockholm that has to accept the possibility of having another group that is working for women but is not necessarily behind all of the objectives of NUEW. But [NUEW members] say no, you have to be part of us or you should not be doing anything. . . . So how can we really convince them that you can have different kinds of organizational set-ups, and as long as they promote women's issues and the Eritrean issues, why should we really insist they have to be at the level of the National Union of Eritrean Women? These kinds of discussions are going on. And that issue, we are trying to entertain it, but it will take time also.[8]

Both NUEYS and NUEW therefore maintained a firm transnational structure inherited from the days of the revolution, although the content of their relationships with their constituents had grown far more complex and much less clear. Of particular interest and debate was the palpable tension between maintaining and facilitating the ongoing integration of exiles into local society through both administrative procedures and nationalist ideology and praxis and encouraging them to address their own particular needs in diaspora. As we have already seen for community associations, NUEYS and NUEW are by no means alone in this dilemma.

The Front, the State, and the Party: From EPLF to PFDJ

EPLF Chapters in the 1980s

Similar to the way in which global mass organization chapters were incorporated into a central transnational structure under the EPLF's leadership, so too were chapters of the front itself set up around the world in the 1980s to strengthen coordination between EPLF and its members and supporters. However, opening such chapters was also an attempt to neutralize fractious political identities by increasing the presence of the EPLF and its nationalist approach abroad. As Gebrehiwet Kahsay, a former chairman of both NUES and the EPLF in North America, explained to me:

[The EPLF] was very concerned that everyone should feel part of the movement, so it was really working very hard from the field. There were people coming out of the field, visiting all these places, having meetings, going and meeting with Eritreans in different areas. . . . So you create people who are conscious everywhere. It was these people who worked together and created organizational support, like the students. . . . But after a stage, when it came to being one organization, it was much easier for EPLF's central leadership to deal directly with things. . . . The main office was in Rome, and before that, Beirut, and before that, at an earlier stage also, in Sudan. . . . And at that [later] stage, economic activities were handled through Rome, the office there. And then we opened offices everywhere later on, EPLF offices in Rome, France, the UK, other places in Europe. Every office was handling what was being done in their regions and then sending it to the field.

In many ways, the kinds of activities these EPLF chapters engaged in did not seem altogether different from the kinds of things mass organizations had been doing for well over a decade. Given the major resettlement of Eritrean refugees abroad, many of them associated with the ELF, it is reasonable to think that the EPLF chose to open chapters around the world to strengthen its transnational administrative presence and draw individual citizens more firmly into its statelike orbit. Throughout the 1980s, EPLF chapters abroad indeed appeared to focus less on overt political work and more on relief measures, to which many former ELF affiliates and nonmembers of EPLF gravitated. These efforts were coordinated with the ERA, which also opened worldwide chapters whose chief responsibility entailed mobilizing resources from NGOs in host countries. Again, Gebrehiwet Kahsay described what these early EPLF chapters did to support the struggle in the field: "Basically, we were buying a lot of stuff like clothes, books—there was a need for books, especially later on—or sending money so [the EPLF] could buy food from Sudan and other places. There was no possibility for buying arms, and no money was used for arms. So our main support was the food and clothes and other items that were available in Sudan. There was an [EPLF] office there, and they used the money for whatever was needed inside Eritrea."

When mass organizations were dissolved in 1989–90, EPLF chapters abroad were able to take up much of the slack, as well as provide an even stronger sense of involvement and ownership over the struggle for those in exile, perhaps offsetting some of the bitterness mass organization activists felt when their associations were shut down. It also helped maintain a level of mobilization, sacrifice, and commitment among Eritreans, including many who formerly supported ELF, upon the achievement of independence in 1991–93. This gradual naturalization of EPLF's administrative presence in diaspora and its major efforts toward relief work helped the front earn trust among former opponents. Gebre, formerly a fighter with the ELF, described how he perceived the EPLF chapters in the United States operating in the months leading up to liberation in 1991: "EPLF started recognizing the contributions of ELF members. Before, during the civil war, we were bandits, bad guys. . . . Later on, the entire thing changed. I remember the ELF martyrs were recognized, and September 1, the day the independence movement started [under the ELF], was recognized. . . . And what happened over the years was some of the ELF members began joining EPLF too."

By the time independence was secured, the EPLF had succeeded in partly neutralizing the political identity conflicts in diaspora, setting the stage for the return of at least some exiles in the immediate period following liberation. Most people, however, both loyal EPLF members and those who did not join the front, remained abroad. And so did the new state, reshaping again its transnational presence to keep Eritrean citizens oriented toward the nation-building process.

From EPLF to PFDJ: A Transnational Transition

Shortly after liberation in 1991, the EPLF began a period of reorganization in which the front transformed itself into a government, the PFDJ.[9] As Pool (2001:162) notes, there were two phases of this transition: the first, in which the Provisional Government of Eritrea (PGE) took over administering the new country from independence until the completion of the national referendum process, and the second, in which the PFDJ was fashioned out of the EPLF and embarked on the making of a new constitutional order. Even prior to the referendum process, however, the PGE announced the Citizenship Proclamation in 1992, which later became incorporated into the constitution as Article 3. This proclamation extended equal citizenship rights to anyone born to one Eritrean parent anywhere in the world. However, as first the National

Charter (1994) and later the constitution (ratified in 1997, though never implemented) also stressed, the guaranteed rights of all citizens also entailed the fulfillment of those citizens' duties and obligations to their nation, families, and communities (see Connell 2001:348; Pool 2001:168).

The processes by which both the referendum on independence and the drafting of the constitution took place evoked the same strategies of large-scale mass education and organizing used by the EPLF throughout the struggle. The two-year, internationally monitored referendum process, which garnered a 98.5 percent total voter turnout around the world (Pool 2001:162) and a 99.8 percent vote in favor of independence, indicated the near-unanimity of Eritreans on the issue of sovereignty. The constitutional process, overseen by the religiously, ethnically, and gender-balanced Constitutional Commission of Eritrea (CCE) and its advisories of foreign legal experts and local elders versed in customary law, also drew upon the familiar processes of political education and democratic centralist debate throughout the constitution's drafting.[10]

During the initial phases of the constitution's drafting, issues ranging from the difference between a presidential and parliamentary system, multipartyism, and the role of the security apparatus and military to the rights of women, the relationship between church and state, and international instruments such as the Universal Declaration of Human Rights and the African Charter on Human and Peoples' Rights were discussed and debated in every urban community and small village, as well as over the radio and through theatrical performances (see Connell 2001:348). During the second phase, a draft of the constitution was again discussed throughout the country as well as in diaspora communities worldwide and several adjustments made. Overall, the Eritrean constitutional process was lauded as a radically democratic approach to popular state making and nation building. Pool (2001:166) wrote, "In many ways, the constitution-making process was unique: political education and information at the rural grass roots level, serious debates and seminars in the urban centers. In the provinces and the capital, as well as in the capitals of Europe and the U.S. where there were Eritrean communities, there was vigorous participation." Critics, however, have pointed out that the process was utterly dominated by the EPLF/PFDJ, and its radical democratic appearance was no more than that: an appearance.

Of course, the central principle of national unity underpinned every decision, perspective, and approach. As Connell (2001), Pool (2001), and Tronvoll (1998a, 1998b) have all noted, there were six guidelines dominating the national charter and the constitution, all of which stemmed from the ideology and praxis of the EPLF during the struggle. First and foremost was national unity itself, which the national charter

constructed in much the same way the EPLF had done in its first document, "Our Struggle and Its Goals." Seeking to "build a national government which . . . rejects all divisive attitudes and activities, places
national interest above everything else and enables participation in all
sectors of Eritrean society," the PFDJ asserted, "All sectarian . . . tendencies must be . . . rejected [as well as] all forms of discrimination and
domination, including ethnic and regional."[11] Complementing and
reinforcing this national unity were the guidelines of broad-based popular participation, the human factor in development (individual dedication and self-sacrifice), self-reliance in all areas, a commitment to social
and economic justice, and strong bonds between the leadership and
population. From the redivision of the country into six *zobatat* (sing.,
zoba), or zones, that undermined existing homologies between ethnicity,
region, kinship, and religion, and the restructuring of land tenure laws,
to the development of mandatory military training and National Service
and the distribution or absorption of major economic assets, the new
government carefully measured each step to adhere to these principles.
And even as former fighters, young people, rural villagers, and Eritreans
abroad all clamored for faster and greater strides to be made toward
development and democratization, the PFDJ insisted that all things
would happen in due course, not a moment sooner, and possibly not at
all.

Convinced that Eritrean society remained as yet too fragile and that
the powerful encroaching forces of international political economy
could stymie the nation-building process, the PFDJ sought to avoid
becoming enmeshed in dynamics that would send Eritrea into the same
post- and neo-colonial tailspin experienced by so many other African
countries. By 1996, the PFDJ's response to the multiple pressures
exerted on it from within and without seemed to be a return to a more
updated version of the EPLF's nationalist-isolationist approach during
the struggle, which some powerful officials viewed as part of a larger
trend sweeping Africa. Connell (2001:368) quotes Zemhret Yohannes, a
former ELF cadre who joined the EPLF in 1981 and served on the
front's political education committee, and later the PFDJ's five-person
secretariat: "We are witnessing a new period, the beginning of a new
stage. . . . There is a regeneration of the old national liberation agenda.
. . . Now we are returning to our roots to create confident African states
with genuinely national culture, regaining national pride. The basis for
this is self-reliance—breaking the vicious cycle of dependency that
Africa has experienced over the past three decades." And while we can
no longer be so sure what this new African agenda means given the continent's exceptionally troubled present, it seems more certain that Eri-

trea has remained on the course that Zemhret describes, for better or worse.

The Transnational Body Politic

Just as the transformation from EPLF to PFDJ expressed continuity between the front and the new party, so too did the state's post independence transnational structure continue operating in much the same way as it had done during the struggle. However, some augmentations did begin taking place in the latter part of the postindependence decade. One of these was the appointment of fifteen officials to the National Assembly who represented different regional diasporas within the Eritrean government. Another was the issuing of the *menenet,* an Eritrean national identity card that functions like a permanent visa and proof of citizenship for Eritreans living abroad. And perhaps most important, the state instituted an annual 2 percent flat tax levied on each adult Eritrean living abroad, the payment of which was coordinated and managed by the embassies of Eritrea and local diaspora chapters of the PFDJ. This steady stream of revenue combined with private remittances sent to family and friends, other kinds of financial donations and investments, and the proceeds from government bonds sold during the Ethio-Eritrean border war to comprise one-third to one-half of Eritrea's total GNP (see Fessehatzion 2005). Much of this financial flow—overseas contributions totaled an estimated $400 million in 2000—is managed and controlled by the PFDJ.[12]

In 1999, a Division of Community Affairs was formed within the consular section of the Ministry of Foreign Affairs. The consular section's central task was to help facilitate the transactions exiles conducted, often in only short visits home, including the buying and selling of property, the initiation of business transactions, and whatever inquiries people made about services they sought or would like to provide. The community affairs department, for its part, created a bridge between Eritrean embassies throughout the world and the Eritrean state, who worked in tandem with PFDJ chapters to mobilize communities in their respective locations. In his bright and airy Asmara office, just a stone's throw from the NUEYS compound and kitty-corner to the Mufti's headquarters, the appointed official explained to me the purpose of his incipient department:

This office was created to really serve the offices of the community associations [abroad] and the embassies, you know. We facilitate them in doing their business. . . . There is a Division of Community Affairs, and a Division of Consular Affairs, and our plan is . . . to give [diaspora Eritreans] very efficient services in terms of facilitating the things they do here. . . . And abroad, we have a plan towards raising communities, you know, they have meetings and we go visit them, like we did before independence, and seek donations. And we have leaders, people who represent the communities and take care of the consular affairs. If we have consular affairs representatives there, then there must be a community affairs representative here, to take care of all the communities. That's what we're planning now, especially in the U.S. and European countries. [The job of the community affairs representative would be] to organize communities, to help form communities [abroad]. For those already there, it would give them some projects to do, such as counting people, gathering data about who they are, monitoring the day to day conditions of our people.

These new departments and other augmentations made to the PFDJ's transnational structure were intended to help integrate diaspora Eritreans into local society and harness their economic potential, while also increasing direct contact between communities, individuals, and the state. The ongoing role of *maHber koms*, or community associations, remained central to this endeavor, where the ideal leaders and representatives of the communities are also affiliated with the PFDJ Party. However, many community associations abroad have resisted the state's attempts to organize them, as discussed earlier.

Whether in Eritrea or exile, not everyone who belonged to the EPLF automatically joined the PFDJ upon its formation in 1994. Similarly, some who had been affiliated with the ELF became members of the new party despite the obvious continuity between the EPLF and the PFDJ. Over the course of its major registration drive, which continued through 1995, more than six hundred thousand Eritrean men and women all over the world signed onto the party (Connell 2001:364). The structure of PFDJ membership included hundreds of local chapters throughout both Eritrea and its diaspora communities. In the midwestern community I studied, the PFDJ sought a major leadership role in the community, including providing important services to local residents and contributing financially to the specific projects being carried out in Eritrea. Most important, the local PFDJ chapter, which carried about fifty names on its roster but revolved around an active and committed core of about fifteen individuals—almost exclusively men—shouldered the very important task of building political consensus through the reproduction of proper national subjectivity among an often contumacious population.

The chairman of the local PFDJ chapter, a soft-spoken man who had been a rank-and-file fighter with EPLF, explained to me the role of the PFDJ in the community as we sat together in the tiny, wedge-shaped office that had been the community's longest fixture, since its veteran days as the EPLF headquarters in the 1980s:

Well, let's first come to Eritrea. You see this big box here? [Points to large metal cabinet.] I will maybe open it one day for you and show you. This is the main place for our culture. It is full of videos, tapes, CDs, books, posters, old cards, everything. Mainly videos and cassettes from home. Songs, political messages, what is going on with the current crisis [border war], what was going on before, the annual Festivals [in Washington, D.C.]. The people come here—and sometimes I put these things in my car, or my friends will also put them in their trunks, and wherever we find people we will sell it, during the festivals or during events, on Independence Day, New Years Eve, whatever, like if we do a festival on Martyr's Day, June 20. We sell a lot. . . . So this has an economic benefit. Also, in distributing culture, keeping ties with people, so they feel a sense of—so they do not feel culture shock, so they feel like they are at home even in America. It looks very small, but in all the cities it is very effective. . . . And it brings money, too. This year, with only the Northeast and Midwest [American zones], we sold 1.5 million dollars. And this went home to help fight [the border war]. . . . And then, we teach people also, [about] all the conflicts and current issues, what is going on, about the war, how we are winning it, what people [in Eritrea] need, like those who are dislocated because of the fighting, what new communities or hospitals or schools are being built, what they need. Or also sometimes selling or distributing *Haddas Ertra* [state-produced newspaper], or information from the Foreign Ministry. We do a lot of things. We also help with collecting materials, for the relief work, or we help with the walkathons. And the 2 percent tax, the forms for the 2 percent tax, I do all the forms, or if somebody wants to do something, like buy a house [in Eritrea], I will do the letter, saying "Mr. [so-and-so] will represent me at home," and I send it to D.C. [the embassy], and D.C. will send it to the individual, and I will say in a letter they have paid the 2 percent and are cooperating with all of us, and the embassy will stamp it and send it, and that guy will send it home, to the person who represents him to build his house. So I help with that too.

Local PFDJ chapters are therefore important conduits for information and goods produced by the state, as well as managers of the bureaucratic procedures required of and by citizens abroad. The main PFDJ representative in each community also becomes an important player, as individuals must conduct their business and communication with the state through that person. Both critics and supporters alike grouse that the system is an outdated holdover from the EPLF days and that going through such designated officials creates problems if there is a conflict of personality, interest, or politics.[13] As we have already seen, however, even more contested is the way in which the PFDJ has mandated the role of local chapters as leaders and organizers of community associations abroad. It is not difficult to see how many Eritreans who do not belong to the PFDJ or oppose the party altogether feel overwhelmed by its presence in their everyday lives and spaces. Included among these are informal gathering places such as coffee shops and diners, favorite hangouts for men of all stripes who like to debate politics and national identity. As the guardians of the nation-state, PFDJ members felt the responsibility to supervise the production and reproduction of national identity in diaspora, build political consensus, and lead communities toward the desirable forms of organization. The individuals who comprise PFDJ chapters were themselves agents of the state, and their belief in its omni-benevolence was both genuine and troubling, especially as the government resorted to more violent modes for achieving compliance after 2001. It later became commonplace for PFDJ members to become spies of sorts, monitoring the activities of their compatriots, including using video and photography, and constructing "blacklists" of "traitors" that were reported to the government (see Conrad 2005).

Religious Bodies: The Orthodox, Catholic, and Protestant Churches

For some, the belief in the PFDJ, and especially in President Isayas Afew-erki, has reached religious proportions. For others, however, religion has surpassed politics in its importance, in part because it provides an alternative construction of national and cultural identity that circum-vents the tenacious distinctions of political identity, and, until recently, enjoyed some autonomy from the state.

As we have seen, throughout the 1970s and 1980s, EPLF actively "sec-ularized" national identity to escape historic tensions between Islam and Christianity within the liberation movement and to weaken the Ethio-pian regime's attempts to foment religious discord. And while the EPLF did not attempt to prevent Eritrean people from worshipping as they chose—indeed, often relying upon churches and mosques as safe havens from Ethiopian violence and drawing inspiration from progres-sive statements made by Catholic bishops against the Derg, for exam-ple—the front did advocate a firm separation of religion and state. It continued to support this separation after independence but in 2001–2 stepped up intervention in religious institutions in order to preempt their capacity to mobilize an independent public sphere, to stem the growth of Pentecostalism, and to limit the kinds of transnational influ-ences religious bodies might attract to Eritrean society. This was quite possibly due to the relative success of churches in achieving some kind of autonomy from the state in both Eritrea and exile, which presented a particularly potent challenge to the state's official, homogenizing con-struction of nationalism and its abilities to direct many aspects of social and civic life both locally and transnationally (Hepner 2003).

While most of Eritrea's Christians are Coptic Orthodox, Catholics and Protestants comprise significant minorities (5 percent and 2 percent, respectively). Catholicism arrived in Eritrea more than two hundred years prior to Italian colonialism, although it grew dramatically during the colonial period and became an important provider of educational and other social services, including the University of Asmara, formerly known as Santa Famiglia. Protestantism, which arrived with Swedish Lutheran missionaries in the 1800s, has since witnessed a proliferation of denominations. Most important in recent years has been the explosive growth of charismatic Christian churches as Eritrea too has been swept up within this acknowledged global trend (Casanova 2001; Cox 1995; Martin 2002), which has won quite a few followers from the ranks of Orthodoxy, Catholicism, and even Islam. The Eritrean Orthodox Church has also contended with the development of its own internal popular movement known as Medhanie Alem that incorporates charismatic elements into traditional worship. Thus, despite the secular orientation of the EPLF/PFDJ and the government's opposition to "new, counter-revolutionary, imperialist-created faiths" such as Pentecostalism (see EPLF 1977), a position first articulated during the liberation war, religious belief and practice remain extremely important in the lives of many Eritreans.

Although small, young, and resource poor, the Orthodox, Catholic, and Pentecostal Eritrean congregations in the midwestern community seemed to show higher levels of activity, commitment, cooperation, and responsiveness to community needs than any other organization in the community's past or present (Hepner 2003). The institutions based on religious identity and practice seemed to mitigate tensions related to political identity that were palpable within organizations based on secular nationalism. Moreover, the relative religious homogeneity of the community cross-cut against other kinds of identities, such as ethnoregional, gender, or generation, fostering a greater sense of unity and mobilizing many more people than the community association, the PFDJ, or NUEW had been able to do. Whether attending Orthodox, Catholic, or Pentecostal worship, cooperation and fellowship among people who had struggled for many years to create the same effects in other kinds of forums was evident. The churches also provided a consistent location for the provision of services that other community institutions had not been able to provide. In particular, children were learning Tigrinya skills through Bible study and worship, connections were being made with American institutions and communities, support for important life events such as weddings, baptisms, and funerals could easily be mounted, and perhaps most important, people came together as large groups on a weekly basis to address other social issues relevant to the community.

Until the government's direct interference into religious institutions, which by 2008 included the closure of at least eighteen evangelical churches, the detention of more than two thousand people for banned practices, and the deposing of the patriarch of the Orthodox Church (see Amnesty International 2005, and annual reports from 2006 and 2007), interdenominational Christianity was perhaps the most depoliti-

cized sphere of Eritrean collective social life. It was also a powerful pur-
veyor of culture, language, and ideas about morality and unity that
superseded profane and contested notions deployed through secular
nationalist demands. Eritrean Orthodoxy and Catholicism in particular
(but also Pentecostalism) remain uniquely embedded in long-standing
cultural and linguistic patterns, allowing congregants to experience and
reproduce Eritrean identity in a sublimely different manner than secular nationalist organizing.

In some ways, this appears to be more related to American realities
than Eritrean ones. As Rhys Williams (2003, personal communication)
suggests, the depoliticization or compartmentalization of religious identity in American society, justified in terms of pluralism and the separation of church and state, establishes conditions for religion to function
as a principle of collective action beyond the realm of politics and political mobilization. In this way, the salience of religion for Eritrean community building is at least partially a response to American sociocultural
and political realities. However, this separation also pertains to the Eritrean state, which (until more recently) provided the Orthodox, Catholic, and at least some Protestant churches more autonomy than virtually
any other kind of institution. As a result, the churches occupied a
unique place within the transnational social field, one that was not thoroughly penetrated or regulated by the one-party state. Until recently,
they represented one of the strongest elements in an otherwise heavily
circumscribed transnational civil society.

Transnational Religious Identities and Institutions

In large part, it is the structural internationalism and ecumenism of
modern church bodies and doctrine that contributed to their depoliticization in exile and challenged the party-state's transnational power. And
while definite similarities obtained between the ways in which different
church bodies engaged transnationally with their diaspora congregations, crucial differences also existed based on the structures of Catholicism, Orthodoxy, and Pentecostalism.

In keeping with its historic transnational orientation (Casanova 2001;
Della Cava 2001), the Eritrean Catholic Church is connected through
the Vatican to a worldwide network of dioceses and parishes, rendering
it less amenable to the circumscribed nationalist projects of particular
states. Accordingly, the Catholic Church's spiritual mandate conflicts
with the jurisdiction of nation building, and especially the Eritrean government's rigorous opposition to any religiously affiliated social development projects, as one priest in Eritrea explained to me: "The
church's stand is very, very universal, all embracing. And the church's

mission is not always very well understood by some states. We were misunderstood very much in this state of Eritrea. The area of education, for example, the area of health and development—there are areas where the church, by its own mission, has to involve itself. To care for the sick? It has been since the time of Jesus, and will always be the church's mission. To say the church will not be involved in this will never work."

Similarly, Pentecostalism was a relatively new incarnation of traditions initiated in the mid-1800s by the Swedish Evangelical Mission and is distinctly modern, eclectic, and international in its outlook. While each Eritrean Pentecostal church remained autonomous, evangelicalism linked born-again Christians together through both informal networks and an all-encompassing discourse of salvation. Incorporating modern music, technology, and a steady stream of international visitors from other evangelical groups throughout the world, Eritrean Pentecostalism retained distinctive elements of language and culture but rejected the perceived traditionalism and parochialism of Orthodoxy and Catholicism. It was also especially appealing to young, educated urbanites and exiles, who tended to associate it with modernity and a cosmopolitan worldview (Hepner and Hepner, in press; see also Treiber 2009).

For example, prior to its closure in 2002 and the arrest of its pastors and many parishioners, the Mulu Wangeel Biet Kristyan Asmara, or Full Gospel Church of Asmara, maintained linkages with the Finnish Pentecostal Church and the Assemblies of God, as well as with other Eritrean Pentecostal congregations in the United States. During services in its two Asmara locations, several thousand people gathered several times a week beneath enormous yellow and white tents. Guests from all over the world—Canada, the United States, and Kenya during my visits—preached and testified in several languages, drawing Eritrean worshippers into a religious community that defied national borders and identities. In the midwestern community, the congregants embraced and practiced Eritrean culture through worship, but many rejected narrow nationalist attitudes, which led others, including many PFDJ members, to regard Pentecostals as insufficiently Eritrean and threatening to the "authentic" religious traditions of Orthodoxy and Islam.

Indeed, the Orthodox Church remains the national church and displayed less internationalism than any of the other denominations. Compared to Catholicism, Orthodoxy cannot easily be characterized as transnational. Consisting of fifteen independent national churches, each possesses its own patriarch and has full autonomy in administrative and pastoral matters (Della Cava 2001:537). In Eritrea, Orthodox Christians are a numerical majority, rivaled only by Muslims. As an institution, however, the Eritrean Orthodox Church in 2001 was just beginning to work out a transnational structure that incorporated diaspora congregations. The mother church in Asmara recognized fourteen congregations in the United States, which were overseen by the North American diocese located in Atlanta, Georgia.

Many more than fourteen Eritrean Orthodox congregations existed in the United States, however, frequently forming around a priest or priests who had arrived by other means. The church disapproved of "unofficial" congregations in exile and mandated that each Orthodox priest accept in full the mother church's written doctrine as well as its structural authority. The church resisted recognizing unofficial diaspora congregations, preferring to send its own selected priests (of which it faced a shortage, thus contributing to the proliferation of unofficial congregations). Part of the church's attempts to control diaspora congregations appeared related to the repression of the Medhanie Alem movement, which adopted charismatic or "foreign" elements into Orthodox liturgy (such as Bible study and modern song and prayer). Fearing the proliferation of such reformist congregations in diaspora especially, the church sought to stem them through a weak but developing transnational structure. Of course, this effort was expedited greatly in 2004, when the government ordered the arrest and detention of three priests who had allegedly coordinated the internal movement. In 2005, following his protest of the arrests, Patriarch Antonios himself was placed under house arrest. He was finally deposed and replaced in mid-2007 with a handpicked patriarch, in contradiction to all church canons.[14] In response, the North American diocese in Atlanta broke with the church in Asmara and asserted its autonomy.

The state's increasing interventions into religious institutions must be understood in conjunction with Eritrea's transnational realities. Not only do religious bodies by their very nature subvert national boundaries, but also their incipient links to exile congregations were beyond the purview of state control. Churches are also connected to wider networks and are strongly supported by Western patterns of religious freedom and church-state separation. Eritreans found it structurally easier to form congregations in the United States than any other type of institution, in part because of their linkages to non-Eritrean institutions and their resonance beyond the national community. Moreover, the vitality of religion and its relative autonomy from the state helped encourage the development of ties between exile congregations and specific churches in Eritrea itself.

The state's recent interference with religious institutions in Eritrea, and the proliferation of human rights abuses based on religious beliefs and practices, seems directly linked to the former autonomy of the churches in the transnational social field, as well as their capacity to mobilize people in ways that prove threatening to official nationalism

(Hepner 2003). However, we cannot assume that the state's crushing of religious autonomy changes political consciousness and loyalty among all believers. In many cases, exiles who belong to proscribed or banned faiths in Eritrea continue to defend the state's practices, indicating the depth of the EPLF/PFDJ's success in propagating its synthetic nationalism and the fear of being labeled a traitor.

Networks of Kin and Friendship

Irrespective of all other transnational institutions, linkages, or identities, each person remains bound to multiple others through affective ties of kin and friendship. Just as Eritreans frequently note that each and every person has at least one martyred family member from the liberation struggle (and now also the Ethio-Eritrean border war), so too, they say, does every Eritrean at home have at least one family member in diaspora.

Kinship among Eritrean Christian highlanders in particular is traced through agnatic (male), segmentary lineages, or *gezawuti*, which form the traditional basis for residence and claims to land in particular villages (Tronvoll 1998a:99). Most Eritreans, including those whose families may have long since left the village and migrated to the city, can generally trace their descent over seven generations. Similarly, the segmentary system engenders a proliferation of patrilineages that all trace descent to a single male agnate (Nadel 1944; Tronvoll 1998a). While Eritrean highland kinship structure is an extremely complex subject I make no attempt to address in detail here, the significance of these relationships among modern urban dwellers nonetheless seems to be twofold. First, every individual knows which village or region his or her family originally comes from and is known by others according to that line, and second, individuals tend to recognize even distant and diffuse kin connections between them.

As Tronvoll has noted (1998a, 1998b), the EPLF-led revolution altered important aspects of traditional kinship structure in the highlands to reorient the tenacious loyalties people felt for their region, village, land, and relatives toward the nation as a whole. More generally, the independence struggle impacted the sense of solidarity traditionally sustained by kinship, drawing on its metaphorical power to re-create blood links between people as members of liberation fronts and as Eritreans (see also Bernal 2000). The reconfiguration of kinship bonds vis-à-vis both political identity and nationalism has generated powerful fictive kin ties between unrelated individuals, who frequently refer to one another by terms like brother, sister, mother, father, or cousin when no biological relationship exists. Thus kinship ties as transnational linkages have not been necessarily limited to actual biological relatives but often include friends, former comrades, and fictive kin.

Despite the fact that the nationalist revolution sought to replace kin loyalties with that of citizen and state, most Eritreans living in exile continued to view their responsibilities and obligations largely in terms of their families and closest friends (see al-Ali, Black, and Koser 2001). During the most radical period of the revolution in the late 1970s, it was common for Eritreans in the United States to shun sending money or goods directly to their families. Rather they sent everything to the EPLF, believing that supporting the front also meant supporting one's family inasmuch as their continuing safety and well-being was entrusted to the EPLF. Today, however, many Eritreans living abroad who pay taxes to the state also send money and other kinds of material items to their families. Unlike the earlier climate among unequivocal EPLF supporters, many increasingly do not believe that the state has the capacity or desire to provide services and economic sustenance to its citizens and therefore have taken it upon themselves to support their loved ones.

Private remittances sent by Eritreans abroad to their relatives and friends at home were generally not monitored by the state, nor did they travel mainly through official avenues such as banks or wire transfer services as in so many other countries with highly developed remittance practices. Rather, most Eritreans relied on the constant stream of people coming and going to physically carry and distribute cash to those for whom it was intended. It was not unusual for someone to travel with ten thousand dollars or more, destined for perhaps dozens of families. Indeed, private remittances have remained central to the Eritrean economy (Bernal 2004; Fessehatzion 2005). They also frequently mean the difference between poverty and sustenance for many people—a difference one man in Eritrea described as being "like sky and earth." Thus remittances have contributed to new class divisions and status markers in Eritrea, as even relatively well-off families have come to expect their relatives abroad—many of whom do not enjoy the same relative standard of living in the United States—to send money, goods, or scarce commodities. This creates dilemmas for both local Eritreans and those living abroad. One government official, a former resident of the United States, felt distressed by what she saw as rampant consumerism developing in Eritrea. Consistent with Eritrea's fierce, do-it-yourself ethic, she explained how turning down remittances was an act of both pride and conscious resistance:

Here, I try to survive with what I need. Like most of my other extended relatives here, they sometimes tell me, "Why don't you buy a big house? You have [relatives] in the U.S. who will help you!" But I say no, I have to be able to survive with whatever I make. They have their own life and I have my own life. Sometimes they might send me some clothes or other small items. And I also send them things—they don't like it, but I send them like gold [jewelry] or something for my nieces. I like to do it, I want to do it. And I also want to make them feel that I can also send things, not just them. And there is also the other way around—sometimes I have fights [with family members here in Eritrea]—I tell them they are like beggars, sophisticated beggars. I can see it if people send money to needy ones. But it's becoming a culture here, you know, to get money from people in diaspora.

Not everyone shared this woman's critical consciousness, however. Many people seemed keen to exploit the sense of responsibility felt by exiles to help their loved ones at home. Moreover, the constant comings and goings of exiles have introduced local society to the cultural tastes, styles, and consumerism of Western societies, and the United States especially. As a result, the existing gap between more well-off families and those who get by on less has continued to widen, while the few families who cannot rely on help from abroad sink ever deeper toward the bottom of Eritrea's evolving class structure. Nonetheless, many Eritreans in the United States feel that it is the very least they can do to help out family members at home, and still others would prefer to live on little in the United States for the peace of mind that their loved ones in Eritrea are doing well. They also enjoy a sense of status and value when they return home (see al-Ali, Black, and Koser 2001:592; see also Basch, Glick-Schiller, and Blanc 1994; Glick Schiller and Fouron 1999, 2001; Levitt 2001). A midwestern taxicab driver explained the commitment so many people feel and how he assists his family:

All members of this community, they don't only help their nation, they help their families at home too. Every three or four months I help my brother, who has four orphaned children. My brother was killed by Ethiopia [in the border war], and these four children, they go to school, they have a few goats and some cows, and they commute like five or ten miles to school. So now, all the people who live in diaspora help their families . . . their mother or father, or both parents, their sister or brother, aunt or uncle, they send something every month, and when they go visit every one or two or three years, they have a good connection. They are welcomed at home and they feel at home, maybe they build a little house for them, or they send them money and they build a place in their grandfather's village.

In addition to the actual money and goods sent from abroad, other messages conveyed in ways both subtle and overt by diaspora kin awaken the consciousness of many Eritreans, particularly young people, to the limited opportunities they face in Eritrea. This awareness of the massive disparities between life in the United States and Eritrea generates frustration, dissatisfaction, and distorted images of life abroad. For, fundamentally, Eritrea remains a country of great sacrifices, where people are expected to endure hardships without complaint and serve their country and the memory of those who were martyred for independence. The differences between life in Eritrea and life in America appear stark: in Eritrea, military training and National Service are compulsory for nearly everyone aged eighteen to forty, and individual choices related to education, career, or family are circumscribed by structural underdevelopment and the social and economic demands placed by the government on its citizens.[15] Life in America, however, offers seemingly endless opportunities and resources, as well as a way to help those left behind, illustrated by the role that exiles play in their relatives' lives.

One young university student, Hintsa, depended on his uncle Tsegai, a midwestern businessman, for assistance with everything from school fees to general living expenses. He remained fixated on the mysterious power he imagined his uncle and aunt must have to bring him to the United States. Bumping along on a country bus from his home village to Asmara, where we had visited his extended family together, Hintsa explained to me how Tsegai was a good man, while his other uncle, Bereket, was bad because he rarely sent money. Later, in an interview, Hintsa elaborated on how he imagined his uncle Tsegai's life in the United States and why he wanted to join him:

Oh, he is the richest man! He owns two businesses. . . . I think they are living a good life in the USA. Everybody is going to America. I think because they are living a good life, they can help their families in this country and every country. You can improve your life there. I like my country, but you know you cannot improve your life here. . . . [Tsegai's wife] was here, she just visited. She sees we are living badly, like sheep. Everything is expensive and there is also the problem of National Service. Because of that problem, I am asking them to help me. I want to get a scholarship and go to the USA.

The kin and friendship ties that obtain between Eritreans at home and in exile contain within them much more than economic or material transfers. As Levitt (2001:11) has pointed out, social remittances—"the ideas, behaviors, and social capital that flow from receiving to sending communities"—have a significant impact on how local people in particular perceive their own status and surroundings. In the Eritrean case, however, the flow tends to occur both ways, in some cases more powerfully from Eritrea to exile than vice versa. Eritreans living abroad depend on their family members and friends for crucial information about everyday living conditions and social and political developments, which in turn shapes their feelings and actions toward Eritrea. Just as during the days of EFLNA when the most coveted news revolved around what EPLF fighters wore and ate, how they lived and where they slept, so too does direct news from home allow Eritreans in exile to feel connected to life on the ground and to make decisions about how to act toward their families, friends, the state, and other institutions.

At the same time, however, a long-developed culture of fear and secrecy, as well as the intense homogenizing pressures of state nationalism, has discouraged people from carrying on detailed or politically sensitive discussions through nonsecure media like telephones, letters, or even e-mail. This self-censorship was especially prevalent among local Eritreans, who possessed sixth-sense awareness of what could and could not be stated and in what context and company one could speak freely. Moreover, self-censorship increased in the years since the Ethio-Eritrean border war, during which time the Eritrean government began repressing internal dissent and other freedoms in the name of national security. Most people I interviewed in Eritrea about the content of their discussions with family members or close friends in the United States refused to discuss whether they talked about politics, insisting that the major content of their discussions revolved around everyday issues such as health, well-being, school, work, National Service, and the weather.

However, even innocuous topics carried a great deal of weight for exiles, who found their own political attitudes influenced by the kinds of situations faced by their relatives. If one's family members or close friends in Eritrea appeared to be unhappy or struggling due to social conditions that have emerged due to government policies, the policies themselves—or the family members—may become subject to critique. Similarly, because so many families were divided by ELF or EPLF political identities, conversations about everyday life under the EPLF/PFDJ were filtered through old grievances and continued to shape ongoing perceptions of the one-party state among exiles who retain (or have adopted) an oppositional stance. For many other Eritreans living abroad and removed from everyday life, however, no manner of disheartening news from home can cool their support for the PFDJ. They remain intensely faithful to official statements about life on the ground and generally dismiss reports that clash with the government's representations or their own beliefs. In turn, they often participate in policing the positions of others who challenge the government line, even if those challenges emerge out of real-life experiences.

Internet Communication and Communities

One of the least regulated but most significant components of the Eritrean transnational social field has been the Internet, now home to hundreds of Eritrean Web sites, chat rooms, and "cybercommunities." Internet mobilization among Eritreans began in exile communities shortly after independence and later encompassed parts of Eritrea itself after the government signed onto the Leland Initiative in 1999, a program designed and implemented by the United States Agency for International Development (USAID) in 1995 to enhance Internet connectivity in Africa. Since then, Internet usage among Eritreans around the world has burgeoned, providing a free and open forum for discussion about countless issues—many of them politically or socially sensitive and therefore not publicly debated in Eritrea itself—as well as the mobilization of resources and other collective efforts. Bernal (2004, 2006) notes how, during the 1998–2000 Ethio-Eritrean border war, Eritreans all over the country used the resources of the Internet to organize fundraising, carry out public relations campaigns, and plan demonstrations at the United Nations. Indeed, this short list but scratches the surface: today, diverse Eritrean online communities accomplish a multiplicity of tasks: they lobby respective foreign governments; disseminate Tigrinya language-learning tools; sell Eritrea-related music, videos, and books; plan and publicize nationwide or regional academic, religious, and sports events; locate assistance from fellow Eritreans (including finding people who can carry items to relatives in Eritrea); post international news about Eritrea and Africa in general; publish statements or open letters on social and political issues by Eritrean authors; and organize the gathering opposition movements and "civic societies" into coalitions. This phenomenon contributes to what Bernal (2000, 2005a, 2005b, 2006) refers to as "a new transnational Eritrean public sphere" sustained largely in exile but penetrating local Eritrean society in definite ways (see also Conrad 2006).

The Eritrean presence in cyberspace dates to 1993, when five academics in the United States founded a discussion list called Dehai, which roughly means "inside chat" or "news." The list rapidly expanded to about five hundred people and became especially vibrant during the 1994 constitutional drafting process, when largely well-educated exiles debated everything from the integration of customary and constitutional law to women's rights and the relationship between religion and the state (Rude 1996). At first the province of those who exclusively supported EPLF, Dehai provided a significant location where Eritreans collectively asserted their national commitment and debated culturally intimate issues. Later, the discussion network grew to include Eritreans around the world of diverse backgrounds and sensibilities, where differing views often clashed against the policed boundaries of proper EPLF/PFDJ nationalist discourse. Rumors abounded that Dehai was a government creation and that high officials, including President Isayas himself, assumed screen names in order to engage in more open, democratic debate (see Bernal 2000). Many discussions carried out in Dehai made their way to Eritrea, as the few people with Internet access prior to 1999 printed out posts that were distributed clandestinely or translated and reprinted in local newspapers. This practice has continued, allowing debates and news available only online to reach a broader audience. I was struck on several occasions by elderly women in both Eritrea and the United States, many of whom spoke no English and were not literate in Tigrinya, discussing with one another the latest news someone found on this or that Web site.

Today, numerous Eritrean Web sites exist that evidence a multiplicity of political views, identities, and interests. The Eritrean government also has an official Web site (www.shaebia.org), where it reports on development-related issues and posts official statements, managing official government positions against information and interpretations available elsewhere. The Web site also contains an entire section devoted to news about the diaspora. Other Web sites (such as www.awate.com) articulate opposition perspectives and identify with ELF positions, highlighting the Muslim- and Arabic-friendly quality of their constituents. One of the most versatile sites remains www.asmarino.com, where people of every persuasion engage in lively debate, advertise all manner of events, and can link up to other Eritrea-related resources and information. Almost all of the sites are moderated by staff members who enforce guidelines of respectability and civility, safeguarding against vituperative ad hominem attacks that ran rampant on early sites like Dehai and remain a feature of Eritrean communication patterns overall.

Among Eritreans, the virtual debates and the real ones clearly overlap (Rude 1996:19; see also Conrad 2006) in many different arenas. All of the components of the transnational social field I have discussed here, from the PFDJ to mass organizations, churches, NGOs, and informal social networks of kin and friends, draw upon the Internet to build and sustain the relationships, material flows, and identities that make up the connective channels between Eritrea and exile. Similarly, the Internet has become the most powerful medium for organizing new global political movements and "vernacularizing" (Merry 2006) concepts such as human rights, democracy, and civil society among Eritreans living all over the world, in part because it reaches far-flung communities instantaneously and also because it cannot be controlled effectively by any authoritative body. It is still important to note, however, that long before the birth of the Internet and other new technologies of globalization, the EPLF had developed a transnational structure nearly as effective in its day.

Clearly, many discussions and debates taking place online often remain stuck there, disembodied and lacking practical impact on Eritrea itself. However, as Rude (1996) noted, early members of Dehai recognized the potential such a network might have for creating real impacts in Eritrea. The successful organization of many efforts over Eritrean Internet networks, from famine and drought relief to briefings by visiting government officials and founding conferences of opposition parties, attests to the validity of the Internet as a facilitator for more concrete interventions. Indeed, even in Eritrea itself, urban dwellers and especially youth gravitate toward the Internet as the main source of information about their country and the rest of the world. Following the closing of the private presses in August 2001, the Internet became the only non-state source of news available in Eritrea. While the television networks and two state-owned newspapers reproduced news available on Eritrean Web sites and about Eritrean activities in diaspora that emphasized support for the government and national loyalty, the Internet allowed access to the critical discussions and independent reports otherwise unavailable. A quick glance at the browser history on any public computer revealed the extent to which local Eritreans accessed Web sites with critical or oppositional content. And familiarity with the users themselves and the paranoia with which some glanced over their shoulders suggested that even free information might come at a price. Indeed, its has become a regular hassle for several Web site managers in exile whose servers have been hacked by government loyalists in an effort to prevent them from posting news and views considered subversive.[16]

The Ties That Choke: Transnationalism's Janus Face

The unevenly institutionalized relationships that form the transnational social field have certainly enabled the ongoing integration of Eritrea and exile into a single entity. But there is another side to Eritrea's transnational reality as well. Inasmuch as the mechanisms of Eritrean transnationalism have contributed to expanding ideas and practices of citizenship, national belonging, identity, and responsibility, they have also limited and repressed certain kinds of practices, institutions, and identities. Because of Eritrea's particular history of nationalism, revolution, and refugee flows, the evolution of its transnational social field has been closely managed by the state, which utilizes its own deterritorialized capacities to intervene in many aspects of everyday life. As a result, the transnational social field has become a battleground where struggles over national identity, belonging, and state-society power take place. Moreover, the financial and moral demands made upon Eritrean citizens in exile prevent the development of stable community institutions in exile. In this way, the ties that bind can also choke.

Transnational Dissonance in the Twenty-First Century

We have already seen how dilemmas arise for Eritreans as they build and engage in transnational institutions and networks. Prior to independence, organizations like EFLNA and chapters of the EPLF faced some unique challenges. For EFLNA, the ability to think and act autonomously, as well as to draw upon lessons and resources not necessarily embedded within local Eritrean realities (such as feminism or internationalist political philosophies) diminished as the organization became more tightly bound to the EPLF. For chapters of the EPLF, reproducing the front's administrative power and nationalist orientation in exile proved difficult in communities numerically dominated by former ELF affiliates. Postindependence, these challenges have only multiplied as Eritreans at home and abroad seek concrete methods for both integration and autonomy amid ever proliferating identities and interests as well as increasing authoritarianism and state violence. Profoundly conflicted questions lie at the heart of the transnational arrangement: In what ways must Eritreans in the United States continue being and becoming Eritrean in order to meet the demands of nationalist identity and belonging, and in what ways should they engage with their societies of settlement? And for whose benefit—the Eritrean party-state's or their own? Can both be accommodated?

The ways in which transnational engagements limit, repress, and disable exile integration into local Eritrean and American society are sometimes subtle and sometimes overt but are almost always related to the Eritrean state's administrative power and nation-building objectives. Moreover, they must be contextualized within the history of the revolution, the structural dynamics of migration, and the EPLF/PFDJ's own synthetic nationalist definitions. These definitions, as I have discussed, remain ambivalent at best toward external political-economic and cultural influences, whether they emanate from the international system of nation-states and associated discourses and ethics or from Eritreans who live abroad. At the same time, however, deterritorialized citizens remain subjects of the Eritrean nation-state, responding to the state's demands in ways that are consistent with the nationalist revolution's goals of self-reliance.

Within the unevenly institutionalized components of the transnational social field I have analyzed in this chapter, these struggles and contradictions materialize both practically and discursively. In NUEW and NUEYS, for example, constituents in diaspora are encouraged by the unions in Asmara to develop relationships with surrounding American communities or institutions and to familiarize themselves with their dual Eritrean and American environments. While defined by both

NUEW and NUEYS as important for diaspora Eritreans, engaging with American civil society or succeeding in education and career goals nonetheless derive their meaning in relationship to the Eritrean state's own objectives. The benefits for Eritrean individuals or communities as "ethnic" populations in the United States remain much less important, except in terms of what a strong ethnic lobby might accomplish on behalf of Eritrea as a whole. Indeed, the realities that Eritreans abroad occupy and what membership in NUEW and NUEYS can do for them as migrants and minorities in their societies of settlement remain largely unaddressed. Rather, the emphasis placed by both NUEW and NUEYS on education and self-improvement both at home and abroad is meaningful in the transnational context largely according to Eritrean realities: skilled Eritreans and strong, capable diaspora communities mean a stronger and more capable Eritrea.

Similarly, as institutionalized avenues that define, direct, and organize the methods by which their constituents engage with local Eritrean society, NUEYS and NUEW are able to deflect the kinds of social remittances that conflict with the state's objectives. For example, one midwestern resident who approached NUEW leaders in Asmara about her idea to found a series of Western-style daycare centers in Eritrea encountered resistance on several levels. First, NUEW officials explained their concern that violence, drug abuse, and other social ills in America could be related to absent parents and the day-care system and that reproducing such a system in Eritrea could result in similar social problems. Second, a lack of support from NUEW, so closely aligned with the PFDJ, signaled major structural obstacles at the state level that circumventing the union would not alleviate. Given the dearth of other independent women's organizations, no other mechanism for fulfilling this woman's dream existed, leading her to abandon it altogether. Moreover, NUEW's stated focus on poor and rural women has led many professional women in the diaspora, who view it as unresponsive to their concerns, away from the union altogether.

A similar situation exists with NUEYS, despite its more proactive efforts to mobilize diaspora youth and take on the often uncomfortable challenges of cultural (re)integration. In this area too, in terms of both culture and skills or technology transfers, NUEYS, like NUEW, privileges Eritrean realities almost to the exclusion of diasporic ones. Although this is not very surprising, many diasporic conditions that diverge from local ones—and yet remain common to Eritrean communities abroad—cannot be addressed through NUEYS's circumscribed objectives. As a result, the kinds of social problems Eritrean youth in diaspora face, including racial and ethnic discrimination, violence, urban gang-related problems, and exposure to drug and alcohol abuse, are generally not acknowledged as important aspects of their lives. Similarly, the positive gains and opportunities available to Eritrean youth in diaspora are valued by NUEYS only insofar as they help achieve the party-state's objectives. Questions about NUEYS's relevance to many diaspora youth inevitably arise, and a sense that diasporic realities are taken seriously only when they converge with Eritrean ones leads many young people to reject involvement in NUEYS.

Finally, many young people who live in places like the United States seem uneasy with the PFDJ's authoritative presence and the very different notion of "freedom" in Eritrea more generally. This uneasiness contributes to a sense of their own otherness in Eritrean society and likely deters some youth from participating in events that bring them in close contact with local peers and the state itself. Institutions like NUEW and NUEYS therefore cannot accommodate—and sometimes actively exclude—certain transnationally constructed practices and identities while blocking associated social remittances that may be at odds with local goals or realities. And while both unions have achieved some success in integrating Eritrea and exile, it is difficult to see at present how far this trajectory will go unless diasporic realities, identities, skills, and objectives are more openly addressed and validated. For while diaspora Eritreans of all ages feel a great deal of national commitment and pride, it seems likely that they will lose interest in the kinds of approaches NUEW and NUEYS have developed thus far if their experiences and abilities are not recognized as authentically Eritrean.

The unions and the PFDJ party itself share obvious structural continuity with the state and are therefore best understood as institutions of governance. As a result, both the integration they enable between Eritrea and exile and the dissonance they generate are linked to the state's own administrative power and the role of official nationalism in defining which practices, identities, and forms of knowledge or skills are desirable and which are not. Through these transnational mechanisms, the state is able to block or ignore certain social remittances, identities, and interests while enabling and even enforcing others. Through the same mechanisms, it seeks to reproduce its own administrative power and nationalist identity in diaspora, through chapters of the PFDJ and the *maHber kom,* or community association. Yet, as I have also discussed, this state presence and authority is deeply contested. From struggles over defining, organizing, and leading "the community" to the role of PFDJ in helping reproduce proper national subjects and citizens, Eritreans abroad—including those who support the government—live with an intense ambivalence about where and how they fit into Eritrean and American society.

In addition, the transnational presence of the state, thoroughly conflated with the PFDJ Party, has encouraged the development of opposition parties and coalitions in exile. In some ways, this trend is a natural outgrowth of Eritrea's own transnational realities and the politics of migration, which deposited abroad much of the existing opposition. In other ways, the growth of Eritrean movements, ranging from staunch opposition to reformism and international human rights and nonviolent social justice agendas, has been a response to the state's increasing power over local and transnational Eritrean society and, more recently, an escalation in political repression and human rights abuses.

But what of those components of the transnational social field that appeared by their very nature to enjoy greater relative autonomy from the state, such as religious bodies, kin networks, and the Internet? Here, too, dissonance often prevails, and the state retains an authoritative presence even if its control is mitigated by the larger transnational structures of religious bodies, the greater privacy of exchanges occurring at the microlevel of family and friends, and the lack of regulations on the Internet. As discussed earlier, the state made several interventions into religious institutions in 2001–2 that have affected their roles in Eritrea and exile. In addition to circumscribing the ability of religious organizations to participate in NGO and other development work, the state also silenced the Catholic bishops for their 2001 pastoral letter, in which they criticized the government's social and political-economic policies since independence, and the Ethio-Eritrean border war in particular. Composed at a time when Eritrea was reeling from the effects of the war and the government had begun curtailing freedoms and altering traditional patterns in the name of nation building, the bishops' critiques were extremely bold. Among their concerns was the notion of freedom in independent Eritrea:

When we talk of the past ten years of independence and freedom in Eritrea we refer to a truly free nation whose freedom is the sum of the freedoms of its nationals. We, therefore, necessarily include freedom of conscience and creed, freedom of speech and the press, freedom of communication, and freedom of association and assembly. Only when all citizens of the nation own this kind of comprehensive freedom can we speak of a truly free nation. . . . So it is that we must ask ourselves some awkward questions: Have we always done what is right for all our citizens? Have we, or how have we, used/abused our freedom? Have we always respected the rights of others? Have we understood justice? Have we used the gift of freedom and independence—attained at such a high price— worthily?[17]

The pastoral letter deeply angered the PFDJ government, who banned its distribution in either Tigrinya or English. One Eritrean Web site, however, managed to publish both the original Tigrinya and an unofficial English translation. For its part, the church insisted on its duty to speak its conscience; one of the priests I interviewed mused aloud about a time when the same officials now silencing the church had once taken great inspiration, as freedom fighters, from the church's critique of the Ethiopian Derg regime.

The state did not limit its intervention to the Catholic Church, however. In early 2002, the government closed indefinitely all new charismatic churches, including the Mulu Wangeel Biet Kristyan Asmara, or Full Gospel Church, which had burgeoned since the Ethio-Eritrean border war, as well as some older ones such as the Seventh Day Adventist Church. In May of that same year, the state denied official status to all faiths except Orthodox Christian, Muslim, Catholic, and the long-established Lutheran Church. Concerned that new religious movements had attracted so many converts from Eritrea's own traditional faiths, introduced foreign beliefs and practices into Eritrean religious life, and established new connections with non-Eritrean religious institutions and sources of capital, the government asserted its authority despite the formal separation of religion and state. In exile locations, however, the churches continued to grow in numbers and strength, far outpacing the community association, NUEW, and the PFDJ as effective community institutions (Hepner 2003). The recent and violent curtailment of religious institutions and practice in Eritrea has all but destroyed the institutionalization of transnational relationships between congregations in diaspora and religious bodies in Eritrea. It also sends a clear message about the power of the state and the ongoing nationalist project to homogenize and subsume all other identities, if not discursively then through repressive policies and practices.

Among family and friends whose networks span Eritrea and exile, informal relationships also provide some autonomy from the kinds of state regulations that shape and limit other aspects of local and exile life. Private remittances, one of the major ways that diaspora Eritreans contribute to local society, have not been regulated by the state to this point. It also remains unclear whether and to what extent the state effectively monitors communications via telephone, letters, and e-mail. Nonetheless, many people believe that the government does intrude on their private conversations, making them reluctant to share certain kinds of information or perspectives with one another. Similarly, some exiles have become skeptical of the transnational institutions sanctioned by the state as appropriate modes of integration and participation. The kinds of on-the-ground reports provided by family members and friends inform exiles' perspectives and activities and sometimes lead them to develop new ways of circumventing the state's transnational presence, if possible. One man in the United States, once an EPLF supporter, confided to me:

I have been getting more letters from home asking for help, reflecting the dire circumstances of the times. I'm trying to mobilize my foreign friends to help me help people. . . . The way the PFDJ has handled its relationships is full of blunders. The diaspora is now totally distrustful and has lost interest in investing in Eritrea. Hence the attempt to somehow empower kin and relatives by directly sending them money. I know quite a few people who sold their homes and property [in the United States] and went home with the intention of permanently settling there. Almost all of them have returned, totally disillusioned and discouraged, and have started building their lives again from scratch. It saddens me in some ways that I can only send money to relatives and friends. I can imagine the pain of those who do not have relatives abroad or whose relatives have chosen to forget them. In some ways, I know that I am contributing to perpetuating the class inequality that is emerging. However, I see no other way around it, under the economic and political reality created by PFDJ.

The presence of the state in virtually every area of transnational political-economic and social life has led some exiles to view private remittances as the only way to truly participate in Eritrean society. At the same time, transformations in local Eritrean consciousness regarding material items and consumerism, largely due to their contact with family and friends in exile, generates new burdens for those who live abroad. Many Eritreans in the United States, partly driven by a sense of guilt over "abandoning" Eritrea for a more privileged existence in the United States, and partly encouraged by the status they achieve through remittances, have lived frugally in America so their families can achieve stability at home. Others who have worked very hard to build lives for themselves in the United States feel overwhelmed by the extent of their families' financial and social crises at home. As Eden explained, with sadness etched in her lovely face:

I always felt so much spirit, so much love for my country. I *loved* Eritrea. Now I'm like—I don't ever want to go back to Eritrea. I associate it with neediness, with everybody wanting something from me, with everyone bringing their child and saying, "Here is my child, take them to America." Like I could just [snaps fingers]. I associate it with people who don't want to try to make the most of what they fought for, what their sons and daughters fought for. I see it as a place people want to run away from. I don't know. I don't like how I feel, but I can't help it. I don't know how to make people understand that just because I live in the U.S. I am not made of money.

Conversely, many local Eritreans are enormously frustrated by their family members in exile who do not seem to grasp the realities that structure local peoples' lives, insisting on reading them from either an idealized, frozen picture of Eritrean life and politics or their own altered subjectivities as denizens of the United States. Another young woman I befriended in Asmara vented her feelings one afternoon as we sipped tea in her family's comfortable living room:

This is a new culture, the idea of raising your voice. Eritreans are not like that, we do not protest when we are unhappy with a situation. Here the government does not like that, and you never know what can happen. The best is to lose your job, at least you still are with family and all of that. If they put you in prison, you are alone and isolated. People are afraid. We do not speak our minds or stir up conflict, but we are all very frustrated. Like my husband. He is nearly forty and is still doing National Service. He is extremely unhappy. He can't do anything else, he has no choice. He has no freedom. We cannot do what we wish, we are bound to do what the government tells us. And these diaspora people, they do not understand what life is like here for us. My husband's sister came for the wedding from the United States and she asked my husband why he didn't just get a job doing something he likes or wants to do. She doesn't understand that your life does not belong to you, you cannot make such choices. And then with politics? She calls and says "Why are the people making President Isayas sad?" and I just want to scream at her that she knows nothing about what life is like here.

In other very important ways the state has also intervened directly into Eritrean families with strong implications for the transnational nation-state. First and foremost, the great sacrifices required of young men and women serving in the military for indefinite periods of time has precluded these same people from fulfilling other important and productive familial roles, such as assisting in the maintenance of the extended household, and even preventing them from being able to get married and start their own families and careers (Treiber 2009). For young women, the problem may be even more acute, as pregnancy out of wedlock has become a strategy for getting out of military service, leaving them saddled with the additional burden—and stigma—of children with absent fathers. And more recently, the government has begun taking more deliberate measures to discourage local Eritreans, and especially those serving in the military, from trying to depart the country illegally by levying on parents or other close relatives an exorbitant fine of 50,000 nakfa (approximately US$3,500). Occasionally, relatives of absconders are taken into custody and held for information or in place of the missing individual. And surveillance of opposition activities by exiles can also come back to haunt those living at home. PFDJ cadres and loyalists regularly monitor the activities of citizens in exile (Conrad 2005, 2006; Hepner 2008), which they report back to the government in Asmara, sometimes leading to threats or harassment against the family members of known "traitors." One unfortunate result of these dynamics is that even those who are unhappy with the current state of affairs have little recourse to protest the government's actions, lest they endanger the lives and well-being of loved ones at home.

Finally, at least some of the tenacious loyalty to PFDJ observable among so many diaspora Eritreans appears related to their material interest in the country. Certainly those who are obedient, supportive, and up to date in their tax payments have a much greater chance of retaining access to purchased and heritable property. To question or criticize the government, despite its increasingly alarming record of rights abuses and its clear turn toward authoritarianism, is for many a leap too perilous to take. For how else can the sacrifices of more than four decades now, and freedom itself, truly make sense? How can the memories of martyrs, and the glorious sacrifices of soldiers, truly be meaningful if all exiles become traitors?

This chapter has explored in detail the structural features of the contemporary Eritrean transnational social field and how they shape communities in exile, as well as Eritrea itself. Many of the patterns that emerged in the 1970s and 1980s continue to reverberate throughout these exchanges. Most important among these is the strength of the Eritrean party-state. At the same time, however, the uneven institutionalization of the transnational social field conjoining Eritrea and exile has created unanticipated opportunities for resistance among both local Eritreans and exiles. It has also revealed the extent to which state nationalism cannot provide an inclusive, meaningful narrative for all Eritreans, and especially those who remain politically at odds with the EPLF/PFDJ. Even for loyal supporters, however, we have seen how the transnational social field is rife with contradictions and limitations, again drawing attention to the inchoate nature of state power and hinting at possible alternatives.

While the state does not necessarily intervene directly in all of the transnational exchanges occurring between Eritreans at home and abroad, it retains a constant presence in the lives and imaginations of Eritreans everywhere. In other ways it does directly intervene, either asserting authority over the form and content of transnational flows or creating obstacles that deflect or delegitimize certain kinds of social remittances. Today the patterns of transnationalism remain a central feature of the modern Eritrean nation-state and carry on the long tradition of coconstructing and contesting the meaning and practice of Eritrean national identity, responsibility, and citizenship. Thus, while Eritrea may provide an excellent example of how nation-states and political communities become transnational, it may also offer some unique and cautionary insights about the dual nature of this dynamic, reminding us how the ties that bind can also choke.

The constraints associated with the Eritrean transnational arrangement under the EPLF/PFDJ, and the long-standing difficulties within exile communities due to the state's presence abroad, have given rise to important forms of resistance already hinted at in this chapter. Whether inspired by former ELF pluralist nationalism and oppositional or subnational identities, or provoked by the recent repressive turn taken by the Eritrean party-state against its citizens, organizations beyond the purview of the transnational social field have also begun seeking intervention into Eritrea for the sake of changing it. These organizations and movements, whether operating on platforms for human rights or alternative political configurations, support the existence of the Eritrean state but are extremely critical of the existing power arrangements both locally and transnationally. Adopting the language of democracy, civil society, and rights, they have reached back into Eritrea's past to locate the roots of these putatively Western features within Eritrean society and culture and now seek to apply them—and lessons they have learned in exile—via the transnational social field that once belonged solely to the EPLF. Meanwhile, the increasingly authoritarian government rejects and punishes such efforts, viewing them as intertwined with historic nationalist grievances and thoroughly co-opted by the neoliberal assumptions and agendas of Western powers and bodies such as the United Nations. The role of Eritreans in exile as a component of transnational civil society is the subject of the final chapter of this book.

Chapter 6
A Painful Paradox
Transnational Civil Society and the
Sovereign State

Meselat

For many Eritreans in the United States, nothing about exile—even the most quotidian details, such as the twang of a *kraar* or the tart sponginess of a well-made *injera* pancake—truly seemed complete in isolation from its referent. It was as though the reproductions of Eritrean life in the United States were but shades of an ideal reality whose Platonic form existed only in Eritrea itself. This was the power that pulled people like Meselat back again and again, forcing her to relish the pain of return as inseparable from the pleasure of reconnection. Because when she returned again to the United States, the pain of isolation was even more acute than the pain of no longer belonging at home. And Meselat didn't belong at home, just as she didn't belong in exile.

Meselat was my accidental friend. We somehow found each other, back to back in a hotel bar where satellite music played and the scene could almost have been Manhattan, she with her male companions and me with mine. I mentioned the Midwest to my friends and her lovely head whirled around. The tickle of her hair sweeping the back of my neck made me turn too, so that we faced each other in the same instant.

"You are from the Midwest?" she said. "So am I." And then she giggled, a throaty and hoarse laugh, her lips held taut against a row of perfect teeth. She was younger than I, beautiful, with an expression suggesting defiant openness. Different from many Eritrean women I knew, who shielded their smiles, averted their eyes, spoke softly, and stayed home at night.

"Really? I don't think we've met before. . . ." I scanned the catalog of faces in my memory, looking for hers. I prided myself on knowing most of the people in the small midwestern community, if not by name then by sight. I would have remembered Meselat, though. She was not in my database of faces.

"Oh, I didn't go out much. I worked all the time. When I wasn't working I was at home with my two little sons." She smiled broadly. "Are you the one they call Terhas?"

I was flattered that she knew who I was. "Well, you know, we *tsAda Ertrawiyen* are a minority," I replied, calling myself a "white Eritrean." Such absurdities did not exist, and Meselat laughed as I hoped she would.

Mesi and I were kindred spirits, as it turned out. We could relate on many levels. Our common link to the same U.S. city implied an immediate friendship that developed into genuine intimacy. She was also a young, married woman without her husband in Eritrea. She was independent and didn't care much about what people thought of her. Like me, she hung around with men because she could talk to them openly and enjoy a beer or two. Drinking in bars and hotel lounges was one of the few outlets for relaxation and conversation in Asmara, that lovely, languid city teeming with tension beneath a calm exterior.

Mesi had left Asmara only a few years before when she married a much older man who had been resettled as a refugee in the 1980s. He was a friend of her uncle's, and a way for her to get to the United States, get out of Eritrea, earn money to send home, move beyond the exigencies of war and militarism. She had two children with him and now spent as much time as possible away from him. He wanted to control her every move, she later told me. Only in Asmara with her extended family and friends did she feel free of his grasp.

But Meselat found Eritrea just as stifling. Once, as we strolled arm in arm through the city, its art-deco facades dappled in sunlight, masking the occasional bullet hole, I succumbed to a feeling of belonging. Turning my face to the sky, I murmured, "I could live in Asmara forever." Mesi looked at me sideways. "No, you couldn't. Don't wish for that," she said flatly. "When you live here, it feels just like a prison."

And so, for Meselat, whose name literally translated to "rights," the bartering of incommensurable freedoms was not so simple. In the United States she was mostly free of Eritrea, except for her husband and those ingrained cultural propensities no one ever really shakes off. But she felt lost there too, cut adrift from herself and especially her family. The paradox drew her back again and again to Asmara, even though reconciling her hard homebound realities with her newly diasporic ones—especially the knowledge that she could leave Eritrea and her family anytime, when her family could not leave Eritrea—pained her deeply.

Our first afternoon together, Mesi and I went to the section of the city where the tailors' shops form rows of small, boxlike hives. Inside each comb was a treasure trove of beautiful cloth: white and eggshell and pale honey cottons, a thick mosaic band of color spun at the bottom. These were the *zurya* shops, where women bought the rich fabrics from which the "traditional" dresses would be custom made by a lone man with a sewing machine. Together we picked out a fabric for my own *zurya*. Then we had lunch in one of the restaurants that catered especially to exiles and tourists; the waitresses all wore *zuryas,* and the clientele sat on low stools, eating *injera* from atop a *mesob*, a colorful cross between a table and a basket. It was there that Meselat told me about her time in military service and why she had left Eritrea for exile.

"It was the best time and worst time of my life," she said. "It was so hard, you know. Like they wanted to cram thirty years of struggle into six months, to teach us what it was like to be a *tegadelay*, a fighter. We were told all the time to remember the sacrifices of the martyrs. They stationed us far out in the desert where we were supposed to be watching for jihadists, you know, crossing from Sudan."

She was smiling and laughing as she remembered. "We never saw a single one! It was so boring! But I was so close to my small group of friends there. All of us were from the city. There was all this tension between the city people and the country people. The country people would sometimes tell the officers, who were also from the country, that we did bad things so we would be punished. Sometimes they would give us only bad food and dirty water to drink. When we got sick, we would take care of each other. My one friend, she carried me when I passed out in the hot sun. And then when I was bitten by a snake and almost died." Even as she told the tales of hardship, she appeared to relish the memories. But there was something deeper behind Mesi's story of military service.

I often walked from my own home in a section of the city known as Mai Temenay, either "my water serpent," or "hoping for water," depending on which way you considered it, all the way to Mesi's neighborhood on the other side of town. Knocking loudly on the metal gate, I would peer through the crack to be sure the blind old dog that once bit me in the knee was nowhere to be seen. Sometimes Mesi wasn't home, and I would spend the afternoon drinking coffee with her mother. Abrehet, the slight, golden-skinned mother of Meselat and eight others, would sit on a tiny stool in front of a tiny stove, fanning the tiny fire that boiled the rich coffee in rounds. She would chat in Tigrinya to me, telling me about each of her children in turn.

On the wall in the comfortable living room, with its overstuffed couches and cool stone floor, was the portrait of a dark-skinned young man,

Mesi's brother number four. Gone, somewhere. Norway? Mexico? Holland? It seemed I had heard different things about him. Mesi said I would meet him one day.

We got together a couple of times after we both had returned home to the United States. But Mesi's life was different there. Her husband didn't like her going out or having friends. Then one day I received a call from her, and she was somewhere else entirely. She had moved herself and her children to another state, but wanted to make sure I was still there.

"Do you remember my brother?" she asked. "The one whose picture was in our living room?"

"Yes," I answered, trying to keep her siblings straight. "Yonas, right?"

"Yonas, yes. He is here. He will be coming to stay with me next week. He is applying for asylum. Can you help him?"

"I can try, Mesi. Send me his lawyer's contact information."

Since returning from Eritrea I had been contacted by numerous attorneys, asking for my expertise as they worked with clients seeking asylum. Sometimes I was contacted by Eritreans themselves, on behalf of their family members, as Mesi had done. I was being drawn into another facet of Eritrean life, a realm apart: the world of untold abuses and subterranean violence, as revealed only by those who had lived—and left—to tell about it.

I received Yonas's statement several months later, that confessional biography meant to render the whole story in all its gruesome detail, mitigated only by cold legal formats. I read it twice. Then I vomited.

Yonas had been an aspiring reporter. He worked with a small group of friends to produce independent stories and float them on "guerrilla radio," captured airwaves uncontrolled by the government. It was a grand idea, and one they copied from the men in power, before they had become the men in power.

Shortly before I had arrived in Asmara in 2001 Yonas had been arrested for his counterrevolutionary activities. He was beaten, tortured, bound, gagged, nearly drowned, starved, and held in an aluminum shipping container until he almost suffocated. He had refused being drafted into the military because he was opposed to the border war with Ethiopia, which broke out in 1998, and for what happened to his sister, Mesi. She had also been abused in the military, assaulted repeatedly by a superior officer to whom she was "assigned." A handmaiden in *shida*, the trademark plastic sandals of the indomitable Eritrean soldier.

This was the dark shadow that hung over her life and her associations with home, why she could never belong in Eritrea again. I had seen it in her sideways glance as I waxed romantic about life in Asmara, the glassiness in her eyes when she told me about her years in military service. I thought maybe it was her unhappy marriage to a man she barely knew, or maybe a seething, inarticulate critique of politics that she could not express, or the way people whispered about her because she hung around with men in bars.

When I saw Mesi at Yonas's hearing, we embraced each other and held on for a long time. Yonas was given asylum on the basis of his credible claims and supporting evidence. Although I had flown two thousand miles for the occasion, I didn't need to testify; the documents I had prepared for the court were sufficient. Later Yonas sent me a book of inspirational poems as a gift. And Mesi sent me a handmade dress from Asmara, spun from the rich cottons we had admired together so many months before. We never spoke directly about her experiences, or Yonas's, again.

Sometime later Mesi told me about her youngest brother, Alemu. The family was hiding him in a well beneath a relative's house so the military could not claim him as a replacement soldier for Yonas, the absconding traitor and exile.

Sovereignty and Its Consequences

In May 1998, just five years after Eritrea secured independence, war again engulfed the Horn of Africa. During the intervening period of peace and relative stability, Eritrea appeared both to itself and to many onlookers around the world—in the words of one high school student I met in the summer of 1995—"the shining new hope for Africa." The energy emanating from the continent's newest nation-state was palpable, infectious. Amid the euphoria of independence, Eritreans threw themselves into reconstruction. With the same resolve, sacrifice, and ingenuity that characterized much of the nationalist revolution, people of all ages and backgrounds participated in building roads, schools, clinics, and homes and reforesting denuded lands and terracing mountainsides as they collectively salved a landscape and consciousness wounded from more than three decades of upheaval. Former members of the ELF as well as longtime EPLF affiliates in exile flocked to be among the first to return, some falling to their knees upon arrival, weeping into the earth. The newly minted state authorities worked as virtual volunteers, explicitly shunning the cults of personality and elitism that characterized so many other postcolonial African leaderships. For Eritreans all over the world, the new nation-state embodied the pent-up aspirations of generations of sufferers.

The explosion of the border war with Ethiopia in mid-1998 therefore descended like another nightmare upon a people just barely recovering from the last. Almost without warning (or so it seemed) a localized spat mushroomed into a full-scale war. Hundreds of thousands of troops were mobilized, and tens of thousands of new land mines laid. As Ethiopia rounded up its citizens of Eritrean heritage and deported them en masse to the Eritrean border in wave after wave of despair, Ethiopians living in Eritrea fled their homes and businesses in fear for their lives.[1] And as the gains of seven years' peace in Eritrea withered for lack of nourishment, a fearsome incarnation of nationalism gathered strength at home and abroad. Responding to the calls of President Isayas Afwerki and the PFDJ, Eritreans all over the world consolidated their efforts to protect what they believed was the very existence of their nation-state.

In the scant two years following the beginning of the border hostilities, more than one hundred thousand Eritreans and Ethiopians lost their lives, and several million more their homes and livelihoods. Drought and famine stalked communities, weeding out the weak and vulnerable, breaking spirits among the strong. Erstwhile economic peaks tumbled to valleys. Families who had already lost several members in the liberation war waited to hear the fate of yet others who had gone to the border. The energy that initially sustained resurgent nationalism began turning in on itself, evoking questions for which no satisfactory answers could be found, and casting doubt upon leaders who revealed themselves to be merely men after all. The lofty ideals to which the PFDJ had held itself seemed all but unfulfilled.

There were many consequences of the Ethio-Eritrean border war and few convincing reasons for why it had happened (see Negash and Tronvoll 2000; Hepner 2000; Tronvoll 1999). As the smoke cleared and the devastation was exposed, many Eritreans found themselves in disbelief that such a thing had occurred. Exiles living in places like the United States drew upon their broadened experience to wonder aloud—many for the first time—about the meaning of government accountability, democracy, constitutionalism, and the rule of law in Eritrea. International bodies such as the United Nations, moreover, and other agencies concerned with aid, development, conflict resolution, and human rights, critiqued Eritrea in ways befitting a member of the world system of nation-states. Besieged from all sides, the Eritrean government retreated into its alter ego as a revolutionary front by reasserting nationalist principles such as self-reliance and democratic centralism. Manipulating the notion of "African solutions for African problems," the African Union's policies of noninterference, and the United States' own landmark policies in the aftermath of September 11, 2001, the Eritrean government imputed nonaccountability for the war through the tautology of national security and defense. After so many years of working to establish international legitimacy for its claims to sovereignty, and then sacrificing so much to protect it, the Eritrean government nonetheless seemed prepared to reject many of the same principles underpinning the logic of statehood. And despite its celebrated constitution, the party-state also appeared to be saying—to its own people and the rest of the world—that it would play neither by those rules nor by anyone else's. The great promise at independence lay in tatters on the battlefield, near a dusty border town called Badme.

The border war had a monumental impact in Eritrea and exile. Although most everyone had responded to the call of defending the nation-state as patriotic citizens, many nonetheless questioned how a genuine, civilly governed state could choose war over extended diplomacy. Among members of the government and former EPLF supporters who felt uneasy with the PFDJ's policies since independence, a nascent reform movement began articulating an alternative political agenda as it sought to reclaim the vision of independence (see Plaut 2002). For those who had long nurtured a critical perspective, especially former ELF affiliates, the vestiges of an organized opposition movement in exile also sprang into action. New chapters of the Eritrean Liberation Front–Revolutionary Council (ELF-RC), headquartered in Germany, began opening up all over the world. Utilizing the Internet and informal social networks, coalitions of proliferating political groups joined together and held conventions from Addis Ababa to Stockholm. Other "civic societies" proliferated at a rate too swift to follow, announcing their formation, mission statements, and upcoming events on various Web sites. Among them were those advocating human and civil rights agendas and democratization through civil society institutions and practices as they searched for authentic examples of these in Eritrean history and culture. Drawing upon the transnational social field that had sustained the Eritrean revolution and emergent nation-state since the 1970s, a new kind of Eritrean public sphere began taking shape (see Bernal 2004, 2005b, 2006; Conrad 2006). Within it, Eritreans began debating for the first time since the BMA years the meaning of the nation and nationalist identity, the arrangement of power and authority in Eritrea, and practices of citizenship that accompanied national belonging.

The emergence of this public sphere, built both deliberately and improvisationally upon the transnational foundation forged between Eritrea and exile, revealed the transculturation of Eritrean specificities and global generalities as they grafted onto one another. Just as the Eritrean state under the PFDJ deployed the ideologies, pragmatic practices, and administrative authority associated with the revolutionary nationalist years to compel its citizens to think and act in certain ways, many of those citizens drew upon their experiences as exiles, and the resources available to them abroad, to make demands upon that state and one another. Similarly, within Eritrea, many people—including journalists, students, intellectuals, activists, and elders—looked toward international constructs of democracy, rights, and civic participation to evaluate the Eritrean condition. And while they have been violently prevented from organizing on those bases within Eritrea itself, those who have fled the country and their clandestine associates who remain behind have utilized the transnational social field to advance visions and platforms that are at odds with the authoritarian nationalist state and increasingly connected to discourses and institutions of non-Eritrean origin. The transnational social field has expanded to include not just networks between and among Eritreans but also those that connect Eritreans to the wider world (see Glick-Schiller 2005).

In the following pages, I step back from the structural and historical details of Eritrea's transnational situation to examine how and why recent movements and claims to democracy and civil society express important dynamics about Eritrea's place in a larger global order. More specifically, I address how Eritreans are responding to perceived failures of the authoritarian nationalist state to deliver on its promises by engaging broader models of citizenship, rights, and belonging. While the party-state has obstructed certain transnational interventions into local society to preserve its own power and nationalist hegemony, it has also encouraged Eritreans abroad to utilize the ideas and resources of their adopted countries for the benefit of Eritrea.

As discussed earlier, transnationalism (and transnational dissonance) have forced Eritreans in exile into a liminal space where they are fully integrated in neither Eritrea nor their societies of settlement. But as classic anthropological analyses by Turner (1969), Douglas (1966), and Leach (1976) showed, liminality can be an especially powerful (and dangerous) location, precisely because it situates people between established social structures or discourses. Thus as Eritreans in exile remain beholden to the nationalist state and its discourses and policies, they also belong—at least partly—to those of their societies of settlement and to the larger global order in which they are positioned. They are what Das and Poole (2004) refer to as a political community "at the margins of the state," simultaneously apart from, and central to, its operations. Exile is therefore a key vantage point from which to study its peculiar patterns of governance and power.

Taking into account both the liminality and marginality of the Eritrean exile condition and the emergence of a new public sphere since the border war, I argue in this final chapter that Eritrea has witnessed the emergence of a transnational civil society that operates across multiple borders and permits mutual, if uneven, interventions between nation and state. This public sphere is comprised of the transnational components I analyzed in earlier chapters and, as I have discussed, con-

stitutes a location wherein the state's structure, authority, official definitions of nationalism, and requirements for belonging are both
reproduced and resisted among exiles, local citizens, and state actors.
The emergence of such a transnational civil society is particularly significant for a marginalized state like Eritrea, which is not only structurally disempowered in the global scheme of nation-states but also too
weak, authoritarian, and militarized to sustain (or allow) a vibrant civil
society in its own right. On a more general theoretical level, moreover,
a concept of transnational civil society helps us better understand how
deterritorialized populations may adopt behaviors and deploy concepts
associated with global civil society's repertoire (democracy, rule of law,
constitutionalism, human and civil rights, religious ecumenism, and the
language of civil society itself) but do so almost exclusively in relation to
the localized territorial realities of their sending states.

Resistance Revisited: The Groups of Thirteen and Fifteen

The year 2001 was an exceptionally significant one in Eritrean history.
Not only was the tenth anniversary of Eritrea's independence celebrated
on May 24, but the months of July to December also witnessed the effer-
vescence of open debate, coupled with swift and unsettling state repression. Following the border war's deescalation in mid-2000, many private
debates were taking place within the PFDJ and among its members and
supporters around the world. Most of these had to do with the government's own conduct during the war, and President Isayas Afwerki's role
in particular.[2] Almost immediately, anyone who expressed reservation or
open disagreement with the way in which the PFDJ had handled the war
was labeled "defeatist" (see Plaut 2002:121; see also Connell 2005a,
2005b). The first to do so were a group of thirteen scholars, nationalist
activists, and professionals—all longtime supporters of the EPLF—who
met in Berlin to draft a letter to Isayas Afwerki regarding their concerns
about what appeared to be an increasingly authoritarian, even dictatorial, tendency in the government. The G-13, as the signatories came to
be called, included among them one of the premier drafters of the constitution, Dr. Bereket Habte Selassie, as well as other prominent Eritreans living abroad. They composed the letter with the intent that it
would reach only the president himself and no one else. Through some
unknown mechanism, however, the letter was "leaked" and before long
was accessible via every Eritrean Web site and the burgeoning independent media in Eritrea.

The "Berlin Manifesto," as it came to be called, created an uproar.
Immediately its signatories were vilified among loyalists for their treach-
ery, deified by budding reformists for their courage, and scoffed at by

staunch oppositionists for being a day late and a dollar short. And despite traveling to Asmara to try to meet with the president himself, the members of the G-13 received little more for their efforts than attacks on their integrity and increasing fear of repercussion on their family members and close associates in Eritrea. In the propaganda wars that followed, they were denigrated for being "diaspora intellectuals" who knew precious little of conditions on the ground and were unduly influenced by "foreign ideas" untranslatable to the Eritrean experience. Moreover, they were portrayed as an isolated group of troublemakers either driven by opportunism or secretly in league with the Ethiopian government. The possibility that they could be part of a larger and longer developing movement or shared consciousness, or that they acted out of patriotic responsibility, was unutterable.

The text of the Berlin Manifesto revealed the dilemma facing so many exiles who have sought to balance their support for the independent state with grounded critiques of the PFDJ party. The letter also revealed the anxiety exiles felt about Eritrea's role and image internationally, where an insistence on either dated revolutionary discourse or exclusivist nationalism may represent a liability for the new, small, and poor African state rather than a source of empowerment and autonomy vis-à-vis the world system. First couching their critique in praise for the historic integrity of the EPLF and the sacrifices made to protect Eritrea's sovereignty in the border war, the G-13 wrote:

Mr. President, To ask why we have come to this impasse, to inquire into what went wrong, and to reflect upon the cause and conduct of the [border] war, and whether it might have been avoided, is not only legitimate, but it is also the duty of every citizen. . . . [W]e wish to assure you, on the basis of close observation, that Eritrea's image has never been as bad as it is today. . . . Much of the world community, including our fellow Africans, perceive the Eritrean government and its leadership as aggressive and irresponsible. Eritrea's leadership has been cast, particularly since the start of the war with Ethiopia, as contemptuous of international law and accepted norms of behavior. . . . Even the commendable policy of self-reliance, which many applauded, has now been portrayed as an aspect of arrogance. . . . Hence, there needs to be a critical reappraisal of policy and praxis.

Concerning the way in which the PFDJ government had handled the important issues of reconciliation with former ELF affiliates, the implementation of the constitution, and the development of institutions for popular political participation since independence, the G-13 also voiced consternation:

We are convinced that we reflect a widely held view among Eritreans that there should be national reconciliation. . . . Wisdom and statesmanship required a call for reconciliation extended to all Eritreans irrespective of belief or political affiliation to join hands in rebuilding a shattered society and economy. It is an opportunity that was lost but that can still be reclaimed. The EPLF (PFDJ) leadership should be willing now to provide political space for groups or individuals. The absence of such space has severely affected the development of civil society and has fostered a feeling of alienation among segments of our society. The Constitution, about which we shall say more below, requires such space in no uncertain terms. . . . A ratified Constitution means that it is already in effect and that the Eritrean people should be enjoying their constitutional rights. We are dismayed to witness the operation of institutions that are clearly and flagrantly in violation of the spirit and letter of the Constitution.

And concluding that "it is no exaggeration to say that, despite some notable progress to its name, the government has failed the nation in some important respect," the authors of the Berlin Manifesto signed off by reaffirming their own duties as citizens and requesting the government to fulfill its own:

On our side, we will spare no effort to help secure Eritrea's territorial integrity and national sovereignty. At the same time, we will endeavor to promote a culture of openness, tolerance, accountability and rule of law. To these ends, we intend to broaden our base by convening a larger meeting which will consider your response to this letter. The idea is to begin to institutionalize a government/civil society dialogue on a continuing basis as a critical part of a healthy development of our future.

Despite the careful crafting of the letter and the spirit of solidarity and concerned citizenship in which it was written, like many other forms of transnational intervention that challenged the authority of the party-state, the Berlin Manifesto was subjected to the same delegitimation and obstruction as other unwelcome social remittances. The leak of the letter to various media, some of it Ethiopian, was perhaps part of this: immediately setting many Eritreans on the defensive, it stymied the G-13's efforts to open such a public debate. As one of the G-13 members explained to me in an interview (much of it off the record), the letter was intended to broach difficult and sensitive issues within a private circle, where it would then expand outward to the public to become a genuine national conversation. By virtue of pressures exerted by transnational civil society, the government would be forced to address certain issues pertaining to its own internal power structure and ostensible plans for political and social democratization. On the record, this interviewee described both the reaction to the G-13 as well as the impetus that brought them together:

There was a violent reaction [to the letter]. People blamed the G-13. . . . I was a bit surprised by the community's reaction here [in the Midwest], actually. I didn't know there was so much anti-intellectual attitude. . . . Some people were triggered by the leak of the letter, some people felt like the country was in danger and we didn't have the luxury to criticize the government, the timing wasn't right, all these things. So there was an anti-intellectual sentiment in the community, especially among ELF people who thought Dr. Bereket and all those guys were supporters of EPLF, and *now* they speak of democracy and reform. For me, it was a welcome change, late is better than never. I never agreed with a lot of things [the EPLF/PFDJ] stands for. . . . Basically the goal was to create a forum for people to discuss the issues. Because we don't have that experience, democratic platforms and so on . . . But all of our plans, to travel from city to city, holding public forums, all of it was upstaged by the leak of the letter.

Indeed, the kind of scenario the G-13 envisioned—a civil debate occurring simultaneously in locations all over the world as Eritreans exercised their constitutional rights and practiced citizenship—drew directly upon the existing transnational social field for its efficacy. However, the content of the conversation, and the objectives for mobilizing such a movement, were quite different from anything seen during the days of the revolution. No longer would the issues be about Maoism, Soviet revisionism, or democratic centralism, but rather democracy, constitutionalism, civil society, and the way in which modern states and citizens should relate.[3] Significantly, the G-13 also called for reconciliation between former EPLF and ELF opposing identities, indicating the extent to which they understood the problem of political identity in exile. The Berlin Manifesto cannot be underestimated for the important shifts it revealed among certain sectors of the Eritrean transnation, in this case longtime supporters of EPLF, who essentially stated that nationalism in situ had failed to engender the kind of society envisioned and that the party-state must now consider Eritrea's place in a global order where democracy and civil society are the dominant forms of political and social power, whatever they might mean in practice.

The G-13 was indeed part of a much larger movement mounting from within the historic EPLF camp (see Connell 2005b). In May 2001, exactly three years after the outbreak of the border war, an open letter composed by fifteen members of the PFDJ's Central Committee was released to the Eritrean transnational public. The document, titled "An Open Letter to Members of the PFDJ," was written collectively by fifteen officials, who later came to be known as the G-15, and was directed toward the president and his most loyal supporters.[4] Nearly all of its esteemed signatories were founding or longtime members of EPLF who had dedicated their lives to the Eritrean struggle. Among them were Haile Menkerios, a founder of EFLNA and Eritrea's former ambassador to the United Nations; Mesfin Hagos, former minister of defense (and current head of the EPLF-DP reform party); and Mahmoud Sherifo, minister of local government (since reported dead after a long period of incommunicado detention). As with the Berlin Manifesto, the letter circulated widely via the Internet, the private Eritrean press, and other underground networks at home and abroad. Many people loyal to the president and PFDJ were scandalized. But perhaps even more looked on with renewed hope and heightening fear about the changes underway.[5]

The letter composed by the G-15 echoed some of the same issues raised by the G-13 in the Berlin Manifesto; however, because state officials themselves wrote it, it was much more difficult for the government to dismiss as the grumblings of dissatisfied exiles. While the letter focused on many important details regarding what the signatories viewed as an ultimately failed transition from the EPLF as liberation front to the PFDJ as a government, it focused on three major issues overall: the lack of proper legal procedures and "accountability and transparency" in the government; the concentration of power in the hands of President Isayas Afwerki; and the urgent need to begin implementing institutional structures that would support a "free and democratic" nation, especially in the aftermath of the border war. Reiterating the initial plans the EPLF had developed for the new state following the 1993 referendum on independence, the authors reminded their colleagues that

the Eritrean Government of transition would have legislative, executive and judicial branches, which provide checks and balances on each other. It would establish the rule of law, consolidate national harmony, uphold political pluralism and ensure transparency, tolerance and accountability. It would be free from corruption, and would develop a common national outlook. It would further develop, as guarantees for a democratic political order, a free and powerful judicial branch, a conscious civil society, a free, reliable, critical and responsible mass media, and other democratic institutions.

Outlining their own position as reformists and contrasting their respect for policies and procedures befitting a modern nation-state with the rigid, revolutionary-era corporatist nationalism being practiced by the president, the G-15 members argued that they were standing up for human and democratic rights, constitutionalism, and reconciliation within the government and society. They charged that the president and his loyal associates were rejecting such changes and justifying them in terms of lack of infrastructure and chronic underdevelopment and the threat of sectarianism and internal disunity, which might be exploited by "enemies" and neoliberal imperialism, and resorting to threats of violence and other "illegal and undemocratic action" to muzzle criticism.

That members of both the G-13 and G-15 shared not only certain opinions with one another but also personal relationships and professional commitments as citizens of Eritrea is evident. The G-13 member

I interviewed explained to me how he and his colleagues in exile were at least partly inspired by conversations held with those same officials who later authored the open letter: "I talked to the people who [later] dissented from within the Central Committee of PFDJ. They were really disgusted at what was going on. We thought we could direct this debate to a more productive course. That was the purpose of the meeting in Berlin. It was not—criticizing the government was secondary."

The G-13 therefore acted not only out of their own genuine concern for what was taking place in Eritrea but also because their intention was to help their like-minded colleagues within the government raise issues for which no effective outlet in Eritrea existed. In the relationship between the G-13 and G-15 incidents, we can detect the same pattern that has characterized much of the Eritrean transnational movement: the way in which the state sought to block a significant transnational intervention by discrediting the Berlin Manifesto and its authors and how exile and local actors nonetheless connected with one another as citizens—albeit imperfectly—to resist state abuses of power. Drawing upon the empowering and more protected location of exile, the G-13 expressed sentiments that their Eritrea-based colleagues could not, despite their own ostensibly powerful positions as longtime leaders in the EPLF and high-ranking officials. That the G-15 formed and com- posed their open letter within a year of the Berlin Manifesto's release suggests that these dissenting officials used the momentum created by the G-13's intervention to initiate an even more powerful one of their own. Moreover, although the G-15 acted in their capacity as government officials, they more importantly believed that they were fulfilling their duty as patriotic citizens. In both the G-13 and G-15 letters, the language of nationalism and the vitality of the liberation struggle as a historical referent remained, albeit blended with the contemporary international- ist discourse of democracy, constitutionalism, rights, the rule of law, and civil society.

Dissent and Punishment: Students, Journalists, and an Anthropologist

In the weeks and months that followed the release of the "Open Letter to Members of the PFDJ," an unsettling blend of social unrest and forced calm enveloped Asmara. As Plaut (2002:122) details, the month of June brought inquiries to the minister of justice regarding the where- abouts of fifteen missing Eritrean journalists. In July, a group of fifty elders sought to mediate the conflicts within the PFDJ only to be rebuffed and several among them arrested. Around the same time, a half-dozen PFDJ officials resigned from their posts, including the ambassadors to Scandinavia, Nigeria, and the European Union, as well as the consul-general in the Netherlands and a senior official in the ministry of foreign affairs in Asmara.

Meanwhile, an independent student movement within the University of Asmara, consciously unaffiliated with NUEYS, began voicing dissent. Semere Kesete, the leader of the movement and a veteran EPLF fighter, was arrested for articulating grievances with the university administration and the government's mandatory summer work programs. Within days, a spontaneous but peaceful demonstration at the courthouse in downtown Asmara resulted in the detention of hundreds of students who had gathered to show their concern. In mid-August, a considerable portion of the student body was instructed to report to the stadium, where they boarded busses bound for work camps at Wi'a and Gel'alo, two of the hottest locations in eastern Eritrea. Human rights groups and international observers criticized the government after two students died, ostensibly from heat exhaustion and lack of medical attention. Back in the capital city, parents and grandparents showed humbling courage by agitating on behalf of the students. Attending to some business at the university one morning, I watched as dozens of elders gathered outside the gates and surrounded the university president as he arrived, pleading with him to bring back the young people. They were forced back by guards and later rounded up and held for hours.

Just one week after the events of September 11 in the United States had captured the world's attention, eleven members of the G-15 were arrested and detained without charge or access to legal representation. Of the remaining four, three were abroad at the time (and remain in exile), and one rescinded his membership. Other individuals suspected of sharing sympathies or direct connections with the G-15 were also arrested, most of them in raids on their homes. At the same time, the government announced the closing of the independent media, including at least eight private newspapers and the Catholic Church's press, the oldest in Eritrea. Scores of journalists were arrested, and several others fled the country altogether, where they have since launched advocacy campaigns on behalf of their imprisoned colleagues.[6]

While the government justified the closing of the presses with the presses' failure to comply with press laws, many understood it as the PFDJ's attempt to silence both dissent and public debate. The private newspapers had become popular as some of the only outlets in Eritrean society for citizens to voice their opinions in a public forum. Moreover, they had been the chief vehicle for disseminating the G-15's open letter, had reprinted numerous postings drawn from Eritrean Web sites, and had published interviews with exile intellectuals who spoke critically of the government's handling of the war. In the aftermath of the border war, however, the PFDJ argued that any form of dissent amounted to a national security threat and extrajudicially charged the G-15 and its supporters, known and unknown, with treason. Reliable information became nearly impossible to find as government television, radio, and newspapers consolidated their monopoly on the production and distribution of knowledge. Internet cafés overflowed as urban young people in particular, who despite their fear of spies watching over their shoulders, signed onto Web sites managed by their compatriots in exile and other independent news sources, searching for analyses of "the current situation."

As a foreigner and an anthropologist, it became increasingly difficult for me to conduct interviews and establish trust with citizens and authorities alike. The sense of fear and uncertainty was palpable and all-encompassing. As Girmay-*Shikor* pursued repeated (and progressively more hostile) meetings with me, questioned Hailu and other close associates of mine, and demanded detailed information about my interview questions and the names of interviewees, I too began feeling the repression sweeping Eritrea in the wake of the war.[7] Despite having the necessary clearances to conduct research, I worried constantly about the safety of people who knew me and felt confused about whether or not I myself could be in danger. The paranoia of Eritrean society was contagious and clearly not unfounded.

Yet, amid all this fear and confusion, friends and acquaintances continued to voice their opinions with astonishing openness. From taxicab drivers who offered unsolicited disquisitions on democracy and the government's abuses of power, to friends who confessed their heartfelt anguish and disillusionment over the turn of events, to local religious leaders who expressed moral outrage about war and human rights abuses, Eritrean people were demonstrating Monga's (1996) assertion that resistance to injustice, patterns of democratic behavior, and forms of civil society in African countries may look markedly different from those of the North/West (see also Comaroff and Comaroff 1999). Whether in everyday behaviors and small, spontaneous acts of resistance (Monga 1996; Scott 1985), or in the larger movements emerging in the transnational social field, I was witnessing Eritreans' attempts to both support their nation-state and "manage and steer [the] communal anger" (Monga 1996:149) provoked by the unhappy circumstances of the present and unresolved grievances from the past.

In these moments, I also felt as though I was observing the same shift taking place as that revealed in the Berlin Manifesto and the open letter, in which Eritreans were acknowledging the ways that official nationalism and the legacy of the revolution had ceased to supply the necessary meanings and practices to sustain the next stage of Eritrea's development as a nation-state. Rather than creating the free and just society it had promised, the postrevolutionary government had instead produced one deformed by rigid controls on power and the perpetual crisis of war. As Eritreans both at home and abroad expressed their dissatisfaction and anger, they repeatedly deployed a flexible—if often normative and idealistic—notion of democracy as the only mechanism for a creating a more inclusive state and national identity. They also used the language of civil society as a model for exercising the rights and social power ostensibly guaranteed to Eritreans all over the world by independence and the constitution. While ideas and discourses emanating from the North/West and communicated transnationally by exiles have shaped much of these debates, other meanings assigned to these terms are also rooted in Eritrea's history and revolutionary experience. In many ways, these debates point to how democracy and civil society may be key symbols and ideological elements as much as, or more than, organizational realities (Verdery 1996 cited in Paley 2002:475).

The Search for Democracy and Civil Society at Home and Abroad

Locating Democracy in Eritrea

While the debate over democracy, civil society, and the state in Africa is not new (e.g., Bayart 1993; Gledhill 2000; Harbeson, Rothchild, and Chazan 1994; Kasfir 1998; Nyang'oro 1999; Nzongola-Ntalaja, Lee, and African Association of Political Science 1998), many scholars are today suggesting that we pay less attention to the definitions of these institutions according to normative, Western formulations and much more to the way in which Africans themselves have understood and practiced them in the past and present (Comaroff and Comaroff 1999; Kasfir 1998; Monga 1996; Schaffer 1998; see also Paley 2002). In Eritrea, the question of democracy has been on the agenda for a long time and is understood to have deep roots in traditional institutions such as the people's assembly, or *baito*, where conflicts were resolved in a public manner and justice dispensed accordingly. This traditional form was adopted and revised by the EPLF during the revolutionary years and was later incorporated into the postindependence state structure, especially at the village level (see Killion 1998:294–95; Pool 2001).

The notion of democracy associated with the post-Enlightenment liberal traditions of Western nation-states also took center stage in Eritrea during the political developments of the 1940s. The years of the BMA (1941–52) in particular introduced to Eritrea many features of multiparty politics and the foundations for (liberal) civil society institutions.

Early nationalist leaders during that era such as Woldeab Woldemariam and Ibrahim Sultan devoted much attention to the idea of democracy. In one 1942 article titled "Democracy and Dictatorship," Woldeab argued that democracy depends on transparency and accountability in government, lest it devolve into dictatorship (Fessehatzion 1999:8). In another article, written in 1948, he thwarted assertions that democracy was only appropriate for "advanced" countries by delving into precolonial Eritrean traditions to locate the roots of practices such as elected leadership and popular political participation (Fessehatzion 1999:8). A decade later, one of the most important claims being made by early nationalists to justify Eritrea's right to self-determination was that the region, unlike the rest of Ethiopia, had already been transformed by these encounters with modern democratic practices.

Throughout the years of the nationalist revolution, the issue of democracy and mass participation also formed an important component in the ideological development of both the ELF and the EPLF. As Chapter 2 discussed, a major justification for the EPLF's own formation was the lack of democratic decision making within the early ELF. In its 1977 *National Democratic Programme*, the front asserted in no uncertain terms its commitment to elected leadership, constitutionalism, equal rights, and freedoms of speech, press, assembly, worship, and peaceful demonstration. It also supported the organizing of youth, peasants, workers, women, and students into civil associations.[8] At its second congress in 1987, the EPLF made yet a stronger case for its commitment to multiparty politics in the postindependence state.

Throughout the years of the revolution, however, the EPLF configured its practice of democratic principles according to those of democratic centralism, a blend of Western-style democracy, Marxist-Leninist collective decision making, and Maoist discipline and absolute respect for authority.[9] Moreover, the configuration of the EPLF's nationalism, with its emphasis on the synthesis and homogenization of identities into a common national one, complemented its structural emphasis on democratic centralism. Accordingly, unified national subjects would participate in the EPLF's efforts to forge "true" democracy, in which state and society merge into an organic whole characterized by solidary interests and a lack of distinction between the political sphere of the state and general public interests (see Bottomore et al. 1983:114). These same commitments have remained operative in postindependence Eritrea under the PFDJ, which, as I have discussed in detail, sought to manage its transnational society and reproduce national identity according to the same mechanisms employed during the revolution itself.

Even during the years of the revolution, however, the EPLF's emphasis on democratic centralism was contested, especially in the transnational arena. As Chapter 3 discussed, EFLNA members broke their association with the EPLF leadership in 1978 because of the antidemocratic and absolutist character they perceived in the front. For these activists, and for others who did not embrace the EPLF's nationalist authority, the centralism in the front's approach was stifling. The range of identities and interests present among EFLNA activists in the United States, and the dissonance experienced by many who returned to the field, illustrates this highly contentious and long-debated relationship between democracy, national identity, and authority. It also highlights how these have been bound up with transnationally constructed identities and institutions since the early 1970s.

Democracy, Political Identity, and Reconciliation

Questions related to the meaning and praxis of democracy in Eritrea have also been extremely important to those whose identities were shaped within the ELF. As explored in earlier chapters, the ELF's nationalist formulation allowed for more pluralist constructions of the nation and national identity, wherein competing political currents and religious, ethno-regional, kin, and other affective loyalties were not subject to the same homogenizing pressures as in the EPLF. While this pluralism led to sectarianism and structural weakness in the front, it also permitted certain claims to a democratic character different from the EPLF's. Although the EPLF's formulation appeared more progressive in its forging of solidarity across broad sectors of Eritrean society, in hindsight members of both fronts recognize that this came at the price of a particular kind of repression—that of nationalist homogenization. In earlier chapters, we heard the voices of both ELF and EPLF supporters who noted that the pluralism and democratization of identity were more prevalent in the ELF during the 1970s.

Today these claims to democracy are even more urgent among members of the new reform movement, initiated by the G-13 and G-15 incidents and the older opposition genealogically related to, and often still aligned with, the ELF. These movements have charged the PFDJ with losing sight of its vision of a democratic, independent nation-state (or having never genuinely held one). For former ELF members and affiliates, moreover, the realities of exile have only exaggerated the importance of concepts like democracy and civil society in the transnational imagination. Not only have Eritreans in places such as the United States been exposed to Western democratic ideologies and practices by virtue of residence, but they were also encouraged by the EPLF during the liberation war to model some of their associational activities on American civic traditions, especially that of ethno-national or diasporic lobbies.

At the same time, however, the struggle of some exiles against the totalizing power of the EPLF heightened the desire to achieve autonomy from the front. Thus the combination of oppositional political orientation, life in exile, and the transnational pressures of the EPLF all helped draw the attention of former ELF affiliates to the usefulness of "democracy" as a tool for resistance and the reimagination of national identity and political praxis in Eritrea. In their own claims to power and belonging, former ELF members envisioned elements of Western democracy transculturated to Eritrea as the only way to truly achieve the kind of "unity" Eritreans collectively desire. At the same time, the consistent application of these practices across both Eritrea and its exile communities was required if they were to become authentically Eritrean. That is, democratization of political and social institutions must take place transnationally if at all. As Asgedom explained:

I think the only way it will work in [the midwestern community] now is if any organization can emerge without restrictions. That is the best way. It's the same thing we are advocating for politics inside Eritrea. It's the same. That's what we are looking for. But in the final analysis, the country has to survive as one nation. It has to be strong. It's the same logic—if you are advocating for multiparties in Eritrea, it doesn't mean the country will be run by many parties. It will eventually be run by some sort of entity that represents the nation. But those are social institutions, not the state itself.

Earlier we saw how the intensive and enduring transnational presence of the Eritrean state in exile, and the manner in which the EPLF/PFDJ sought to control the activities and identities of exiles (and especially those formerly belonging to the ELF), created further fragmentation in exile communities. These same impulses have led to organized resistance among exiles who now reject the state's transnational authority and, like their reformist counterparts, see reclaiming Eritrea from a corrupt regime as their new patriotic duty. Utilizing democratic ideals such as freedom of speech, association, and assembly, exiles have staged demonstrations across the United States to draw attention to the antidemocratic nature of the PFDJ in Eritrea and to call for reconciliation between former EPLF and ELF political identities. These acts of resistance are not only justified in terms of defiance against a regime that refuses such freedoms for its people at home, however. They also represent a creative reversal of the transnational pressure applied by the EPLF/PFDJ to have their populations abroad lobby the U.S. government and stage demonstrations on behalf of the state's interests. One author on a popular opposition Web site wrote scathingly about the PFDJ's transnational power and the concomitant need for exile agitation as a catalyst for change in Eritrea and, ultimately, reconciliation between EPLF and ELF:

Eritreans do not need PFDJ's permission to meet. Repeat: Eritreans do not need PFDJ's permission to meet. The PFDJ, which claims a guardian's role for itself in the lives of Eritreans who, according to it, do not have the maturity of children, detests the idea of Eritreans meeting without its knowledge or permission. That's why it calls meetings "conspiracies," "secret cells." That's why it works so hard to disrupt them. . . . That's why Eritreans should form associations (no matter how modest the agenda or few the membership). This is how the Civil Society is formed. Eventually, there will be natural coalitions and critical mass will be reached to challenge the coercive powers of PFDJ. Eventually, something that is far-fetched now will be a reality in the course of time: a "Parliament in Exile," as suggested by one of Eritrea's former National Assembly members, Herui T. Bairou. Networking includes a recognition of resolution that will establish a healthy respect for reconciliation.[10]

According to this formulation, which resembles Asgedom's ideas about democratizing the midwestern community, agitation in exile contributes to democratic change and the growth of civil society institutions in Eritrea by putting these into practice within communities that remain transnationally bound to Eritrea. The connection between the reconciliation of former ELF and EPLF political identities and democratization in Eritrea is also central to these goals, as former ELF affiliates and other opposition activists acknowledge that creating spaces for their political participation in Eritrea depends on broader recognition of their contributions to the liberation struggle and their non-EPLF identities as authentically Eritrean. The late Seyoum Ogbamichael, former leader of the ELF-RC based in Germany, commented:

The way out is for the system to move out and open the stage for all the people. All political forces in Eritrea should establish a unity transitional government. This transitional unity government will take our country to democratization. We believe that the transition to democratization is based on national reconciliation. This is the way out. If there should be a workable process of democratization, it should be based on a broad base of reconciliation; if not, it could not be workable and cannot escape the risk of civil war.[11]

For those who continue to nurture their distinctive experiences, nationalist orientation, and political identities in relation to the ELF, democracy at least partly means that they will be provided (or will claim by force) a genuine role in Eritrea's political and social arena. But it also means an honest revisiting of, and new consensus about, the constitution of national subjectivity. The exclusion felt by many former ELF affiliates from structures of power, the lack of genuine recognition for their contributions to the revolution, and the increasingly intolerance of the EPLF/PFDJ's synthetic and homogenizing definitions of national identity have led many to suggest that the ELF's more pluralist construction may offer an alternative (or at least a platform for revision). Speaking in a meeting of the ELF-RC in the midwestern region, Seyoum Ogbamichael advocated the recognition of different identities within the political landscape, acceptance of opposing viewpoints, tolerance and mutual respect, and building from the common ground shared by all Eritreans as a major objective of the opposition movement.[12] Thus reconciliation and democratization go beyond objective measures taken in the course of governance; they include an expansion of nationalism to accommodate identities and solidarities based on religious, ethno-regional, kinship, and alternative political sensibilities that have otherwise been repressed by the EPLF/PFDJ. Utilizing the resources, rights, and freedoms of host countries offers opportunities for exiles to not only obtain skills in the practices of democracy, citizenship, and civil society but also to develop culturally specific ideas about their meanings and how to implement them transnationally in preparation for doing so in Eritrea. As Paley (2002:485) writes, "Social movements strategically and selectively appropriate and transform transnationally circulating discourses, sometimes filling foreign words with their own meanings."

Practicing Democracy, Citizenship, and Constitutionalism

Having established their presence in the United States more than forty years ago, Eritreans have had much occasion to participate in American democratic and civic institutions. In addition to staging demonstrations and experimenting with the mobilization of action groups around specific issues, such as the implementation of the constitution, the human rights of political prisoners, and freedom of expression, Eritreans have been influenced by other kinds of experiences with Western democracy and citizenship as well. For some, the ability to participate in elections; to exercise one's free speech, assembly, and religion; and to live within a relatively coherent and predictable sociopolitical environment has influenced their perspectives and behaviors vis-à-vis Eritrea.

One respondent in Asmara, a priest, had pastored an immigrant congregation in the United States for thirteen years before returning to Eritrea. Part of his work entailed empowering his congregants by encouraging them to become citizens and to vote. To set an example, he applied for U.S. citizenship, was sworn in alongside his parishioners, and organized trips to the polls during local and national elections. Drawing on the experience of voting as a U.S. citizen, he then described to me how it felt to vote in the Eritrean referendum on independence in 1993:

In 1993, when the referendum was done, even though I wasn't here in Eritrea, it was a particular experience for me, because it was the first time in my life I was able to vote as an Eritrean. Imagine, from 1981 to 1993 I lived in the States, where people really take for granted the power to vote. For me, what was—I have no words to express the joy and feeling I had about what many Americans had at their fingertips and some did not even really appreciate. So just to show the contrast—I was living in a country that is so open democratically, and to have had this experience for the first time. I'm not saying every aspect of America is good, but it was very powerful, and particularly great that day. . . . I would like to have the opportunity to vote as an Eritrean many times. But the process has not gone that way, and it has become harder for me because of that earlier experience. Harder for me than most people here in Eritrea, probably. . . . That kind of experience and being very much involved in the political organization there [in the United States] changed me a lot.

Similarly, the ability to predict certain outcomes based on the "rule of law" also appears important to many Eritreans who use their rights as citizens or residents of Western countries to draw attention to the lack thereof in Eritrea. Amid the torrent of articles posted daily on Eritrean Web sites, one finds frequent references to the freedoms available in the West as compared with those of Eritrea. During a series of demonstrations held by critics of the PFDJ across the globe in 2001 and 2002 protesting the treatment of dissidents, journalists, students, and others, several of the events were reportedly disrupted by PFDJ members and loyalists as they tried to prevent their compatriots from speaking out against the government. In one article, already cited earlier in this chapter, the author noted that demonstrators were essentially protected from the repressive behavior of the Eritrean transnational state by the fact that they were subject only to the laws of the United Kingdom—and not the PFDJ's—regarding their right to demonstrate:

Unfortunately for [supporters of PFDJ], the UK actually thinks the rule of law overrides the rule of the mob and the hoodlums [who disrupted the demonstration] will be persecuted [*sic*]. . . . [Their associates] can all raise funds for them and visit them in jail because, unlike Eritrea, the UK does grant its prisoners visitation rights. . . . Our brothers and sisters in Eritrea live in FEAR but there is absolutely no reason why those of us who reside in nations with rule of law should. Our Eritrean families look to us to speak for them, to articulate their fear, their anger, their helplessness, and we should.[13]

During meetings of the newly formed ELF-RC in the midwestern region, which I attended on several occasions, some concern arose among members of the opposition that PFDJ supporters would also attempt to disrupt their events. While no one turned out in person to do so, a flyer did circulate within the wider community charging the ELF-RC with connections to Osama bin Laden and Islamic terrorist groups. ELF members were outraged, and some even talked about threatening the PFDJ members with lawsuits. When I asked one leader of the group if his oppositional activities could create problems for him if he returned to Eritrea to visit, he responded vehemently that he was an American citizen and would use his rights as an American, including seeking safe haven in the U.S. embassy in Asmara, if the government threatened him. For this man, American citizenship afforded him at least the theoretical access to rights and legal representation that he could wield against the Eritrean government if necessary.

The idea that a democratic environment—like those of many host countries in which exiles reside—guarantees certain basic freedoms and rights according to the rule of law has become increasingly important to Eritreans in recent years. As rights and freedoms that were valorized during the revolutionary era (though not necessarily upheld in practice) are increasingly eroded or violated, people have focused intently on the Eritrean Constitution as a necessary blueprint for instituting important changes. One of the most important issues for reformists and oppositionists alike has been the failure of the PFDJ to implement the constitution, despite its ratification in 1997 and the popular democratic practices employed in its drafting. For many, this has been a key signifier of the regime's lack of commitment to models of democracy and civil society in Eritrea that they believe are appropriate to modern nation-states, such as guaranteed constitutional rights and multiparty elections. These models, moreover, have already been grafted onto Eritrea's own realities via the constitution itself, which drew upon those of other nation-states around the world (including the United States') for structure and inspiration. The failure of the PFDJ government to implement the constitution therefore suggests that the regime is in fact opposed to the rights and freedoms contained within it, and perhaps always has been. Moreover, the issue of elections evoked yet further questions about what this key component of "democracy" would mean unless coupled with a sincere consideration of multipartyism and important political developments taking place in exile, many of which appeared to be both a product and a cause of the government's reticence to implement the constitution. Bereket Habte Selassie wrote:

Who will participate in such an election? Will the field be open only to the PFDJ, as some diehard cadres would have it, or will it be open to other parties? If the former, where is the reform? If the latter, how will that come about and who will be the likely opposition parties that would contest the election? . . . Some Eritreans, including the present writer, expected the EPLF to permit the formation of multi-parties after independence. The fact that this did not happen has given ground for exiled opposition groups, most of them former ELF cadres, to charge the PFDJ leadership with being obsessed with the monopoly of power.[14]

In addition to issues such as electoral politics, constitutionalism, and ELF-EPLF reconciliation as important features in a democratic Eritrea, the issue of what constitutes a "citizen" and how citizens should behave, is also important. We have seen some examples already of how the G-13 and G-15 expressed their criticisms of the Eritrean government in terms of their duties as patriotic citizens. We have also seen how those participating in public demonstrations, or in American voting procedures, consciously recognized the way they were exercising the rights associated with citizenship in the United States and what this meant for them as Eritreans. Common to all of these cases is the idea that citizenship affords individuals and groups certain claims to empowerment within a given state and the ability to criticize or mobilize against its government (or on its behalf).

However, the model of citizenship that the Eritrean one-party state has put into practice since independence is based almost solely on the definitions of nationalist subjectivity developed by the EPLF during the revolution. According to that formulation, proper national subjects were those who identified first and foremost as Eritrean rather than as members of ethno-regional, religious, or kin groups. They were also highly obedient to the structures of authority created and deployed by the EPLF as a liberation front and were expected to make enormous sacrifices on behalf of the nation. Today these same definitions of the proper subject have been transposed to the proper citizen, who largely exists to support and serve the state. Mandatory government programs such as National Service and indefinite military conscription, or the summer work programs for high school and college students, illustrate the way in which the state defines Eritrean citizenship in terms of the responsibility individuals bear to the state rather than in terms of the state's responsibility to serve its citizens. Similarly, the often extreme repressive measures taken against those who criticize or resist the state's demands reveal how strongly the state insists upon its own definitions of citizenship while rejecting the idea of the "social contract" central to liberal democratic traditions as they emerged in the West.

Resistance to the state's definitions in Eritrea and exile, however, shows that ideas about belonging, rights, and responsibility that are proper to a nationalist revolution may be inappropriate for an independent nation-state. The state's taxation of exiles, for example, has caused an outcry among those who have come to value the notion that representation and other rights should accompany taxation. Again, drawing upon their experiences as citizens of Western countries, exiles in particular have mobilized around the idea that citizenship entails at least the right, if not the duty, to criticize one's government. As a young exile named Daniel put it:

A lot of things have to be done. . . . [The government's] gotta be open to the public, people gotta, see, hear, listen, and know about it. They might not be exposed to a whole lot of politics, but they have common sense and an idea of what's good for the country. Just because people aren't intellectual doesn't mean they're dumb. They do know and understand what's good for the country and what's not good for the country. So it should be open to discussion. Then people can criticize if they need to criticize the government. Being a leader, you need to be criticized, you need to be pushed around. That's how it should be. Not just sitting and doing whatever you want to do, and whatever you do the people have to take it. You should do for the people, not the people should do for you.

Daniel's perspective is attuned to those aspects of citizenship that entail structured, popular participation in politics and government accountability to citizens. This same idea is echoed by an anonymous writer on an Eritrean Web site, who pushes this logic one step further to suggest that citizens bear an additional complementary responsibility to voicing criticism, that is, if citizens do not exercise their right or duty to speak up, then they actually forfeit their own claims to empowerment and democratic representation:

If we are serious about constitutionalism and democracy, then we have to start exercising our responsibility as citizens and take a government to task when it is violating its bond with the citizens. Governments—all governments—should be rewarded and punished for how well they live up to their contracts with the citizens. They shouldn't be allowed to milk the goodwill of the citizens indefinitely. This is what a nation should expect from its citizens—particularly its youth and students. If we fail to do this, then the government has every right to say, "the people are not ready for democracy."[15]

Whether or not the concept of citizenship being invoked by many Eritreans as they struggle with the state's authority is based on actually existing conditions in their countries of residence, or on a more idealistic formulation belonging to the realm of normative political theory and democratic ideology disseminated in the United States, is clearly debatable. The point, however, is that changing constructions of citizenship and political subjectivity with which Eritreans engage as members of host societies, or more broadly as members of a global order, are being brought to bear upon a state that continues to insist on nationalist formulae increasingly at odds with the expectations of its population both at home and abroad. Moreover, these constructions have as much to say about the collective past and the injustices Eritreans have inflicted upon one another in the course of the independence struggle as they do about the contemporary conditions facing Eritrea as both a territorial, and transnational, nation-state.

Democracy and Transnational Dissonance

The claim that Eritrea has learned from the experiences (and errors) of other nation-states and governments, both in Africa and internationally, has been important to the PFDJ's narrative. Whether or not this claim is based on any objective fact, or can be measured as such, is another matter. Concerning the transnational debate over the meaning of democracy and the nation-state in Eritrea, however, the issue of "local" definitions specific to Eritrean culture and history versus those that are based on eighteenth- and nineteenth-century Europe (or more contemporary models associated with globalization) has been a major dimension of the struggle between the PFDJ and dispersed Eritreans. This dilemma is by no means unique: the question of shaping postcolonial African nation-states according to Western-dominated formulations (or not) has been among the most pressing concerns for Africans and for scholars of Africa since decolonization (see Laakso and Olukoshi 1996; Mamdani 1996), not least of all as a result of neoliberal, transnational pressures from Western governments, donors, and other agencies engaged in development and structural adjustment lending (Ferguson 2006).

As we have seen, Eritreans at home and abroad have coconstructed national identity and the nation-state since the inception of the independence struggle. Today they are doing the same with concepts like democracy, civil society, constitutionalism, and citizenship. In all cases, this process has been characterized by contradictions, power struggles, and both failed and successful interpenetrations. The tension between "trans" as an international or global signifier and "national" as one of local Eritrean specificities, while productive in certain ways, also generates such dissonance as to render elusive a consensual definition of democracy's meaning and praxis in Eritrea to this point. Moreover, this tension unfolds in a global context beset by massive power differentials that have historically been detrimental to poor, postcolonial, and reconstructing states like Eritrea.

According to the PFDJ's official position, Eritrea is in fact on the long and uneven path to democratization. However, given the history of sectarianism within the nationalist movement itself, the trauma of the border war, and ongoing threats from "external enemies" such as Ethiopia and now the United States, the PFDJ believes that the country must proceed very slowly toward democratic institution building. Moving away from an earlier emphasis on "participatory democracy," the PFDJ has come to favor the notion of "guided democracy," wherein through the course of economic development and social stabilization directed solely by the government, Eritreans will become more capable of sustaining the multiple pressures that democratic practices inevitably exert. The clamoring for more rapid progress among many Eritreans, and especially those in exile, has caused consternation among those who insist that Eritrea's present and future cannot be dictated by forms or concepts not firmly grounded in local experience.

Among Eritreans at home and abroad who support the PFDJ, the kinds of engagements with democracy that exiles have introduced appear disingenuous at best and dangerous at worst. Many midwestern Eritreans who continued to support the PFDJ during the time I conducted fieldwork felt that exiles should not primarily concern themselves with political participation in Eritrea. Rather, their role should be one of economic and technical support in development efforts, which over time would help contribute to the conditions necessary for an effective democratic society. One active leading member of the PFDJ party argued passionately:

The issue is not democracy. The issue is survival. Basic living. You cannot discuss things like this with the diaspora. They only see things in their own environment. To them, how many political parties? To me, it's not the parties. In every house, most of the mothers, three, four, or five of their children are at the war front. They don't know when their children are coming back. Reintegration is the most important factor, the basic living is the most important factor, and we go from there. It is a process. Then we can move into the implementation of other things. . . . The people, many of them can't even write. They don't discuss things based on issues—they only discuss politics in terms of the revolution or religion or regionalism. I myself, I would call it a democracy when they can read the paper, sign the paper, and identify their leaders. Timing is crucial. Am I going to [institute democracy] right now because I am threatened by some group in Germany or the diaspora? Or wait and finish the infrastructure?

A close colleague of his also noted, somewhat contradictorily:

First, we have to look at ourselves. What can we really contribute to the country? I mean, we don't live the day-to-day life of the people in Eritrea. We are living in a different country, a different society. And we are also challenged by the day-to-day life of where we live. So we shouldn't have a say. We should have only a minimal say of what goes on in Eritrea. . . . We cannot decide the fate of the Eritrean people because we don't live their life—we can only support them. If I'm not mistaken, Eritreans are the only people from the African continent who are actively involved in the political life of their country. We were involved in the creation of the constitution. The committee came here and we voiced our opinions like everyone else, we argued. . . . I think the government of Eritrea relies heavily on the diaspora. Not only in economic terms, but in big political decisions. We were involved in the referendum, we voted. . . . But we cannot govern the Eritrean people from the U.S. We have to live there.

According to this perspective, which reflects that of the PFDJ generally and betrays the particular ambivalence the party-state feels toward its exiles (and that exiles feel toward transnationalism), Eritrean society simply cannot sustain the introduction of democratic institutions or multiple political parties at a time when the country has been weakened economically and is still recovering from both the border war and the thirty-year independence struggle. Only when important strides toward reconstruction and development have been achieved can such things as political parties, elections, free press, and other associated practices be instituted safely. Moreover, the kind of democracy that will emerge in Eritrea is unlikely to duplicate the features common in Western nation-states like the United States. And while the one-party state quite clearly needs its exiles, especially for financial reasons, allowing them to participate too freely may damage Eritrean society by allowing them to impose "foreign" ideas or structures that are inappropriate to Eritrean realities.

Few, if any, Eritreans who advocate democratization, however, would argue that Western institutions or practices should be imposed on Eritrea. Indeed, many are quite critical of how democracy has been practiced, and its meanings manipulated, in and by countries like the United States. They are also acutely aware of the contradiction presented by Eritreans who live in the United States and enjoy its freedoms and yet refuse to advocate the same in Eritrea due to a narrow nationalist perspective or interests such as property or investments. According to one incisive interviewee who defined himself as a patriot rather than a nationalist:

I can't deny it. I live in this society and am pretty much influenced by the democratic institutions, the practices, that go on in here. But I do not subscribe to the mainstream views of what democracy is. I was involved with African American movements, the civil rights movement. . . . We understand the issues of minorities here, of oppressed groups. We understand discrimination, because we've lived it. So it is not by normal American standards of democracy—it has faults and limitations. We are not trying to duplicate it, to just take it and put it into Eritrean society. We know what influences our way of thinking. Most Eritreans here have liberal social views. But when it comes to Eritrean society, they seem to deny that right for the people who speak out, to have a democratic society. It's very hard to tell how sincere they are when you talk to them about democratic principles and so on, because when it comes to Eritrea they seem to feel like, well, we don't want to do this, the country is going to go to chaos, our unity, our stability. People say, "oh, democracy can wait." That makes me furious! I say, why do you live in this country then? If you believe in those rights for yourself, why are you denying your own people the right of liberty, and to have legal, social, and civil rights?

Considerable dilemmas have arisen for Eritreans as the many different meanings assigned to democracy and other accompanying features such as constitutionalism and citizenship have collided within the transnational social field. Some of these meanings are embedded within Eritrean history and experience, while others emanate from specific Western traditions or from more general global trends wherein terms like *democracy* and *civil society* are constructed as ideal features of contemporary nation-states. However, the task of defining and applying democracy in Eritrea is not simply about the particular realities with which Eritreans contend, such as the legacy of ELF-EPLF political identities, a history of sectarian struggle, a growing and restive exile population, and the existence of identifiable democratic impulses within traditional Eritrean culture. It is also about the challenges facing a marginalized nation-state as global pressures—many of them embodied by its own population—push the limits of revolutionary nationalist discourse and praxis toward the hegemonic political and cultural models of nation-statehood and governance in the contemporary world. The next section discusses these global pressures vis-à-vis Eritrean transnational civil society and the "sovereign" state.

Transnational Civil Society and Dilemmas of Sovereignty

Civil Society, Modernity, Globalization

While the notion of civil society does not possess as long a history among Eritreans as that of democracy, the concept in and of itself has been a subject of considerable interest in the West since classical and medieval times (Ehrenberg 1999). It has become a particularly dominant category of political thought since the birth of the modern nation-state and has undergone several revivals around the world as new states have formed or experienced major political and social transitions. This was particularly the case in the 1980s, when Eastern European countries were experimenting with social movements and democratization efforts under "actually existing socialism" (Cohen and Arato 1992; Ehrenberg 1999; Paley 2002; Verdery 1999). In these modern manifestations, the concept of civil society has been closely linked to democracy; indeed, it has been viewed as the driving force behind democratization everywhere, including in postcolonial Africa (Mamdani 1996:14). Since the 1990s, moreover, it has become increasingly linked to neoliberal strategies for development (Ferguson 2006; Paley 2002; see also Callaghy, Kassimir, and Latham 2002). However, like democracy, civil society has seen a broad and changeable usage that has varied across places and time periods, rendering it at least as polysemous and perhaps even more nebulous in its definition. For some besieged leaderships and populations, moreover, it appears another weapon in the Western, and especially American, arsenal for global consumer-capitalist hegemony.

Once thought to belong exclusively to the Western Enlightenment project and the liberal political traditions of industrializing, capitalist states, the notion of civil society has since become a highly pliable one that actors across a variety of historical and social milieus have found "especially 'good to think,' and signify with, at moments when the conventional connections between the political and the social, state and public, are perceived be unraveling" (Comaroff and Comaroff 1999:12). Accordingly, the concept has captured the attention and imaginations of scholars and actors enmeshed in studies and conditions of globalization, wherein parts of the world once thought to be removed from the kinds of histories and traditions out of which civil society first emerged have now staked claim on it as a useful concept and model for sociopolitical action. Indeed, one important aspect of globalization (whose roots can be traced to Western imperial expansion, colonialism, and capitalism since the sixteenth century) has been the export of ideas and structures associated with the Western nation-state form and institutions of governance and sociopolitical empowerment (see Balandier 1970; Gledhill 2000; Wolf 1982). Among those seeking to forge and interpret the modern nation-state form in Africa, the concept of civil society has been tackled from a variety of perspectives and disciplines.[16]

While different orientations in political theory and social science have produced unique definitions, the most common characterization of civil society is that of an intermediate, semipublic sphere between family and the state, comprised of differentiated institutions such as schools, religious bodies, trade unions, nongovernmental organizations, voluntary associations, and ad hoc social movements. In more liberal, normative political thought, civil society was thought to comprise a "third realm" distinct from both the state apparatus and the economic sphere, that exerted a democratizing force vis-à-vis the often antagonistic state (see Cohen and Arato 1992). In contrast, the Marxist tradition construed civil society as a sphere of largely unregulated human needs and desires that required the state to direct and control it (Bottomore et al. 1983; Cohen and Arato 1992; Ehrenberg 1999). More recently, some scholars have decried civil society as a useful category for analyzing social movements at all. As Shefner (2007) has argued for Mexico, far from a panacea, civil society is a basis from which elite class interests support the state and political-economic patterns that, in turn, disproportionately benefit elites under conditions of neoliberal globalization.

To be sure, much of the contemporary debate about civil society has focused on what it is and how to measure it rather than the historical or cultural specificities surrounding its articulation and efficacy or the substantive meanings and practices assigned to it by actors (Comaroff and Comaroff 1999; Kasfir 1998; Mamdani 1996; Monga 1996; Pratt 2006). A major critique among Africans and Africanists, then, has been that the concept's formulation in both liberal and Marxist political theory is unable to analyze civil society according to its actual manifestations or culturally imbued meanings in African societies. In many treatments of civil society in Africa to date, African nation-states were said to either lack civil society institutions altogether or to possess a deformed version of a Western standard.

More recently, however, as anthropologists and others interested in the meaning of civil society to non-Western societies have entered the debate, elements of liberal and Marxist political theory have proven useful as interpretive tools. In particular, ideas derived from the work of Antonio Gramsci (1971, 1977) have demonstrated their versatility across a variety of culturally disparate milieus. Gramsci developed a conception of civil society and its relationship to the state that is flexible and nuanced in its ability to understand political, cultural, and historical phenomena as mutually constituted. Gramsci viewed civil society as the semiprivate (or semipublic) "ethical root of the state" (Bobbio 1987:150), where hegemony and popular consent were produced. The legacy of Gramsci's analysis for social science has been an understanding of the ongoing dialectical engagement between state and society, where each penetrates the other and the distinctions between them are sometimes blurred (Bottomore et al. 1983:73).

More specifically for anthropology, Gramsci's conception of civil society has been useful because it focuses on how the state-society relationship is founded as much in ideological and cultural relations as it is in material ones (Bobbio 1987:148; see also Pratt 2006). This approach broadens civil society's interpretive scope beyond Marxist analyses of class conflict to include issues of race, ethnicity, gender, and other aspects of identity and social differentiation as central to society's relationship with political economy and the state (see Hall 1990; Holub 1992; Laclau and Mouffe 1985; Marshall 1994). Moreover, Gramsci's ability to account for power as a relation, one that pervades society but is not possessed or deployed equally among differentiated groups, has influenced scores of later theorists interested in social inequality, social movements, nationalism, "governmentality," and the state (see Holub 1992:92). This perspective is not incompatible with analyses that foreground how class interests are expressed and rooted in civil society (see Shefner 2007). However, it does presuppose that class, like other identities, is culturally constructed as well as materially grounded (Medina 1997, 2004).

Gramsci's legacy has also been important to contemporary scholars interested in the resurgence of civil society discourse and praxis in non-Western or nondemocratic contexts and, more broadly, under conditions of globalization that foster the exportation and local adaptation of

Western models for nation-state relations or require them as a precondition for development lending. African countries and populations are no exception: the global resurgence of civil society as a fertile category for thought and action (Burawoy 2001; Casanova 2001; Kaldor 1999) has also influenced the African imagination in definitive ways (Comaroff and Comaroff 1999). As in the case of the democracy concept's popularity, this fixation on civil society is related to the way in which the nation-state form has been constructed around the world as the most "natural" unit of human and social organization in the world today (Gledhill 2000; Glick-Schiller 1999; Glick-Schiller and Fouron 2001; Herzfeld 1997; Malkki 1995b; Nagengast 1994) and the associated political patterns that accompany the post–Cold War world after the decline of socialism. Similarly, the growing interest in the state as a subject of ethnographic inquiry (Das and Poole 2004; Gledhill 2000; Greenhouse, Mertz, and Warren 2002; Hansen and Stepputat 2001, 2005; Paley 2002) has resulted in a renewed interest in how and why concepts like sovereignty, democracy, and civil society are being reconstituted across the globe.

However, as numerous scholars have pointed out over the past decade, globalization has also transformed many patterns long associated with the territorial nation-state form. Categories that were previously understood to be aligned, such as national identification, state sovereignty and administrative authority, citizenship, political participation, national economies, and cultural boundedness, have all shifted under conditions of globalization. These conditions include extensive international migration, the spread of multinational capital, flexible labor markets, and communication technologies such as the Internet. The appearance of "deterritorialized nation-states" (Basch, Glick-Schiller, and Blanc 1994), or states from whom their nations have been decoupled and then regrouped according to new cross-border practices and institutions by social actors and governments alike, is also a major feature of globalization. As Casanova (2001:423) has put it:

Globalization is . . . continuous with the world system of states, but it alters radically that system by dissociating the elements which were clustered together within the nation-state: administrative territorial state, political society or body of citizens, market economy, civil society, and nation, all embedded territorially within a system governed by the principle of undivided and exclusive sovereignty. Globalization limits and relativizes state sovereignty; frees capitalist market and civil society from its territorial-juridical embeddedness in state and nation; and as a result dissolves the particular fusion of nation and state which emerged out of Western modernity and became institutionalized worldwide, at least as a model, after the French Revolution. Globalization does not mean the end of states or the end of nations and nationalism, but it means the end of their fusion in the sovereign territorial nation-state.

It is this last point that remains of particular importance for Eritreans and for other populations who remain bound by nationalist ideologies or other dramatic commitments to the territorial nation-state and yet also participate in discourses and practices that challenge or explode the previously taken-for-granted homologies upon which modernity—and modernist ideologies like nationalism—rest (see Glick-Schiller and Fouron 2001). Because of this tension between hallmarks of modernity and those of globalization, the reevaluation of formerly "stable" components of social and political organization has become more pressing.

It is within this context that a resurgence of civil society discourse and associated practices has taken place among scholars and actors alike. One example is the notion of "global civil society," which has achieved popularity as researchers develop tools for understanding the emergence of human and moral communities or movements that transcend national identities and territorial nation-states to appeal to common concerns of social justice, ecological sustainability, and human rights (see Kaldor, Anheier, and Glasius 2003; Keane 2003; Walzer 1997). As a concept, global civil society refers to the way in which people across varied national and juridical contexts unite in discernible ways to press particular entities (including states and international bodies) into policies and practices that address the common dilemmas of large groups of concerned citizens. These dilemmas typically transcend the nation-state itself to include issues of global scope and importance, such as the spread of HIV/AIDS, terrorism, war, corporate responsibility, environmental degradation/sustainability, and international criminal courts, among others. At their core, the objectives of global civil society tend to be a decrease in violence, enhanced democratization in terms of power sharing and decision making, and an emphasis on the well-being of humanity regardless of national or state affiliation. The phenomenon of global civil society, moreover, has only been augmented by the heightened mobility of people (whether voluntary or forced) and the resulting multiple subjectivities that individuals form as members of more than one nation-state.

More than any other body of literature, contemporary studies of transnational movements, processes, and identities highlight all of these issues simultaneously, whether in relation to specific nation-states or clusters of several at once. In addition, they provide valuable ethnographic insight into the unevenness of globalization as a process, one that is "produced and consumed not in thin air, not in some virtual reality, but in real organizations, institutions, communities" (Burawoy 2001:148), and often with contradictory effects. Thus studies of transnationalism remain ultimately concerned with the consequences of globalization for specific populations or locations, although few have incorporated the concepts of civil society or global civil society in their analyses. It is a central argument of this book that a conception of transnational civil society—one that draws upon concerns similar to those articulated by global civil society but exclusively in reference to circumscribed national conditions—contributes to a more critical, nuanced, and dialectical understanding of the dilemmas facing nationalist states as they relate to their increasingly transnationalizing societies under conditions of globalization.

Sovereignty and Transnational Civil Society in Eritrea and Exile

The ambivalent relationship among Eritreans and the transnational nation-state must also be understood with respect to an additional, but no less pressing dilemma: how a small, poor, and young nation-state must defend its relative autonomy amid the multiple pressures of neoliberal models of political-economic development and other aspects of foreign intervention. As I have suggested earlier, as well as argued elsewhere (Hepner and Fredriksson 2007; Hepner 2008; O'Kane and Hepner 2009), the Eritrean government remains obsessed with controlling the form, shape, and scope of processes of globalization in order to prevent the hollowing out, or outsourcing, of the policies and technologies that underpin modern forms of governmental power. As Glick-Schiller and Fouron have noted for Haiti (2001), nationalism and long-distance nationalism articulate important critiques about the domination of poor countries by rich ones and entail efforts on the part of governments and citizens to ameliorate the consequences of structural inequality. Certainly, the impact of neoliberal models of economic development, which often go hand in hand with political reforms such as democratization and the development of civil society, as Ferguson (2006) most recently reminds us, has been uneven and largely negative for postcolonial African countries. Thus the PFDJ government's efforts to maintain control over its transnational citizenry by both institutionalized and ideological means are part of a deliberate and long-developing strategy.

This strategy, forged during the revolutionary era, is intended to facilitate and maintain the centralization of power in the party-state by extending its ideological and administrative control over its populations at home and abroad. It is also intended to prevent transnational citizens, and exiles in particular, from exposing Eritrea to the forces of Western imperialism in its cultural, political, and economic guises. While discourses and practices associated with democracy, constitutionalism, citizenship, rights, and the rule of law are modes through which exiles work through conflicts deeply embedded in the history of the nationalist movement and through which contemporary authoritarianism is challenged, they also suggest strategies that have long been used by Western countries, donors, and international lending agencies to measure Africa's "deviation" and to compromise the control of national governments over their own societies.

Thus anxieties over sovereignty and security lead the party-state to rebuff the efforts of its transnational civil society, even as the latter grows larger and more sophisticated in exile as a result of repression. As we have seen, transnational processes were instrumental in the achievement of that state and the rise to power of the EPLF/PFDJ regime, and until recently, the latter seemed well in control. Since the border war with Ethiopia, however, the transnational social field has proliferated in many directions, spurring Eritreans to build linkages with a plethora of international organizations with rights-based platforms, such as Amnesty International, Reporters without Borders, and a variety of evangelical Christian organizations that advocate religious freedom. Moreover, in addition to those exiles who lobby foreign governments such as the United States for better policies toward Eritrea, other transnational citizens frustrated with the imperviousness of the PFDJ regime have taken to pressuring the U.S. State Department as it considers whether Eritrea should be designated a state that sponsors terrorism due to the government's recent support for members of the Somali Islamic Courts Union. The party-state's concerns with respect to the dangers of transnational intervention by its own citizens, then, are not unfounded. While transnationalism historically enabled the achievement of independent statehood, it may also be a key factor in eroding state sovereignty, both for better and, inevitably, for worse.

However, there is an additional dimension to the dilemma of sovereignty that must be noted if we are to fully grasp the painful paradox of transnational political struggle in Eritrea and exile. In recent anthropological explorations of the concept of state sovereignty (Das and Poole 2004; Hansen and Stepputat 2006; O'Kane and Hepner 2009), interest has especially focused around ideas drawn from the work of Italian scholar Giorgio Agamben (1998, 2000). Das and Poole (2004), following Agamben, define sovereignty not so much as control over policies and administration as more simply, and starkly, the power over life and death itself. That is, the sovereign state, by its very definition, retains the ability to determine which members of the political community are sufficiently "outside the law" so as to render them expendable without legal procedure or consequence. "Because the sovereign cannot by definition be bound to the law, the political community itself becomes split along the different axes of membership and inclusion that may run along given fault lines . . . or may produce new categories of people included in the political community but denied membership in political terms" (Das and Poole 2004:12).

Indeed, insofar as the party-state has operated since independence with no clear political or juridical blueprint for the division and accountability of powers, and has instead intensified processes of militarization and authoritarian rule, the definition of sovereignty as being prior to the law and beholden to no constraints on the configuration or exercise of power seems to be the most salient one in Eritrea today. As the party-state claims to defend sovereignty in terms of territory, national policies, and economic development, the real exercise of its authority seems to pivot on the capacity to surveil, discipline, and punish. The party-state has long identified those who fall within the political community, and those without, by reference to the categories of soldiers, martyrs, traitors, and exiles. Most vulnerable to the sovereign power of the state at this juncture, and those whose experiences render it most visible, are the thousands of men, women, and children who by virtue of their religious beliefs, their political views, or their failure or refusal to submit to the full authority of the state, have been reduced to "bare life" (Agamben 1998) in police stations, military camps, and secret prisons. In addition, there are the tens of thousands of others who have become new refugees.

The many costs of sovereignty, whether rooted in the preindependence period or stemming from recent developments, point up the painful paradoxes of transnational political struggle. As many Eritreans look on the current political situation with disbelief and disillusionment; as some seek to carve out autonomous modes of sociopolitical organization, or ways of being Eritrean that diverge from official nationalist patterns; and as others deny the suffering of so many of their compatriots to protect the sanctity of the nation-state and current government, they simultaneously challenge and entrench all that is precious, and all that is terrible, in the unfolding drama that is their beloved country.

Notes

Chapter 1

1. For background on Eritrea's nationalist struggle for independence, see Connell 1997; Iyob 1995; Killion 1998; Markakis 1987; Pateman 1998; Pool 2001; Wrong 2005.

2. All names of interviewees and some details of their lives have been changed to preserve their confidentiality.

3. See Verdery (1991) on the anatomy of socialist states in Eastern Europe and Pratt's (2006) analysis of corporatist nationalism in the Middle East for interesting comparisons.

Chapter 2

1. The factionalization of ELF following exile into Sudan was complex and rife with personal and political rivalries. Abdallah Idris was expelled from the core leadership of the ELF, known as the Revolutionary Council (RC) in 1981, in part for his developing anti-Christian tendencies. He attempted a coup in 1982 against his secular colleagues and proclaimed himself the leader of the RC. The RC then split into two: an Islamist wing under Abdallah Idris with strong ties to Saudi Arabia and a secularist wing under Ahmed Nasser and Habte Tesfamariam known as the Tayara, or "General Trend." Each claimed to be the genuine RC, though the secularist Tayara group generally retained that designation, and Abdallah's group was seen as the splinter. Repeated attempts were made—often brokered by Arab North African states like Sudan and Tunisia—to reunite the factionalized RC. However, a third faction known as Saghem, meaning "return to home," also formed, which favored reunification with the EPLF. In 1985, Saghem itself splintered into factions, one of which merged completely with the EPLF in 1987 and two others that eventually took up residence in Ethiopia and supported the Tigrayan Peoples Liberation Front (TPLF) fighting in Northern Ethiopia. (See Killion 1998:25–26, 192–94, 365.) The ELF today remains the most significant Eritrean opposition movement, albeit still debilitated by factionalization and confined to exile.

2. See, e.g., Aretxaga 1997; Das and Poole 2004; Donham 1999b; Giddens 1985; Gledhill 2000; Gupta and Ferguson 1997; Greenhouse, Mertz, and Warren 2002; Herzfeld 1997; Kertzer 1988; Lavie and Swedenburg 1996; Malkki 1995a, 1997; Müller 2005; Nagengast 1994; Scott 1998; Verdery 1999.

3. It is telling that no full-length comprehensive study of the ELF yet exists

in any language. However, bits and pieces of the history of the ELF are under construction in various places, chiefly found on Web sites such as www .awate.com and www.nharnet.com.

4. The issue of Muslim-Christian relations in Eritrea over the *longue durée* remains important, complex, and, in my opinion, poorly understood. Overall, relations between the two major religious groups have been characterized by peaceful coexistence and mutual interaction. There have also been undeniable episodes of violence and persistent feelings of hostility and alienation, however. Most important perhaps, at various points in Eritrea's history, the character of Muslim-Christian relations has been framed differently to underpin specific political objectives. Throughout much of the civil conflict between the ELF and the EPLF, the nature of Muslim-Christian tensions was likely exaggerated in order to legitimize the EPLF's unique program. Today it has become more common among EPLF/PFDJ loyalists to understate religious tensions in the past and present, including within the historic split between the ELF and the EPLF. This is largely due to the fact that the PFDJ regime has come under intense international criticism for the persecution of new religious movements, and the imprisonment and torture of Pentecostal Christians in particular. Reemphasizing Eritrea's history of religious tolerance and underplaying the role of religion in the ELF-EPLF conflict thus serves the contemporary purpose of portraying the PFDJ government as especially tolerant of religious diversity and Eritrea as an inherently peaceful society were it not for the foreign-inspired machinations of new religious movements.

5. The political developments surrounding the formation of the EPLF are exceedingly complex and not within the scope of this work. For detailed analysis, interested readers are directed to Iyob 1995; Markakis 1987; and Pool 2001. Killion 1998 is also a useful resource.

6. While the translation from Tigrinya means "We and Our Objectives," the document is commonly referred to in English as "Our Struggle and Its Goals."

7. Some sources attribute sole authorship to Isayas Afwerki.

8. "Our Struggle and Its Goals," from the English translation printed in *Harnet* (Eritreans for Liberation in North America) 2, no. 3 (March 1973): 5–23.

9. Ibid.

10. Ibid.

11. For analyses of central Ethiopian expansionism and cultural hegemony, see Holcomb and Ibssa 1990; Donham 1999b; and Levine 1974.

12. Drawn from Chinese Maoism, democratic centralism involves a pattern of ostensibly open democratic discussion among large groups, after which the leadership makes final and unquestionable decisions (see Connell 1997:42).

13. The extent to which EPLF actually achieved these goals and the degree to which mass organizations functioned in their intended capacities is somewhat unclear, perhaps even more so today than during the independence war and postliberation period. Authors who have written favorably about EPLF's programs in the field, and pro-EPLF nationalists themselves, have perhaps overstated the progressivism and success of mass organizations. Critics have perhaps done the opposite, claiming that mass organizations were actually coercive institutions rather than voluntaristic ones. I claim agnosticism on this point; I do not think we have achieved the dispassionate distance, or been provided the necessary freedom and autonomy in terms of research, to draw firm conclusions. Whether the institutions themselves are coercive or not, many people engage with them willingly, thus striking that classic balance between coercion and con-

sent that Gramsci (1971, 1977) identified as key to hegemony. Nicola Pratt (2006) has analyzed a remarkably similar process in Arab nationalist states of the Middle East and North Africa.

14. An essay by Awet T. Weldemichael (2009, in press) helps fill this historical gap.

15. The decision to exterminate the dissidents did meet with some resistance among other ELF cadres, chiefly those who later formed the Eritrean Democratic Movement (EDM), another dissident faction in ELF led by Hiruy Tedla Bairu. The EDM actually first emerged in 1976 and was labeled *falool*, "anarchist," by the ELF leadership. They called for organizational reforms within ELF and advocated a change in leadership. Many EDM members were arrested and executed by the ELF leadership, while others went into exile (Iyob 1995:120). Hiruy Tedla Bairu went to Sweden, where he remained active in Eritrean politics. In October 2002 he was elected chairman of the National Democratic Alliance (NDA), a now-defunct and renamed umbrella coalition of ELF and other forces that oppose the PFDJ regime and organize against it in exile. See Chapter 6 for more discussion.

16. The TPLF was a rebel movement comprised of Tigrinya-speaking peoples of northern Ethiopia, who in 1975 began fighting against the Derg regime. Although EPLF and TPLF had their differences, they also cooperated with one another and largely supported one another's aims. In 1991, a coalition of rebel groups led by TPLF overthrew Mengistu and the Derg regime and took control of Ethiopia as the Ethiopian Peoples Revolutionary Democratic Front (EPRDF) under Meles Zenawi. See Young 1997 for an analysis of the TPLF.

17. Most notably, Ibrahim Totil and Zemhret Yohannes.

Chapter 3

1. An earlier and more detailed version of this chapter is published as "Transnational *Tegadelti*: Eritreans for Liberation in North America and the Eritrean Peoples Liberation Front," *Eritrean Studies Review* 4, no. 2 (2005): 37–84. The material in this chapter appears with the kind permission of the Red Sea Press.

2. The names of interviewees have been redacted or changed to preserve their confidentiality.

3. For a detailed, albeit ideologically charged, description of these positions, see AESNA/AEWNA 1978, chap. 5. For ESUNA's view on Eritrean self-determination and the "nationalities question" in Ethiopia, see "The National Question in Ethiopia: Proletarian Internationalism or Bourgeois Nationalism?" *Combat* 5, no. 2 (August 1976): 2–94.

4. One Eritrean leader in ESUNA was Haile Menkerios, who returned to Eritrea to join the EPLF in the early 1970s where he became a member of the EPLF Politbureau and, upon independence, the permanent representative of Eritrea to the United Nations.

5. *Harnet* 2, no. 1 (January 1973): 6. *Harnet* was largely the project of Yemane Gebreab, its chief editor, and Kassahun Checole, who produced much of the writing for the magazine.

6. Letter from Eritrean students to U-Thant, Secretary General of the United Nations, December 20, 1970 (Research and Documentation Center archives, Asmara).

7. *Harnet* 2, no. 1 (January 1973): 8.

8. See *Harnet* 2, no. 1 (January 1973).

9. Among them were Haile Mekerios, Naizghi Kiflu, Andeberhan Woldegiorgis, Tsegai "Dinesh" Tesfatsion, Yemane Gebreab, Hagos "Kisha" Gebrehiwet, Gebremikael "Lilo" Mengistu, Seyoum Seium, and Alemseged Tesfai.

10. *Harnet* 2, no. 1 (January 1973).

11. Ibid.

12. *Harnet* 2, no. 3 (March 1973).

13. EFLNA later published an analysis of its relationship with various international groups and movements: *Zmdena Enasa ms gesgesti wudebat, tmaHayshu zweTse* [The Relationship between EFLNA and Progressive Parties, rev. ed., 1977] (Research and Documentation Center archives, Asmara).

14. Ibid., 9.

15. See, e.g., *meTsanHi medeb, Sene* [June] 1, 1977, a reading roster that included works such as *History of the Communist Party of the Soviet Union* (1939) coupled with the EPLF's own writings. See also *medeb politikawi tmherti, Miyazya* [April] 9, 1975, another political education syllabus that includes selections from Marx and Engels's *The Communist Manifesto*, essays from the *Peking Review*, writings by Mao Tse-tung, and analyses of Eritrean political history by foreign authors as well as by the ELF, EPLF, and EFLNA itself (Research and Documentation Center archives, Asmara).

16. A cooperative effort among members and the Wisconsin chapter in particular, but reportedly penned mostly by Yemane Gebreab, Gebremikael "Lilo" Mengistu, and Petros Yohannes, building upon an earlier paper cowritten by Alemseged Tesfai and Lilo in Madison, Wisconsin. Other major contributors included Paulos Tesfagiorgis and Gebre Hiwet Tesfagiorgis.

17. See, e.g., letter from the education committee regarding the general report on labor and academic skills, 1977 (Research and Documentation Center archives, Asmara).

18. Equivalent to about one million dollars today.

19. See, e.g., *debdabie n'he.g.Ha.E. meda, kab akayadit shmag'le Enasa* [Letter to EPLF in the field from EFLNA executive committee, dated November 29, 1976], stating, "We have some criticisms of the latest issues of *Vanguard* and *Spark*, especially *Vanguard*, because it seems to us that it is an official bulletin but doesn't reflect the development of the people's front" (Research and Documentation Center archives, Asmara).

20. *National Democratic Programme of the Eritrean Peoples Liberation Front*, January 1977, p. 34.

21. See, e.g., *Tsebtsab meda Tehasas 1976–Tiree 1977* [Field Conditions report, December 1976–January 1977]; *Tsebtsab meda, Hamle 7, 1978* [Field Conditions report by EFLNA, July 7, 1978]; *Tsebtsab meda, June 1981* [Field Conditions Report by AESNA, June 1981, from observations made March 26, 1981–May 20, 1981] (Research and Documentation Center archives, Asmara).

22. Dimtsi Hafash programs are also available to Eritreans abroad via the Internet.

23. Andemikael Kahsai, who served various posts in the EPLF and after independence. In 2001, he ended his term as mayor of Asmara.

24. Letter to EFLNA leaders from EPLF organizing committee, Rome, June 14, 1977 [*Debdabie n'akayadit komiti Enasa kababal wedeb ab weTsaee, Roma, Sene 14, 1977*] (Research and Documentation Center archives, Asmara).

25. *Eritrea: Revolution or Capitulation?* AESNA and AEWNA (1978), p. 2.

26. Ibid., 1.

27. Ibid., 9.

28. Ibid., 10. Excerpt from EFLNA, *Tasks of EFLNA*, September 1974, quoted in original.

29. Ibid., 27–28.

30. See, e.g., *Resistance* 1, no. 2 (November–December 1978), and any other issue released in 1978 and 1979.

31. See, e.g., *Fuluy tewesakhi TsHuf, tebleTsti ba'ulom teQale'om (1978)* [Special Additional Writing: Opportunists Exposed Themselves]; *Entaynet 9 Hafashawi gubaie Enasa, kde'At meraHti Enasa* (1978) [Concerning EFLNA's Ninth General Congress: The Betrayal by EFLNA Leaders; Boston Chapter]; *Qlu'e debdabie bza'eba 9 gubaie nay Enasa (1978)* [Open Letter to EFLNA concerning the Ninth General Congress, Madison Chapter]; *Qlu'e debdabie, Tsere demokrasiyawi Hluf Tsegamawuyan falulnat meraHti (1978)* [Open Letter Concerning the Anti-Democratic Ultra-Leftist Renegade Leaders; Minnesota Chapter] (Research and Documentation Center archives, Asmara).

32. See, e.g., *T'mre- temekoro nay wusanietat 9 Hafashawi gubaie Enasan gobrawi wuTsitun, Hamle 1979* [Collective Experiences of EFLNA's Ninth Congress and Plan of Action, July 1979]; *Awontaw'n alutaw'n temekorotat Enasa (Tehasas 1979)* [Pros and Cons of EFLNA's Experiences, December 1979] (Research and Documentation Center archives, Asmara).

33. Memo from EFLNA, Seattle chapter, undated (Research and Documentation Center archives, Asmara).

34. See *Fuluy tewesaKi Tsuhuf* [Special Additional Writing], *Ertra ab Qalsi* 1, no. 3 (February 19, 1979): 1–15.

35. Transcript of speech made by Gebremikael Mengistu, undated and unpublished, approximately 1979 (courtesy of Gebremikael Mengistu).

Chapter 4

1. I have not named the particular community in an effort to protect the privacy of those who willingly participated, as well as the community as a whole, which neither endorsed nor objected to my research.

2. Given the fact that the vast majority of Eritreans supported independence despite conflicts of political identity, most Eritrean adults are thought to have participated in the referendum. However, it is reasonable to expect that some did not, either because they did not support independence or failed to register with the embassy.

3. The 1992 Proclamation on Citizenship claims any person born to an Eritrean mother or father, either within the state of Eritrea or abroad, as an Eritrean citizen. See Chapters 5 and 6 for further discussion of citizenship.

4. This man was also elected chair of the NUEY in 1978 and was stationed in the EPLF's Rome office. After the split between EFLNA and the EPLF later that year, he returned to the United States to help clean up the mess. He remained in the United States after Eritrean independence and only returned to Eritrea to serve in the government in the mid-1990s.

5. In Tigrinya, *maHber kom* literally means "community association." The word *kom* is an adaptation from the English "community" or "committee." Tronvoll (1998:120, 130) and Pateman (1998:161) also note that EPLF administrative militias instituted in the liberated and semiliberated areas and responsible for implementing various reforms, including land tenure, were also known as *koms*.

6. Several months before I conducted this interview in Asmara, Mahmoud

Sherifo had been sacked during the earlier stages of a power struggle within the PFDJ that came to a head in 2000–2001. He later was signatory to the G-15's Open Letter to the PFDJ, which criticized the president and called for democratic reforms. He was arrested with his colleagues in September and remained incommunicado thereafter. A clandestine report ostensibly written by former prison guards at the secret detention center known as Eira'Eiro and released to Eritrean networks in 2006 indicated that Sherifo had died in prison for lack of medical treatment and possibly as a result of torture.

7. "MaHber Komen Temekoro Ertrawiyen ab Sedeten" ["Eritrean Exiles and Their Community Experience"], *Hagerey* (1989): 12–19 (Research and Documentation Center, Asmara).

8. *Hagerey* (June 1989): 12, trans. from Tigrinya.

9. Ibid., 17, trans. from Tigrinya.

10. "Me'ebale Eritrawi MaHber Kom B'Kemey?" ["Eritrean Community Development: By What Means?"], *Hagerey* (1990): 29–37 (Research and Documentation Center, Asmara).

11. *Hagerey* (January 1990): 30, trans. from Tigrinya.

12. Ibid, 32.

13. Ibid., 37.

14. Ibid.

15. Ibid. (June 1989): 12.

16. These ambivalent attitudes have taken on new significance since 2002, when the Eritrean government forcibly closed most new churches and began engaging in systematic persecution of Pentecostal Christians in particular.

17. In fact, there were several stages of fund-raising that took place during the border war. In addition to special events, where large sums of money were raised in several hours, the Eritrean state launched its "dollar a day" campaign. Eritrean citizens throughout the world were asked to contribute "a dollar a day to keep the Woyane [Ethiopian government] away." All payments were made through the embassy of Eritrea in Washington, D.C., and were coordinated by local PFDJ chapters throughout the United States.

18. "Blueprint for Action," November 5, 2001, www.awate.com, accessed January 6, 2002.

Chapter 5

1. Isayas Afwerki, the president of Eritrea, is quoted as saying of the postindependence period, "It's not like the liberation war, where you have one major obstacle and other problems are simply secondary. . . . Now it's completely different. You have to face challenges in all directions, and their magnitude is tremendous in terms of the frustrating effect on what you want to do and what you can do" (Connell 1997:281).

2. NUEYS originally formed in 1978 as the AES. In 1987, at the EPLF's second congress, it became the NUES, and in 1994 it became the NUEYS. In this chapter I refer to it as only NUEYS for the sake of clarity.

3. NUEYS information pamphlet, Asmara, January 2000.

4. "National Union of Eritrean Women," Eritrean Relief and Rehabilitation Association (ERRA), August–September 1994, reprinted from *The Horn of Africa Bulletin* 6, no. 5 (September–October 1994).

5. NUEYS information pamphlet, Asmara, January 2000.

6. *Keremti*, the rainy season, corresponds to summer months in the United

States and Europe and is the most heavily traveled time of the year for exiles returning to visit. Diaspora Eritreans are often referred to as *beles,* after the seasonal cactus fruit that also makes its appearance during *keremti.*

7. "About the National Union of Eritrean Youth and Students in North America, Washington DC Chapter," http://denden.com.nueys/brochure.htm, accessed February 18, 2001.

8. Of course, the resolution to such a dilemma would require greater democratization at the level of the state and the broadening, rather than shrinking, of a public sphere. The chairperson's comments seem to place the responsibility for allowing nonaffiliated groups back onto NUEW members themselves, when clearly the problem emerges from the interdependence of mass organizations with the EPLF/PFDJ.

9. The front's transition to a government deserves a more complex treatment than is possible here. For more thorough analyses, rReaders are directed to Connell 1997, 2001; Pool 2001; and Tronvoll 1998a, 1998b..

10. The CCE was led by the esteemed Eritrean lawyer Dr. Bereket Habte-Selassie, a resident of the United States, and also included former individual members of the ELF, largely drawn from those who had joined the EPLF in 1981 or had returned to Eritrea at independence. No organized ELF groups were permitted to participate in any aspect of the constitutional and state-making processes, however (Pool 2001:166, 180). See also Habte-Selassie 2003.

11. "A National Charter for Eritrea: For a Democratic, Just and Prosperous Future" (EPLF, February 1994), quoted in Pool 2001:164.

12. During the 1998–2000 Ethio-Eritrean border war, U.S. Eritreans contributed $25 million in donations to the state.

13. Even those critical of the current government must play by its rules if they wish to do much of anything in Eritrea besides visit their families from time to time. Similarly, national commitments that supersede political identity compel virtually everyone to participate in fund-raising, especially when Eritrea is in turmoil, while bonds of kin and friendship encourage a constant flow of remittances. Hence the very high rates of revenue generated by exile communities despite the ambivalence many feel toward the current government.

14. It is worth recalling here the Ethiopian Derg regime's persecution of Pentecostals in Ethiopia in the mid to late 1970s, following Mengistu Haile Mariam's ascent to power, and the subsequent interference into the Orthodox Church (see Donham 1999b; Eide 2000; Hepner and Hepner, in press; Larebo 1988).

15. National service (*agelgolot*) often drags on for as long as the government instructs people to continue. Conscripts, whose work ranges from construction to serving in government ministries, are remunerated with about 140 nakfa per month, or about fifteen dollars. Random sweeping of city streets and constant checking of paperwork by armed soldiers have also become more common, signaling an intergenerational conflict between the former fighters who make up the bulk of the government and the restless young people they charge with laziness, ingratitude, and lack of national commitment. Indeed, National Service is an important tool of nationalist reproduction intended to enculturate young people with the values of the former guerrilla fronts. Similarly, the summer student campaigns, or *keremtawi ma'etot,* in which I participated in 1995 as a volunteer, acclimates high school students to similar values of hard work and sacrifice for nation building.

16. See Conrad 2006 for an excellent recent ethnographic analysis of Eritrean politics on the Internet, with specific reference to the German Eritrean diaspora.

17. From the official translation of the 2001 Pastoral Letter of the Eritrean Catholic Bishops, article 3, pp. 2–3.

Chapter 6

1. The forced removal of Eritreans and Ethiopians on both sides of the border has been one of the most deplorable and damaging aspects of the war. For various accounts see Hepner 2000; Legesse and Citizens for Peace in Eritrea 1998; Negash and Tronvoll 2000; Tronvoll 1999; and Woldeselassie 2000.

2. See Connell 2005a for rich documentation of the political events of 2001, including interviews with now-imprisoned government officials and a discussion of the clandestine Peoples Party at the core of the EPLF.

3. Mahmoud Mamdani (1996:19) has cogently noted that, in Africanist circles, the discourse on civil society (and democracy) since the 1980s both resembles and seems to have replaced the earlier discourse on socialism.

4. See Connell 2005b for the full text of the letter.

5. I discovered a range of reactions among local Eritreans during the G-15 affair. Some were upset and defensive of the president. Some evaded speaking about it at all. Many others, however, expressed support for the message the G-15 sought to convey. I was in fact quite surprised at how many people agreed with the letter, including individuals who had been highly supportive of the PFDJ and of the president on my earlier trips to Eritrea.

6. Among the arrested was Fessehaye "Joshua" Yohannes, a personal friend, veteran EPLF fighter, celebrated playwright, children's theater director, and writer with *Setit* newspaper. After languishing in a secret prison location for more than six years, he reportedly died in January 2007 of torture-related injuries. Eritrea continues to have the highest number of journalists in prison on the African continent and is the only African country with no independent media.

7. Although I cooperated in providing information about my research design and major questions, I refused to reveal to authorities the identities of private citizens I had interviewed or relate the content of our discussions as per the terms of informed consent procedures. Authorities were unfamiliar with and highly suspicious of these procedures. I stopped holding interviews or meeting individuals in public places for fear of being followed.

8. See Article 1, "Establish a Peoples Democratic State," *National Democratic Programme of the Eritrean Peoples Liberation Front* (1977:23)

9. This democratic centralism was coordinated and enforced, as Connell (2005b) has shown, by the recently unmasked Eritrean Peoples Revolutionary Party (EPRP), or the Peoples Party, within the EPLF.

10. "Blueprint for Action," November 5, 2001, www.awate.com, accessed January 6, 2002.

11. "Interview with Seyoum Ogbamichael," June 29, 2001, www.awate.com, accessed February 21, 2002.

12. It is important to note that these values are more or less also shared by those who are not affiliated with the ELF opposition movement. Many Eritreans who belong to none of the existing political movements are doubtful that any will offer a truly democratic alternative. That part of doing politics includes the manipulation of concepts and terms such as *democracy* and *freedom* is undeniable. My analysis of the use and meaning of these among various Eritrean political movements is not an endorsement of their claims to power.

13. "Blueprint for Action," November 5, 2001, www.awate.com, accessed January 6, 2002.

14. Bereket Habte-Selassie, "The Disappearance of the Constitution and Its Impact on Current Politics in Eritrea," January 20, 2001, www.news.asmarino .com, accessed January 22, 2001.

15. "Misplaced Loyalty," November 19, 2002, www.awate.com, accessed November 21, 2002.

16. See, e.g., Bingen, Robinson, and Staatz 2000; Callaghy, Kassimir and Latham 2002; Comaroff and Comaroff 1999; Gledhill 2000; Guyer 1994; Harbeson, Rothchild, and Chazan 1994; Hepner 2003; Kasfir 1998; Mamdani 1996; Monga 1996; Nyang'oro 1999; Pratt 2006.

Glossary of Tigrinya Terms and Phrases

There is no widely accepted standardized system for transliterations from Tigrinya to English. Here, the glottalized (or ejective) consonants are reflected by capitalization, as is the voiceless pharyngeal fricative "h." An apostrophe is used for glottal stops and for the voiced pharyngeal fricative sound that is commonly compared to the Arabic 'ayn.

aboy. My father.
adetat. Mothers (pl.).
'adi. Village .
agelgolot. National service.
akayadit shumagalle. Executive committee.
b'selam yerakhbena. May we meet in peace.
bado-seleste. Rumor mill (lit., "zero-three").
baito. Traditional people's assembly.
beles. Cactus fruit (lit.); summer visitors from the diaspora.
berbere. Red pepper spice blend, a staple in Eritrean cooking.
Dimtsi Hafash. Voice of the Broad Masses (radio programming).
dirar tegadelay. Dinner for a fighter.
Enasa. Tigrinya acronym for Eritreans for Liberation in North America (EFLNA).
enda Hazen. Funeral wake.
equb. Rotating, informal mutual credit.
Ertra Kom. Eritrean community.
falool. Anarchist.
ferenji. Foreigner.
ga'at. Starchy porridge with yogurt, butter, and *berbere*, considered a healing food.
gabi. White spun-cotton wrap or shawl, also used like a blanket.
gezawuti. Segmentary lineages (lit., "houses").
gwyla. Circular group dance, or party.
Habesha. A person from highland Eritrea or Ethiopia (lit., "Abyssinian").
Hadde hizbi, Hadde libi. Eritrean national slogan, "one people, one heart."
Hafash. Masses.
hagerey. Motherland (lit., "my country").
Hamadi'e. Tigrinya acronym for National Union of Eritrean Women (NUEW).
Haray. Okay, all right (colloq.).
Harnet. Liberation.
Hegdef. Tigrinya acronym for Peoples Front for Democracy and Justice (PFDJ).

Hibrete-seb. Community (lit., "a unity of people").

Hijab. Women's Islamic dress.

injera. Spongy pancake-like bread made of fermented teff (native grain) or wheat flour.

Jebha. Familiar name for Eritrean Liberation Front.

kebessa. Highlands.

kemey allekhi, me'arey. How are you, honey (fem. sing.)?

keremtawi ma'etot. Student summer campaign (work program).

keremti. Rainy season, corresponding to summer in the Northern Hemisphere.

Kifli Hizbi. Department of Mass Administration (lit., "people's section").

kraar. Traditional stringed instrument.

ma'etot. Work programs.

maHber. Association.

maHber kom. Community association.

MaHber Show'ate. Association of Seven (early nationalist organization).

meda. The battlefield and attendant social environment of the independence war (lit., "the field").

Medhanie Alem. Internal charismatic movement within the Eritrean Orthodox church (lit., "savior of the world").

menenet. Identity (also, identity card, issued by the government).

Menk'a. Internal dissident movement of the Eritrean Peoples Liberation Front (lit., "bat").

mesob. Large woven basket with flat surface and lid, used as a table.

m'ezuzat. "Obedients."

mua!. Utterance to indicate strong feelings of agreement or disagreement.

Mulu Wangeel. Full Gospel Church.

nakfa. Eritrean national currency, named after location of the EPLF's most dramatic victory over Ethiopia.

NeHnan 'Elaman. "Our Struggle and Its Goals," document produced by the leaders of EPLF in 1970.

netsela. White spun-cotton shawl, with colorful threads on the edges, worn by women over their clothing.

n'tay meselkha. What do you think? (lit., "What does it seem like to you?").

semay-teqes. Skyscraper.

Sha'bia. Colloquial name for both EPLF and PFDJ.

shida. Plastic or rubber sandals worn by guerrilla fighters during the independence struggle, now a symbol of national identity.

shiger yellen. No problem.

shikor. Lit., "sugar," also used as a term of endearment ("sweetie").

Taliano. Colloquial for "Italian," often used to refer to white people.

tariqa. Islamic brotherhood.

tchenfer. Chapter or branch.

tegadelay. Fighter (sing.).

tegadelti. Fighter (pl.).

Tilfi. Embroidered white spun cotton.

tsa'da Ertrawiyen. Lit., "white Eritreans."

tsebtsab meda. Conditions in the battlefield.

warsay. Postindependence generation (lit., "inheritors").

wedi Asmara. Urban man (lit., "son of the city of Asmara").

wushtawi andeHeki. Internal rules (of an organization).

wushtawi gudayat. Internal security (secret service).

Yamin. Name of internal dissident movement in EPLF (lit., "rightist").

yike'alo. The generation of fighters who carried Eritrea to independence (lit., "those who can do all things").

zemecha. Ethiopian student national service campaign, post-1974 revolution.

z'Hafley. My sister (lit, "this [you], my sister").

zilzil Tibs. Dish made of sautéed beef strips with peppers and onions.

zoba. Zone.

zurya. Women's traditional dress, usually white or cream-colored cotton with colorful spun threads.

References

AESNA/AEWNA. 1978. *In Defence of the Eritrean Revolution.* New York: Association of Eritrean Students in North America/Association of Eritrean Women in North America.

Agamben, Giorgio. 1998. *Homo Sacer: Sovereign Power and Bare Life.* Translated by D. Heller-Roazen. Stanford, Calif.: Stanford University Press.

———. 2000. *Means without End: Notes on Politics.* Minneapolis: University of Minnesota Press.

Al-Ali, Nadje, Richard Black, and Khalid Koser. 2001. "The Limits to 'Transnationalism': Bosnian and Eritrean Refugees in Europe as Emerging Transnational Communities." *Ethnic and Racial Studies* 24:578–600.

Al-Amin, Muhammad Said. 1992. *Al-Thawra al-Iritiriyya* [The Eritrean Revolution]. Asmara.

Ammar, Wolde-Yesus. 1997. "The Role of Asmara Students in the Nationalist Movement: 1958–1998." *Eritrean Studies Review* 2:59–84.

Amnesty International. 2005. "Eritrea: Religious Persecution." AI Index: AFR 64/013/2005.

Andall, Jacqueline. 2002. "Second-generation Attitude? African-Italians in Milan." *Journal of Ethnic and Migration Studies* 28:389–407.

Anderson, Benedict. 1991. *Imagined Communities: Reflections on the Origin and Spread of Nationalism.* London: Verso.

Aretxaga, Begoña. 1997. *Shattering Silence: Women, Nationalism and Political Subjectivity in Northern Ireland.* Princeton, N.J.: Princeton University Press.

———. 2003. "Maddening States." *Annual Review of Anthropology* 32:393–410.

Arthur, John A. 2000. *Invisible Sojourners: African Immigrant Diaspora in the United States.* Westport, Conn.: Praeger.

Balandier, Georges. 1970. *Political Anthropology.* Translated by A. M. Sheridan-Smith. New York: Pantheon Books.

Balsvik, Randi Rønning. 1985. *Haile Sellassie's Students: The Intellectual and Social Background to Revolution, 1952–1977.* East Lansing: African Studies Center, Michigan State University, in cooperation with the Norwegian Council of Science and Humanities.

Bariagaber, Assefaw. 2006. "Explaining Fresh Refugee Movements out of Eritrea." Paper presented at African Studies Association–UK meeting, London, September 12.

Barth, Elise Frederikke. 2001. "Female Fighters in Eritrea: A Study of Soldiers and Socialization." MA thesis, Oslo University College.

Basch, Linda, Nina Glick-Schiller, and Cristina Szanton Blanc. 1994. *Nations Unbound: Transnational Projects, Postcolonial Predicaments, and Deterritorialized Nation-States.* Luxembourg: Gordon and Breach.

Bauman, Zygmunt. 2001. *Community: Seeking Safety in an Insecure World*. Cambridge: Polity Press.

Bayart, Jean Francois. 1993. *The State in Africa*. London: Longman.

Bernal, Victoria. 2000. "Equality to Die For? Women Guerrilla Fighters and Eritrea's Cultural Revolution." *Political and Legal Anthropology Review (PoLAR)* 23:61–76.

———. 2004. "Eritrea Goes Global: Reflections on Nationalism in a Transnational Era." *Cultural Anthropology* 19(1):3–25.

———. 2005a. "Digital Diaspora: Conflict, Community, and Celebrity in Virtual Eritrea." In T. R. Hepner and B. Conrad, eds., *Eritrea Abroad: Critical Reflections on the Global Diaspora* (special issue of the *Eritrean Studies Review*) 4(2):185–209.

———. 2005b. "Eritrea On-line: Diaspora, Cyberspace, and the Public Sphere." *American Ethnologist* 32(4):660–75.

———. 2006. "Diaspora, Cyberspace, and Political Imagination: The Eritrean Diaspora Online." *Global Networks* 6(2):161–79.

Bingen, R. James, David Robinson, and John Staatz, eds. 2000. *Democracy and Development in Mali*. East Lansing: Michigan State University Press.

Bobbio, Norberto. 1987. *Which Socialism?* Minneapolis: University of Minnesota Press.

Bottomore, Tom, L. Harris, V. G. Kiernan, and R. Miliband, eds. 1983. *A Dictionary of Marxist Thought*. Cambridge, Mass.: Harvard University Press.

Bundegaard, Christian. 2004. "The Battalion State: Securitization and Nation-building in Eritrea." Programme for Strategic and International Security Studies (PSIS), Geneva, Switzerland.

Burawoy, Michael. 2001. "Manufacturing the Global." *Ethnography* 2:147–59.

Calhoun, Craig J. 1997. *Nationalism*. Buckingham: Open University Press.

Callaghy, Thomas, Ronald Kassimir, and Robert Latham, eds. 2002. *Intervention and Transnationalism in Africa: Global-Local Networks of Power*. Cambridge: Cambridge University Press.

Casanova, José. 2001. "Religion, the New Millennium, and Globalization." *Sociology of Religion* 62:415–41.

Chatterjee, Partha. 1986. *Nationalist Thought and the Colonial World: A Derivative Discourse?* London: Zed Books.

———. 1993. *The Nation and Its Fragments: Colonial and Postcolonial Histories*. Princeton, N.J.: Princeton University Press.

Cohen, Jean L., and Andrew Arato. 1992. *Civil Society and Political Theory*. Cambridge: MIT Press.

Comaroff, John L., and Jean Comaroff, eds. 1999. *Civil Society and the Political Imagination in Africa: Critical Perspectives*. Chicago: University of Chicago Press.

Compton, Kaila Morris. 1998. "The Strength to Travel Together: Eritrean Experiences of Violence, Displacement, and Nationalism in a Global Network." Ph.D. diss., Harvard University.

Connell, Dan. 1997. *Against All Odds: A Chronicle of the Eritrean Revolution*. Lawrenceville, N.J.: Red Sea Press.

———. 2001. *Rethinking Revolution: New Strategies for Democracy and Social Justice: The Experiences of Eritrea, South Africa, Palestine, and Nicaragua*. Lawrenceville, N.J.: Red Sea Press.

———. 2005a. *Conversations with Eritrean Political Prisoners*. Trenton, N.J.: Red Sea Press.

———. 2005b. "Eritrea." *Countries at the Crossroads 2005*. New York: Freedom House Books.

Conrad, Bettina. 2005. " 'We Are the Prisoners of Our Dreams': Exit, Voice and Loyalty in the Eritrean Diaspora in Germany." *Eritrean Studies Review* 4(2):211–61.

——. 2006. " 'We Are the Warsay of Eritrea in Diaspora': Contested Identities and Social Divisions in Cyberspace." In Leif Manger and Munzoul A. A. Assal, eds., *Diasporas within and without Africa*. Uppsala: Nordiska Afrikainstitutet.

Cooper, Derek. 1992. *Urban Refugees: Ethiopians and Eritreans in Cairo*. Cairo: American University in Cairo Press.

Cox, Harvey G. 1995. *Fire from Heaven: The Rise of Pentecostal Spirituality and the Reshaping of Religion in the Twenty-first Century*. Reading, Mass.: Addison-Wesley.

Das, Veena, and Deborah Poole, eds. 2004. *Anthropology in the Margins of the State*. Santa Fe: School of American Research; Oxford: James Currey.

Della Cava, Ralph. 2001. "Transnational Religions: The Roman Catholic Church in Brazil and the Orthodox Church in Russia." *Sociology of Religion* 62:535–52.

Donham, Donald L. 1999a. *History, Power, Ideology: Central Issues in Marxism and Anthropology*. Berkeley: University of California Press.

——. 1999b. *Marxist Modern: An Ethnographic History of the Ethiopian Revolution*. Berkeley: University of California Press.

Douglas, Mary. 1966. *Purity and Danger: An Analysis of the Concepts of Pollution and Taboo*. London: Routledge.

Eco, Umberto. 1989. *Foucault's Pendulum*. San Diego: Harcourt, Brace, Jovanovich.

Ehrenberg, John. 1999. *Civil Society: The Critical History of an Idea*. New York: New York University Press.

Eide, Oyvind M. 2000. *Revolution and Religion in Ethiopia: The Growth and Persecution of the Mekane Yesus Church, 1974–1985*. Oxford: James Currey.

Eritrean Catholic Bishops. "God Loves This Country." 2001 pastoral letter, English version.

Eritrean Peoples Liberation Front (EPLF). 1977. *National Democratic Programme of the Eritrean Peoples Liberation Front*.

Farah, Nurrudin. 2000. *Yesterday, Tomorrow: Voices from the Somali Diaspora*. London: Cassell.

Ferguson, James. 2006. *Global Shadows: Africa in the Neo-Liberal World Order*. Durham, N.C.: Duke University Press.

Fessehatzion, Tekie. 1999. "Eritrean Public Intellectuals and the Making of National Identity." Keynote address to the Association of Eritrean Professionals and Academics for Development (AEPAD), Washington, D.C. August 22.

——. 2005. "Eritrea's Remittance-based Economy: Ruminations and Conjectures." In Tricia Redeker Hepner and Bettina Conrad, eds., *Eritrean Studies Review* 4(2):165–83

Foner, Nancy. 1987 [2001]. *New Immigrants in New York*. New York: Columbia University Press.

Gebremedhin, Jordan. 1989. *Peasants and Nationalism in Eritrea: A Critique of Ethiopian Studies*. Trenton, N.J.: Red Sea Press.

Gellner, Ernest. 1983. *Nations and Nationalism*. Ithaca, N.Y.: Cornell University Press.

Giddens, Anthony. 1985. *The Nation-State and Violence*. Cambridge: Polity Press.

Gledhill, John. 2000. *Power and Its Disguises: Anthropological Perspectives on Politics*. London: Pluto Press.

Glick-Schiller, Nina. 1999. "Transmigrants and Nation-States: Something Old and Something New in the U.S. Immigrant Experience." In Charles Hirschman, Philip Kasinitz, and Josh DeWind, eds., *The Handbook of International Migration: The American Experience*. New York: Russell Sage Foundation.

———. 2005. "Transnational Social Fields and Imperialism: Bringing a Theory of Power to Transnational Studies." *Anthropological Theory* 5(4):439–61.

Glick-Schiller, Nina, and Georges Fouron. 1999. "Terrains of Blood and Nation: Haitian Transnational Social Fields." *Ethnic and Racial Studies* 22:340–66.

———. 2001. *Georges Woke Up Laughing: Long-distance Nationalism and the Search for Home*. Durham, N.C.: Duke University Press.

Gluckman, Max. 1940 [2002]. "The Bridge: An Analysis of a Social Situation in Modern Zululand." In Joan Vincent, ed., *The Anthropology of Politics*. London: Blackwell.

Gramsci, Antonio. 1971. *Selections from the Prison Notebooks of Antonio Gramsci*. Edited by Quintin Hoare and Geoffrey Nowell Smith. London: Lawrence and Wishart.

———. 1977. *Selections from Political Writings, 1910–1920*. Edited by Q. Hoare. New York: International Publishers.

Greenhouse, Carol. 2002. "Introduction: Altered States, Altered Lives." In Greenhouse, Mertz, and Warren, eds., *Ethnography in Unstable Places: Everyday Lives in the Context of Dramatic Political Change*.

Greenhouse, Carol, Elizabeth Mertz, and Kay B. Warren, eds. 2002. *Ethnography in Unstable Places: Everyday Lives in the Context of Dramatic Political Change*. Durham, N.C.: Duke University Press.

Gupta, Akhil, and James Ferguson, eds. 1997. *Culture, Power, Place: Explorations in Critical Anthropology*. Durham, N.C.: Duke University Press.

Guyer, Jane. 1994. "The Spatial Dimensions of Civil Society in Nigeria: An Anthropologist Looks at Nigeria." In D. Rothchild, J. Harbeson, and N. Chazan, eds., *Civil Society and the State in Africa*. Boulder, Colo.: Lynne Rienner.

Habermas, Jürgen. 1981. *The Theory of Communicative Action: Reason and the Rationalization of Society*. Translated by Thomas McCarthy. Boston: Beacon Press.

Habte-Selassie, Bereket. 2003. *The Making of the Eritrean Constitution*. Trenton, N.J.: Red Sea Press.

Hall, Stuart. 1990. "Cultural Identity and Diaspora." In J. Rutherford, ed., *Identity: Community, Culture, Difference*. London: Lawrence and Wishart.

Hansen, Thomas Blum, and Finn Stepputat. 2006. "Sovereignty Revisited." *Annual Review of Anthropology* 35:295–15.

Hansen, Thomas Blum, and Finn Stepputat, eds. 2001. *States of Imagination*. Durham, N.C.: Duke University Press.

———, eds. 2005. *Sovereign Bodies: Citizens, Migrants and States in the Postcolonial World*. Princeton, N.J.: Princeton University Press.

Harbeson, John, Donald Rothchild, and Naomi Chazan, eds. 1994. *Civil Society and the State in Africa*. Boulder, Colo.: Lynne Rienner.

Harvey, David. 1996. *Justice, Nature, and the Geography of Difference*. Oxford: Blackwell.

Hegel, Georg Wilhelm Friedrich. 1975. *Lectures on the Philosophy of World History*. Translated by H. B. Nisbet. Cambridge: Cambridge University Press.

Hepner, Tricia Redeker. 2000. "Pride, Prejudice, and Ethnicization of the Eritrean Nation." *Ufahamu: Journal of the African Activist Association* 28:87–103.

———. 2003. "Religion, Nationalism, and Transnational Civil Society in the Eritrean Diaspora." *Identities: Global Studies in Culture and Power* 10:269–93.

———. 2005. "Transnational *Tegadelti*: Eritreans for Liberation in North America and the Eritrean Peoples Liberation Front." In Tricia Redeker Hepner and Bettina Conrad, eds., *Eritrean Studies Review* 4(2):37–84.

————. 2008. "Transnational Governance and the Centralization of State Power in Eritrea and Exile." *Ethnic and Racial Studies* 31(3):476–502.

————. 2009. "Seeking Asylum in a Transnational Social Field: New Refugees and Struggles for Autonomy and Human Rights." In David O'Kane and Tricia Redeker Hepner, eds., *Biopolitics, Militarism, and Development: Eritrea in the 21st Century*. New York: Berghahn Books.

Hepner, Tricia Redeker, and Lynn Fredriksson. 2007. "Regional Politics, Human Rights, and U.S. Policy in the Horn of Africa." *Africa Policy Journal* 3(Spring). http://www.hks.harvard.edu/kssgorg/apj/issues/spring_2007_issue/Article. hepner.htm

Hepner, Tricia Redeker and Randal L. Hepner. "Arresting Faith: Religion and State Repression in Contemporary Eritrea." In Günther Schlee, Data Dea, and Christiane Falge, eds., *New Religiosity and Intergenerational Conflict in Northeast Africa*. In press.

Herzfeld, Michael. 1997. *Cultural Intimacy: Social Poetics in the Nation-State*. London: Routledge.

Hobsbawm, Eric, and Terence O. Ranger, eds. 1983. *The Invention of Tradition*. Cambridge: Cambridge University Press.

Hodgin, Peter. 1997. "An Introduction to Eritrea's Ongoing Revolution: Women's Nationalist Mobilization and Gender Politics in Post-War Eritrea." *Eritrean Studies Review* 2:85–110.

Holcomb, Bonnie, and Sisai Ibssa. 1990. *The Invention of Ethiopia*. Trenton, N.J.: Red Sea Press.

Holtzman, Jon. 2000. *Nuer Journeys, Nuer Lives: Sudanese Refugees in Minnesota*. Boston: Allyn and Bacon.

Holub, Renate. 1992. *Antonio Gramsci: Beyond Marxism and Postmodernism*. London: Routledge.

Itzigsohn, José. 2000. "Immigration and the Boundaries of Citizenship: The Institutions of Immigrants' Political Transnationalism." *International Migration Review* 34:1127–53.

Iyob, Ruth. 1995. *The Eritrean Struggle for Independence: Domination, Resistance, Nationalism, 1941–1993*. Cambridge: Cambridge University Press.

Jameson, Frederic. 1984. "Postmodernism, or the Cultural Logic of Late Capitalism." *New Left Review* 146 (July–August):59–92.

Kaldor, Mary. 1999. "Transnational Civil Society." In T. Dunne and N. Wheeler, eds., *Human Rights and Global Politics*. Cambridge: Cambridge University Press.

Kaldor, Mary, Helmut Anheier, and Marlies Glasius, eds. 2003. *Global Civil Society 2003*. Oxford: Oxford University Press.

Kasfir, Nelson, ed. 1998. *Civil Society and Democracy in Africa: Critical Perspectives*. Portland, Ore.: Frank Cass.

Keane, John. 2003. *Global Civil Society?* Cambridge: Cambridge University Press.

Kertzer, David I. 1988. *Ritual, Politics, and Power*. New Haven, Conn.: Yale University Press.

Kibreab, Gaim. 1985. *African Refugees: Reflections on the African Refugee Problem*. Trenton, N.J.: Africa World Press.

————. 2003. "Citizenship Rights and Repatriation of Refugees." *International Migration Review* 36(4):24–73.

————. 2005. "Urban Eritrean Refugees in Sudan: Yearning for Home or Diaspora?" In Tricia Redeker Hepner and Bettina Conrad, eds., *Eritrean Studies Review* 4(2):115–41.

————. 2006. "Eritrea: The National Service and the Warsai-Yikaalo Campaign as Forced Labour." Paper presented at African Studies Association–UK meeting, London, September 12.

Killion, Tom. 1997. "Eritrean Workers' Organization and Early Nationalist Mobilization: 1948–1958." *Eritrean Studies Review* 2(1):1–58.

———. 1998. *Historical Dictionary of Eritrea.* Lanham, Md.: Scarecrow Press.

Koehn, Peter. 1991. *Refugees from Revolution: U.S. Policy and Third-World Migration.* Boulder, Colo.: Westview Press.

Laakso, Liisa, and Adebayo Olukoshi. 1996. "The Crisis of the Postcolonial Nation-State Project in Africa." In Adebayo Olokoshi and Liisa Laakso, eds., *Challenges to the Nation-State in Africa.* Uppsala: Nordiska Afrikainstitutet.

Laclau, Ernesto, and Chantal Mouffe. 1985. *Hegemony and Socialist Strategy: Towards a Radical Democratic Politics.* London: Verso.

Larebo, Haile Mariam. 1988. "The Ethiopian Orthodox Church and Politics in the Twentieth Century: Part II." *Northeast African Studies* 10(1):1–23.

Lavie, Smadar, and Ted Swedenburg, eds. 1996. *Displacement, Diaspora, and Geographies of Identity.* Durham, N.C.: Duke University Press.

Leach, Edmund. 1976. *Culture and Communication.* Cambridge: Cambridge University Press.

Legesse, Asmerom, and Citizens for Peace in Eritrea. 1998. "The Uprooted: Case Material on Ethnic Eritrean Deportees from Ethiopia Concerning Human Rights Violations." Eritrean Human Rights Task Force, USA.

Leonard, Richard. 1988. "Popular Participation in Liberation and Revolution." In Lionel Cliffe and Basil Davidson, eds., *The Long Struggle of Eritrea for Independence and Constructive Peace.* Trenton, N.J.: Red Sea Press.

Levine, Donald. 1974. *Greater Ethiopia.* Chicago: University of Chicago Press.

Levitt, Peggy. 2001. *The Transnational Villagers.* Berkeley: University of California Press.

Levitt, Peggy, and Rafael de la Dehesa. 2003. "Transnational Migration and the Redefinition of the State." *Ethnic and Racial Studies* 26(4):587–611.

Louie, Andrea. 2000. "Re-territorializing Transnationalism: Chinese Americans and the Chinese Motherland." *American Ethnologist* 27:645–69.

Malkki, Liisa H. 1995a. *Purity and Exile: Violence, Memory and National Cosmology among Hutu Refugees in Tanzania.* Chicago: University of Chicago Press.

———. 1995b. "Refugees and Exile: From 'Refugee Studies' to the National Order of Things." *Annual Review of Anthropology* 24:495–523.

———. 1997. "National Geographic: The Rooting of Peoples and the Territorialization of Identity among Scholars and Refugees." In Gupta and Ferguson, eds., *Culture, Power, Place: Explorations in Critical Anthropology.*

Mama, Amina. 1992. "The Need for Gender Analysis: A Comment on the Prospects for Peace, Recovery and Development in the Horn of Africa." In Martin Doornbos, Lionel Cliffe, Abdel Ghaffar M. Ahmed, and John Markakis, eds., *Beyond Conflict in the Horn: The Prospects for Peace, Recovery, and Development in Ethiopia, Somalia, Eritrea, and Sudan.* Trenton, N.J.: Red Sea Press.

Mamdani, Mahmoud. 1996. *Citizen and Subject: Contemporary Africa and the Legacy of Late Colonialism.* Princeton, N.J.: Princeton University Press.

Marcus, Harold G. 1994. *A History of Ethiopia.* Berkeley: University of California Press.

Markakis, John. 1987. *National and Class Conflict in the Horn of Africa.* Cambridge: Cambridge University Press.

Marshall, Barbara. 1994. *Engendering Modernity: Feminism, Social Theory, and Social Change.* Boston: Northeastern University.

Martin, David. 2002. *Pentecostalism: The World Their Parish.* Oxford: Blackwell.

Matsuoka, Atsuko, and John Sorenson. 2001. *Ghosts and Shadows: Construction of Identity and Community in an African Diaspora.* Toronto: University of Toronto Press.

Medina, Laurie Kroshus. 1997. "Defining Difference, Forging Unity: The Co-Construction of Race, Ethnicity, and Nation in Belize." *Ethnic and Racial Studies* 15:757–80.

———. 2004. *Negotiating Economic Development.* Tucson: University of Arizona Press.

Merry, Sally Engle. 2006. "Transnational Human Rights and Local Activism: Mapping the Middle." *American Anthropologist* 108(1):38–51.

Monga, Celestin. 1996. *The Anthropology of Anger: Civil Society and Democracy in Africa.* Boulder, Colo.: Lynne Rienner.

Müller, Tanja R. 2004. "'Now I Am Free': Education and Human Resource Development in Eritrea; Contradictions in the Lives of Eritrean Women in Higher Education." *COMPARE* 34(2):215–29.

———. 2005. *The Making of Elite Women: Revolution and Nation Building in Eritrea.* Boston: Brill.

Murtaza, Niaz. 1998. *The Pillage of Sustainability in Eritrea, 1600s–1990s: Rural Communities and the Creeping Shadows of Hegemony.* Westport, Conn.: Greenwood Press.

Nadel, Siegfried F. 1944. *Races and Tribes of Eritrea.* Asmara: British Military Administration.

Nagengast, Carol. 1994. "Violence, Terror, and the Crisis of the State." *Annual Review of Anthropology* 23:109–36.

Negash, Tekeste. 1997. *Eritrea and Ethiopia: The Federal Experience.* New Brunswick, N.J.: Transaction.

Negash, Tekeste, and Kjetil Tronvoll. 2000. *Brothers at War: Making Sense of the Eritrean-Ethiopian War.* Oxford: James Currey; Athens: Ohio University Press.

Nyang'oro, Julius. 1999. *Civil Society and Democratic Development in Africa: Perspectives from Eastern and Southern Africa.* Harare: Mwengo.

Nzongola-Ntalaja, George, M. C. Lee, and African Association of Political Science. 1998. *The State and Democracy in Africa.* Trenton, N.J.: Africa World Press.

O'Kane, David, and Tricia Redeker Hepner, eds. 2009. *Biopolitics, Militarism and Development: Eritrea in the 21st Century.* Oxford: Berghahn Books.

Paley, Julia. 2002. "Toward an Anthropology of Democracy." *Annual Review of Anthropology* 31:469–96.

Pateman, Roy. 1998. *Eritrea: Even the Stones Are Burning.* Trenton, N.J.: Red Sea Press.

Plaut, Martin. 2002. "Briefing: The Birth of the Eritrean Reform Movement." *Review of African Political Economy* 29:119–24.

Pool, David. 1998. "The Eritrean Peoples Liberation Front." In C. Clapham, ed., *African Guerrillas.* Oxford: James Currey.

———. 2001. *From Guerrillas to Government: The Eritrean Peoples Liberation Front.* Oxford: James Currey; Athens: Ohio University Press.

Portes, Alejandro, and Rubén Rumbaut. 1996. *Immigrant America: A Portrait.* Berkeley: University of California Press.

Pratt, Nicola. 2006. *Democracy and Authoritarianism in the Arab World.* Boulder, Colo.: Lynne Rienner.

Reid, Richard. 2005. "Caught in the Headlights of History: Eritrea, the EPLF, and the Post-war Nation-State." *Journal of Modern African Studies* 43(3):467–88.

Riggan, Jennifer. 2009. "Avoiding Wastage by Making Soldiers: Technologies of the State and the Imagination of the Educated Nation." In David O'Kane and Tricia Redeker Hepner, eds., *Biopolitics, Militarism and Development: Eritrea in the 21st Century.*

Rude, John. 1996. "Birth of a Nation in Cyberspace." *The Humanist*, March–April, 17–23.

Saulsberry, Nicole. 2002. "The Life and Times of Woldeab Woldemariam." Ph.D. diss., Stanford University.

Schaffer, Frederic C. 1998. *Democracy in Translation: Understanding Politics in an Unfamiliar Culture.* Ithaca, N.Y.: Cornell University Press.

Scott, James C. 1985. *Weapons of the Weak: Everyday Forms of Peasant Resistance.* New Haven, Conn.: Yale University Press.

———. 1998. *Seeing Like a State: How Certain Schemes to Improve the Human Condition Have Failed.* New Haven, Conn.: Yale University Press.

Selassie, Wubnesh W. 1992. "The Changing Position of Eritrean Women: An Overview of Women's Participation in the EPLF." In Martin Doornbos, Lionel Cliffe, Abdel Ghaffar M. Ahmed, and John Markakis, eds., *Beyond Conflict in the Horn.* Trenton, N.J.: Red Sea Press.

Shefner, Jon. 2007. "Rethinking Civil Society in the Age of NAFTA." *The Annals of the American Academy of Political and Social Science* 610(1):182–200.

Silkin, Patricia. 1989. "New Marriage Laws and Social Change in the Liberated Areas of Eritrea." *International Journal of the Sociology of Law* 12:147–63.

Smith, Michael P., and Luis E. Guarnizo, eds. 1998. *Transnationalism from Below.* New Brunswick, N.J.: Transaction.

Teklemariam, Tesfamariam. 2002. "Eritrean Immigrants: Correlates of Satisfaction and Cultural and Social Adaptation." M.A. thesis, DePaul University.

Thieman-Dino, L., and J. A. Schechter. 2004. "Refugee Voices: The Missing Piece in Refugee Policies and Practices." In C. Nagengast and C. Vélez-Ibañez, eds., *Human Rights: The Scholar as Activist.* Oklahoma City: Society for Applied Anthropology.

Tolstoy, Leo. 1957. *War and Peace.* Translated by Rosemary Edmonds. London: Penguin.

Treiber, Magnus. 2005. *Der Traum von guten Leben. Die eritreische warsay-Generation im Asmara der zweiten Nachkriegszeit.* Münster: LIT-Verlag.

———. 2009. "Trapped in Adolescence: The Postwar Urban Generation." In David O'Kane and Tricia Redeker Hepner, eds., *Biopolitics, Militarism and Development: Eritrea in the 21st Century.*

Tronvoll, Kjetil. 1998a. *Mai Weini: A Highland Village in Eritrea.* Trenton, N.J.: Red Sea Press.

———. 1998b. "The Process of Nation-Building in Post-War Eritrea: Created from Below or Directed from Above?" *Journal of Modern African Studies* 36:461–83.

———. 1999. "Borders of Violence: Boundaries of Identity; Demarcating the Eritrean Nation-State." *Ethnic and Racial Studies* 22:1037–60.

Turner, Victor W. 1969. *The Ritual Process: Structure and Anti-Structure.* London: Routledge and K. Paul.

United States Committee on Refugees (USCR). 2001. *Refugee Reports.* Washington, D.C.

Verdery, Katherine. 1991. "Theorizing Socialism." *American Ethnologist* 18(3):419–39.

———. 1996. *What Was Socialism, and What Comes Next?* Princeton, N.J.: Princeton University Press.

———. 1999. *The Political Lives of Dead Bodies: Reburial and Postsocialist Change.* New York: Columbia University Press.

Walzer, Michael, ed. 1997. *Toward a Global Civil Society.* New York: Berghahn Books.

Weldemichael, Awet T. 2009. "The Eritrean Long March: The Strategic Withdrawal of the EPLF, 1978–1979." *Journal of Military History.* In press.

Williams, Brackette F. 1991. *Stains on My Name, War in My Veins: Guyana and the Politics of Cultural Struggle.* Durham, N.C.: Duke University Press.

Wilson, Amrit. 1991. *The Challenge Road: Women and the Eritrean Revolution.* Trenton, N.J.: Red Sea Press.

Woldemikael, Tekle M. 1993. "The Cultural Construction of Eritrean Nationalist Movements." In C. Young, ed., *The Rising Tide of Cultural Pluralism: The Nation-State at Bay?* Madison: University of Wisconsin Press.

———. 1998. "Eritrean and Ethiopian Refugees in the United States." *Eritrean Studies Review* 2(2):89–109.

———. 2005. "Bridging the Divide: Eritrean Muslims and Christians in Orange County, California." In Tricia Redeker Hepner and Bettina Conrad, eds., *Eritrean Studies Review* 4(2):143–64.

Woldeselassie, Melles. 2000. *Deportation of Eritreans from Ethiopia: A Lesson to the World.* Asmara: Sabur.

Wolf, Eric. 1982. *Europe and the People without History.* Berkeley: University of California Press.

Wrong, Michela. 2006. *I Didn't Do It for You: How the World Betrayed a Small African Nation.* New York: Harper Perennial.

Young, John. 1997. *Peasant Revolution in Ethiopia: The Tigray Peoples Liberation Front, 1975–1991.* Cambridge: Cambridge University Press.

Index

Acknowledgments

In addition to the hundreds of Eritreans who participated in the writing of this book, I wish to thank the following individuals and institutions. I am most deeply grateful for the support of my beloved soul mate, Randal Hepner; my parents, Nancy and Jim Redeker; my parents-in-law, Maxine and Terry Hepner; and our extended clans. The research on which this book is based was generously funded by the National Science Foundation, the Social Science Research Council, the Wenner-Gren Foundation for Anthropological Research, and Michigan State University. The following mentors and friends were invaluable: Lynne Goldstein, Laurie Medina, Bill Derman, Andrea Louie, Judy Pugh, David Robinson, the late Harold Marcus, the MSU African Studies Center faculty and staff, Iskias Naizghi, Asmeret Asefaw Berhe, Mesfin Asgedom, Megan Plyler, Heather Van Wormer, Debra Budiani, Tim Carmichael, Ellen Foley, and Janice Harper. At the University of Tennessee I am especially grateful to Andrew Kramer and Lily Harmon-Gross. I also thank Victoria Bernal, Bettina Conrad, Celeste Giampetro, David O'Kane, Awet Weldemichael, the late Ken Sokoloff, Ghislaine Lydon, Judy Wittner, John Sorenson, Don Donham, Nina Glick-Schiller, and Dan Connell; colleagues at the Max Planck Institute for Social Anthropology in Halle, Germany; the two anonymous reviewers whose helpful comments strengthened this book; the University of Pennsylvania Press; and the Exhibit, Performance, and Publications Fund at the University of Tennessee. Ezana Tekeste and Tsegaye Arrefe offered their friendship and assistance with some difficult Tigrinya documents and concepts. My colleagues and friends at Amnesty International have remained a source of courage and a candle in the dark. In Eritrea and exile, I am indebted to countless people, including all those in the "midwestern community"; the one called "Hailu"; and faculty, staff, students, and researchers at the University of Asmara and the Research and Documentation Center, especially Peter Schmidt. There are so many others I would like to thank, including "family" and friends in Asmara who remain so dear to me. While I wish to name each and every one, I would prefer they not be held accountable for the ideas and interpretations that are my sole responsibility. *B'selam yerakhbena.*